The Grea Sა

Open *The Great Sales Book* at any page and you will find ideas that
you can use today to help you sell more of whatever it is you sell.
Jack Collis's masterpiece on the art of gentle persuasion is packed
tight with common sense techniques that have withstood the test of
time. A great read for anyone wanting to improve their sales results.
JOE ROBERTSON, MANAGING DIRECTOR, HEALTHY BUILDINGS
INTERNATIONAL PTY LTD

Jack Collis's book lives up to its title because it truly is
comprehensive. It is not *Another Great Sales Book*; it is **The** *Great
Sales Book* because it is truly the most definitive of its kind in
Australia at this point in time.
LOWELL TARLING, EDITOR, *FRANCHISING MAGAZINE*

I have been in the selling profession for over 30 years. For
10 consecutive years I was the leading life insurance salesman
in Australia. I achieved this by reading and learning everything
I could about selling. *The Great Sales Book*, which is easy to read,
is the best, most definitive and informative on the
art of selling. It's the salesman's bible.
JOE LANGLEY, MANAGING DIRECTOR, ELECTRONIC ENTERPRISES

The Great Sales Book is great. What the sales industry needs,
and we'll use it as our sales bible for all existing and future sales
and customer service people.
ROB MATHEWS, MANAGING DIRECTOR,
BRILLIANT IMAGES PTY LTD

Not only is this book cram-packed with useful sales guidelines and
strategies, it is also totally absorbing and inspirational. For any
business involved in sales, this book will be invaluable.
KERRY WONKA, MANAGING DIRECTOR, FUTUREMEDIA PTY LTD

The
Great
Sales
Book

The Great Sales Book

JACK COLLIS

HarperBusiness
An imprint of HarperCollins*Publishers*

Harper*Business*

An imprint of HarperCollins*Publishers*, Australia

First published in Australia in 1996
Reprinted in 1997
This edition printed with corrections in 1998
Reprinted in 1999, 2000, 2001 (twice), 2002
by HarperCollins*Publishers* Pty Limited
ABN 36 009 913 517
A member of the HarperCollins*Publishers* (Australia) Pty Limited Group
www.harpercollins.com.au

HarperCollins*Publishers*
25 Ryde Road, Pymble, Sydney, NSW 2073, Australia
31 View Road, Glenfield, Auckland 10, New Zealand
77-85 Fulham Palace Road, London W6 8JB, United Kingdom
Hazelton Lanes, 55 Avenue Road, Suite 2900, Toronto, Ontario M5R 3L2
and 1995 Markham Road, Scarborough, Ontario M1B 5M8, Canada
10 East 53rd Street, New York NY 10022, USA

National Library of Australia Cataloguing-in-Publication data:

Collis, Jack.
The great sales book.
ISBN 0 7322 6634 3.
1. Selling — Psychological aspects. I. Title.
658.85

Set in Goudy 10/12
Printed and bound in Australia by Griffin Press on 80gsm Econoprint

11 10 9 8 7 6   02 03 04 05

FOREWORD

WHENEVER I MEET Jack Collis I feel a new confidence in the practice of personal sales and the ongoing opportunities for sales professionals. His immense knowledge of sales practice and salespeople development provides an invaluable skills resource and practical insights for meeting the challenges of operating in the sales arena today.

In a highly successful sales and sales training career spanning over 35 years, Jack Collis has personally influenced over 100 000 salespeople in face-to-face training. Through his many books and training seminars he has made a profound difference to people's lives and careers in contributing to the success of salespeople across Australia and New Zealand, and in other countries where his books and tapes have carried that influence internationally. Jack's programs are focused on providing workable personal solutions that create operating structures for immediate and long-term success.

In *The Great Sales Book*, Jack Collis provides a practical guide that I can recommend to all levels of salespeople seeking to create new confidence in themselves and to develop improved career success in selling and personal communications in these technical and super-competitive times.

Jack Collis delivers refreshing, practical and dynamic insights for creating real solutions for successfully operating in the competitive sales environment. He is a legend in successful sales performance in today's hectic chase for instant success and quick fix, technology-based solutions.

In this essential skills and development book for salespeople, Jack Collis provides a major opportunity for finding a better way to achieve success and personal satisfaction through selling as a career. He delivers the link for salespeople to fully understand the dynamics of their role and personalities and so quickly develop personal strength and performance skills for ongoing success in their life and sales work.

As a result of the rapid changes in business today, salespeople often develop a lack of confidence in their abilities and can suffer extraordinary stress through their failure to develop clearly defined goals, build ongoing skill resources and understand the parameters for their success. Because technology-based sales solutions, often installed as cost-saving measures, frequently fail to properly exploit the energies, enthusiasm and intuitive elements of the personal sales approach, salespeople feel alienated and so their performance, and therefore the success rates for their organisation, declines.

Many businesses are increasingly disenchanted with sales performance through technology-based solutions and are gaining new appreciations of the importance of effective personal salespeople in supporting the sales and marketing effort.

Jack Collis shares my view and teaches that there is no magic solution to becoming expert in selling, that success depends on learning and applying a host of different skills backed up by positive attitudes based on consistent good work habits. He also teaches that 'People do business with people' and that in our technology-driven world, professional salespeople hold a critical responsibility as the organisation's personal communicator and change agent. The role of the sales representative has never been more critical in converting prospects into profitable sales and in ensuring that the organisation has both the ear of and a clear voice with its customers.

The Great Sales Book provides a major opportunity for salespeople to grasp the solutions offered with both hands, follow the directions of experience, and take immediate steps to create a new level of personal strength for improving performance in an increasingly competitive operating environment.

W.D. (Bill) Leigh, FASI, *Australian Sales Institute*

CONTENTS

INTRODUCTION

*Striving for excellence is the ideal. If one has the
talent to try for the top, then that should be the
aim. Talent is a gift which should not be wasted.*
CHRIS EVERT

The Great Sales Book is a unique sales book — first,
because it covers the subject more thoroughly and expertly than any
other sales book available in this country today, and second, because it
is written for this market. You can use every one of the hundreds of ideas
and be confident that they will help you to develop strong and enduring
relationships with your prospects and clients that will ensure you
succeed and prosper in this exciting and rewarding business of selling.

This book doesn't outline a system that you must follow from start
to finish. The issue of selling is too complex for a one-system
approach. What may be helpful to one person may be useless to
another. You have to choose what is important to you at any given
time. For that reason, each subject is dealt with in a separate chapter
so that you can go directly to whatever is your current concern or
interest. Whether it is getting started in the business and needing
basic skills, or refreshing your skill level, or wanting to bring yourself
up to date in negotiating, there is a chapter for you. *The Great Sales
Book* is about giving you worthwhile choices. It is filled with practical,
results-oriented methods, strategies, techniques and tactics that work
and are working today for thousands of salespeople who have listened
to my cassettes, attended my seminars, or read my articles on personal
motivation, goal achieving and how to sell successfully.

If you buy this book, read it, put it on the shelf and forget it, you
won't get your money's worth. However, if you adopt the ideas, learn

the principles, practise the techniques and implement them as methods in your everyday sales activity, this book can represent the beginning of a rewarding growth experience for you.

The Great Sales Book is about strategies, techniques and tactics that have been proven to be successful in the only way that counts, and that is by making sales in the everyday marketplace in which we salespeople work. It covers the whole field of selling. From skills that we must master if we are to be a truly successful salesperson, to attitudes and habits that either push us forward to success or hold us back until failure runs us down. It explores the habits that are essential to our sales success, because many salespeople are very skilful and have strong positive attitudes but their success is limited because they have never developed the day-to-day habits that are necessary to ensure a high level of success on a continuous basis.

So important are these attitudes and habits that not only are they dealt with throughout the book, but a separate chapter (Chapter 29) has been specially written on them by my good friend and associate, Dr Alec Dempster, who is a psychiatrist practising in Collins Street, Melbourne. Alec has written on why so many salespeople are held back by attitudinal problems and how they can overcome them. This is another part of the book that not only makes it unique among sales books, but also makes it required reading for those who are finding it difficult to reach their true potential.

Another unique feature of *The Great Sales Book* is that it includes interviews with eight business and media personalities, all of whom are nationally known and recognised as leaders in their field of endeavour, on what they consider are the most important issues for salespeople in terms of successful selling. Each person has been interviewed on a separate topic, and their comments have been included at the end of the chapter on that topic. I am sure you will be very interested in what Alex Hamill, Cyndi Kaplan, David Koch, Bob Miller, Harry M. Miller, Allan Pease, Imelda Roche and Carla Zampatti have to say about what they believe will help you to become a peak performer.

This book is not about being king of the heap, the winner of every sales trophy on offer or the richest person in the business, unless you want to be. It is essentially about how to be a peak performer and how you can reach the level of your potential while at the same time having some balance in your life. The view expressed is that there are many phases of success, all of which are important to our wellbeing and our ability to continually perform at the peak of our potential. Life is to be lived and enjoyed not endured, and it is not necessary to be frenetic about success to enjoy it. The world includes many people who have defined success so narrowly that, apart from work, they lead empty lives. There are also many who are highly successful in their chosen field of work who lead a life full of meaning and enjoyment, because they know that balance in life is critical to fulfilment.

Peak performance is not a system or a method; it is a state of mind which results in very high standards of personal performance, which are evidenced by the following characteristics. Peak performers:

◆ Are sure of their ability and are not willing to perform at a lower level.
◆ Are always willing to be involved in the day-to-day business in which they work. They are pro-active, not reactive.
◆ Are willing to accept targets and objectives, while at the same time continually setting their own goals, mostly above the requirements of their organisation.
◆ Have high moral and ethical standards.
◆ Don't have to be driven, but always work at personal levels of productivity that truly reflect their current potential.
◆ Accept that in order to achieve personal success, it is necessary to be involved with others so that they too can be successful.
◆ Constantly search for new ideas, trends and changes that are taking place, and adapt and change their presentation to include and accommodate them.
◆ Are leaders, not followers.
◆ Are confident of their own abilities, but humble in the way they reflect that confidence in their own activities.
◆ Network constantly to create influence with and value for their clients and prospects.
◆ Exercise strong discipline in their life and pay attention to ongoing learning, for they accept the challenge of continual self-development.

The sales philosophy of this book is simple and direct and is based on the following beliefs.

Selling and marketing are the most important functions in any organisation because that organisation either sells its way to success or it withers and dies. Throughout the book, wherever selling is mentioned it should be understood that marketing is implied, and vice versa. The belief that nothing happens until someone sells something has been around for generations, but it has been voiced more as a platitude than a belief. Today, change driven by technology is the force most affecting every organisation. Businesses can't afford to wait around until the consumer discovers them. Someone has to be out there in the marketplace selling their products and services, or they will fail.

Salespeople need to be more than someone who sells and takes orders; they should understand marketing as much as selling. They need to be expert not only in finding and selling prospects, but must also develop relationships that endure and bind the customer to their organisation. The best way to do that is to deal with every prospect and customer on a win/win basis and to use the technique of negotiating more than selling. What's the difference? A car salesperson sells a car, but negotiates the value of the trade-in.

This book will put forward selling strategies, techniques and tactics that are soft sell but very effective, because they are based on sound ethical practices of persuasion and effective communication. They will develop relationships and mutual trust, and foster the interests of your customers as much as they will benefit your organisation. Soft selling should not be interpreted as weak selling. Persistence and commitment are critical to success, and they are therefore seen as attitudinal traits that are just as critical to sales success as are selling skills.

Selling is not seen as a function of outsmarting anyone, but as a responsibility to add value to whatever offer we are making and to whomever it is being made. Selling is supplying first-class information in a creative way that will support the prospect or customer in making a sound decision that will develop a future relationship that is beneficial to all parties.

This book supports the adage that if you provide a person with fish you may save them from starving, but if you teach that person to fish you give them a living. In this book you will find plenty of ideas on what to say and do in a given situation, but more importantly you will find principles that, if learned and implemented, will enable you to create your own solutions with the certainty that you will then be completely in charge of your own future.

The information contained in this book will present the view that selling today has to be different from in the past, and it will demonstrate that difference by the way it suggests salespeople act in this new market. At the same time it will acknowledge that, according to the Small Business in Australia survey for 1995, there were 785 800 small businesses in Australia whose salespeople work mostly on a one-to-one basis or are largely face-to-face salespeople dealing with prospects who come to them.

The Great Sales Book focuses on the need for every salesperson to become as expert as possible in the art of selling and negotiating. It promotes the view that successful selling is essentially a matter of being a first-class communicator, and that each sales situation is a unique experience brought about by the mix of buyer and seller needs, wants, attitudes and habits, all impacted upon by location, time constraints and the expectations of other interested and involved parties.

Yet the process of selling and buying can be simplified by perceptive participants, and each has to select what they consider is the best course of action to achieve their objective for each particular sale. Perception is a critical issue in every sales presentation. The ability to correctly identify issues as they unfold and select the right response is a skill not every salesperson can claim. Not everyone learns from experience or consistently practises the multiple sales skills that must be mastered if they are to become a peak performer in terms of perception.

There are all types of selling needs, ranging from a simple face-to-face, one-call, single-need sale, to multi-call team negotiation presentations of complex multi-solution sales. They range from the non-technical to high-tech. They can be commercial or industrial and anything in-between, and the sale can be of a product, a service or an idea. Whatever the make-up of the saleable item, someone has to sell it, and the sale can be made to an interested party or an expert buyer. The need of the salesperson for particular skills supported and reinforced by suitable attitudes and habits will not only change from sale to sale but also according to the development of that salesperson. This book is structured so that each individual can locate and turn directly to the area in which they need help at any particular time.

To get the most from this book, be an active reader. Read with a pencil or pen in your hand. When you come across a key idea, strategy or tactic that applies to you, underline it or make notes in the margin. After reading each chapter make a list of selling ideas, concepts or skills that will help you in your sales career and set a plan to put them into practice. Don't wait. Decide what you want to do and go for it.

Have confidence in the ideas that appeal to you and implement them as soon as the opportunity to do so arises. Peak performers know that positive action generally pays off and that the penalties of procrastination are very high, so they consistently focus on what they can do and they do it.

Finally, the changes currently taking place in our working environment are altering our world forever. They are massive and constant, and the future promises no respite. Technology is driving the change in a relentless push that cannot be stopped. The swifter communications become, the more relentless the change. All of this activity is producing new opportunities for each of us if we can see them. The challenge is to see with new eyes, to perceive with new wisdom, and to act with speed and purpose to claim our share of these new and exciting times. Go for it!

ACKNOWLEDGMENTS

My special thanks to Dr Alec Dempster, Consultant Psychiatrist, who so generously contributed to this book by writing Chapter 29, 'Making Personal Progress', and to Bill Leigh for writing the Foreword and providing help and advice on many aspects of today's sales scene. My thanks also go to Des Arcus, Marie Gannon and Ivan Silink who so willingly shared their views on special areas of selling with me, and to Barry Carsons for his kind permission to adapt five of his sales graphics for use in the chapters on communicating and negotiating.

I want to thank the following people for giving their time and sharing their knowledge with my readers by agreeing to be interviewed for this book. Their willingness to help is an inspiration in itself and I am deeply grateful to them:

Alex Hamill	The Gentle Art Of Communicating
Cyndi Kaplan	Presenting Yourself
David Koch	Creating Wealth
Bob Miller	Why People Buy
Harry M. Miller	Negotiating Your Way To Sales Success
Allan Pease	Making Powerful Presentations
Imelda Roche	Selling Buyer Benefits
Carla Zampatti	You, Yourself Incorporated

PART 1

THE

PSYCHOLOGY

OF SELLING

CHAPTER 1

THOUGHTS ON SELLING

*What we think is what we get, so be sure that
what you are thinking is positive and reflects
your current aspirations.*

LET ME SHARE with you some thoughts I have on selling. These thoughts reflect my many years of selling and marketing in one capacity or another, ranging from retailing, through wholesaling, to direct marketing, as well as my careers as a full-time salesperson, marketing manager of one of the world's largest and most successful financial institutions and, now, international speaker and author.

During this time I have trained thousands of people in the art of selling and sales negotiation. They have come from all types of occupations in industry, commerce and government. They have held all levels of positions within their organisation, from driving the delivery van to general manager of the whole organisation. They have sold products and services that have covered all sections of the market, from low-price, basic everyday products and services to high-priced, exclusive products and services — from money to motor cars, lipsticks to lollipops, in country and city locations, selling to all sections of the community.

I believe that . . .

Selling is an exciting, interesting, absorbing and rewarding occupation in which it is possible to decide one's own future. People who are successful in selling have a lifestyle that is the envy of many. Selling makes it possible to become financially successful in a manner and time frame not available in many occupations. Above all, it is possible to be independent and creative without the shackles that many occupations impose.

The business of selling has changed dramatically in the last decade, but this has largely been due to technological advances, not changes in human nature. Technology has supplied us with the means to communicate with prospects and customers in ways that were not previously possible. Computers enable us to organise our work more effectively, and provide creative and flexible ways of demonstrating our ideas and creating *what if?* solutions at the point of sale. Mobile phones, computers and faxes have revolutionised sales communication. They have opened the way to full-scale direct marketing of products on a personal basis. They make it possible to harvest customers in a cost-effective way that is being accepted by many forward-thinking sales organisations.

Technology has also brought many changes to the way sales teams are managed and has made sales individuals more accountable for their performance. It allows salespeople to increase their productivity through the more effective use of their time.

At the same time as technology has been changing the sales scene, the values of the community have changed and are being reflected in government legislation aimed at recognising and protecting the rights of consumers. In some industries it is now mandatory for salespeople to meet specific requirements in terms of evidence of certain types of disclosure. It would seem that this will become the norm in most sales situations.

Changes in communication have seen the community become better informed about products and services in the marketplace, with the result that their expectations have risen greatly. Value for money is just one of the prime expectations of today's consumer. Almost every business is trying to make it easier for the consumer to buy from them, which means that ease of buying has to be considered in the competitive nature of the marketplace.

Even though many people accept technological change and enhancement, there are those who see the changes as a threat instead of an opportunity. Let me assure those people that there really is no cause for worry. You may feel uncomfortable at first, but it is only a change, not a prison sentence, and those who are swift to embrace change as an opportunity will reap the benefits. The timeless saying, 'You have to be in it to win it' applies as much to life as anything else. As Mike Porter said: 'Life is like an ice-cream cone — you either lick it or it drips on your shoes.'

The changes that have come about impact more on our procedures, systems, values and methods of presentation than on the act of making a sale. People's basic nature hasn't changed; their fundamental emotions are still the same. They still desire things for the same reasons. They still resist ideas for the same reasons. They still love, hate, envy, fear, succeed, fail and persist for the same reasons. No amount of change is likely to alter that. If you confuse technological issues with basic human emotions you will limit your success. It matters little whether you make a sales offer by advertising (either by TV or print), letter, phone or face-to-face; it will be emotions that will decide whether you succeed or fail. The communication method is the technology by which you make the offer. The sale will be made, or lost, on human emotion.

Many people think that technology is the ultimate answer to sales success, or that direct marketing to a customer base is the best way to increase sales productivity. Such views fail to answer the core question, which is how to get the most business from existing customers. Whatever advances there are in technology, the three 'Ds' still apply to customers: they die, they desert, they depart. They will always need to be replenished with new customers. That is why prospecting is so critical to sales success.

I have learned that . . .

In selling, offering advice and suggesting courses of action is a very real responsibility. As people will often do as we ask, our commitment must be to discharge that responsibility to the best of our ability so that what we do and sell benefits our prospects and customers.

We can all do and become whatever we are willing to do or become; the only limiting factors are those we place on ourselves. There is no obstacle we cannot overcome if we set our minds to it.

Creative thinking — being able to see threats as opportunities — pays highly, because the world pays a higher price to those who are willing to think and express themselves differently and constructively. Salespeople who think differently have a tremendous advantage over those who don't. Playwright Neil Simon has some wonderful advice on the subject of creativity: 'Don't listen to those who say "It's not done that way" — [if Michelangelo had, he] would have painted the Sistine floor and it would surely be rubbed away by today.'

Personal achievements derive from the power of the human spirit. Life really is a self-fulfilling prophecy, and the greatest sin we can commit is to fail to build the life we want.

Success goes hand-in-hand with hard work, persistency and dedication. Positive, enthusiastic, self-motivated, highly committed, goal-oriented individuals display humankind's greatest qualities.

Adversity strikes most of us at some time in our lives; when it does, the strong grow stronger and the weak wilt and leave. There is nothing too tough to stop some people, while others are simply not strong enough to stand for anything.

People enter jobs in search of a future. They do so with ambition and hope, but many leave with excuses and failure. These people haven't learned that the difference was, and always will be, up to them. As William Feather said: 'Success seems to be largely a matter of hanging on after others have let go.'

Making good plans, writing them down and making a commitment to carry them out has no substitute as a vehicle for success.

In selling, as in life, people see things from their own point of view. The most successful people are those who understand when to compromise and what compromises to make.

The truth is rarely black or white, but tends to lie somewhere in the middle greys. I have learned that trying to *do* everything and *be* everything is a very tough job. But if we get most things right and constantly try to improve, we will build a wonderful life for ourselves and those we love and care for.

If you want a greater measure of success than you now enjoy, if your objective is to get more, see more, be more, do more or have more, whether it is time, money, recognition or travel, your chances of getting it will increase if you turn your desire into a goal. Decide what you want, when it is you want it, agree what it is you'll give in return for what you want, because there are no free lunches, work out a plan and then do it. If you can prepare such a plan, commit to it and see it through with enthusiasm, then you've got it made. Commitment is the key. Winning is the motivation.

It has been said many times that ideas are a dime a dozen, but remember that the ideas you have and don't use are no more effective than the ideas you have never had and can't use.

There is no mystery about what makes organisations successful. It is selling. No organisation ever saved or shrank its way to success; it *sells* its way to success, or it fails. The fuel that fires an organisation's sales system is marketing, advertising and salesmanship, and each of us has a vested interest in all three of these factors. You and I, the people who sell, supply the fuel that fires the sales system, and as long as we supply it in abundance we and the organisations we represent will grow and prosper.

The final ingredient needed to make our success possible is time. Time to make it all happen. Today you have the time — 24 hours, the same as everyone else. What you do with it depends on what you believe. Today you have the time and the opportunity that selling offers to build the life you want. The greatest time of your life awaits you here and now if you want it enough. The opportunities you seek, the rewards you want, can be yours now if you set yourself realistic goals and recognise that work, not time alone, will bring them to reality. If you do all these things, then you are entering a new era of opportunity, happiness and prosperity. Go for it!

CHAPTER 2

INCREASING YOUR SALES PRODUCTIVITY

*Increasing sales productivity
is the constant challenge
for every salesperson.
It strengthens those who embrace it
and weakens those who resist it.*

THERE ARE ONLY three ways to improve your personal sales productivity other than employing someone to do your work for you:

1. Increase the value of your prospects.
2. Improve your selling performance.
3. Work harder.

No matter what you do, or how you do it, it will have to fall into one of these three categories. Let's look at an example. The ratios used may not bear any resemblance to your actual ratios, but the principles are the same as those you contend with every day.

HOW TO IMPROVE YOUR PERSONAL SALES PRODUCTIVITY

Let's use the following example. Say your current ratios are as follows: You call on 100 people over a given time. That's your work effort. You make 10 sales from these 100 calls, so you sell 1 in 10. That's your level of sales skill. Each sale produces $1000 in sales revenue. That's your prospect sales value. From the 10 sales you make, you receive $10 000 in revenue. The value of each of your 100 calls is $100 in revenue. The value of each prospect is $100 in revenue.

If you want to increase your personal sales productivity, you have three choices: increase your prospects' value, become more expert at selling, or work harder.

Increase the value of your prospects

If you work no harder, still see 100 prospects, don't improve at selling and still make 10 sales by selling 1 in 10, but you ask for more when you close each sale and raise your sales value to $1250 per sale, you will have *increased your prospecting productivity by 25 per cent.*

By asking for and receiving more, you have automatically upgraded your prospecting results. If you not only ask for more, but also improve your prospecting skills by taking more care in selecting and qualifying your prospects, then you might get an additional 25 per cent. Thus, by simply asking for more each time you close a sale and at the same time raising the quality of your prospects, you could increase your productivity by 50 per cent.

If you upgraded the quality of your prospects to such an extent that you could get an average of $2000 per sale, then you would have achieved your objective of doubling your sales productivity in one simple process. Before you decide that it can't be done, write down what you would have to do to increase your prospecting results by 100 per cent. You will be surprised at how easy it is to increase your sales productivity by employing this method. It may also be helpful to read the chapter on prospecting as you evaluate your prospecting possibilities.

Improve your selling performance

Let's say you work no harder, you still see 100 people, you don't improve your prospecting and you still receive $1000 per sale, but you do improve your selling skills and now make 12.5 sales: your ratio of selling skills is now 1 in 8 instead of 1 in 10. You have raised your sales productivity by 20 per cent, simply by selling 1 in 8 instead of 1 in 10.

How might you do this? Are you going to improve your ability to get interviews? Will you become better at answering objections and reaching agreement? Will you use a prepared sales presentation and visual aids, where presently you do it off the top of your head? Are you going to learn a new questioning technique? Are you going to close more sales by improving your ability to ask for the order?

Whatever you do to improve your selling skills has the potential to increase your sales productivity by 50 per cent or more. Before you review your present selling skills, read the chapters in this book which relate to the areas you want to focus on — you'll be surprised at how many useful ideas you will find.

If you improve your prospecting skills by 33⅓ per cent and your selling skills by 33⅓ per cent, then you will improve your sales productivity by more than 66 per cent. This result can often be achieved by simply changing your attitudes. Go for it!

Work harder

You can work harder in one of two ways. The first way is to ask more people to buy what you sell. Don't work longer hours, but in the same amount of time ask more people to buy. The other alternative is not to increase your asking rate but to work longer hours.

Let's say you still get $1000 per sale and still sell 1 in 10 (so your prospecting and selling skills haven't improved), but instead of seeing 100 prospects you see 125: you will increase your productivity by 25 per cent by working harder.

How might you do this without working longer hours? You can do it through better planning and preparation, by using your time more effectively, by planning your sales calls so that you don't have to travel long distances between calls, and by adopting seminar selling methods so that instead of talking to one prospect at a time you talk to 20 or 50. Use the available technology to increase your asking rate.

As before, assess what you would need to do, and how you would have to change, in order to see 125 people in the time it now takes you to see 100. If you achieve this, you will have increased your sales productivity by 25 per cent.

Let's say you have increased the value of your prospects by 33⅓ per cent, improved your selling skills by 33⅓ per cent and see 33⅓ per cent more prospects: you will have doubled your sales productivity. In many cases this can be done by simply changing your attitude, brushing up on your selling skills and using time more effectively.

THE IMPORTANCE OF ATTITUDE

The principles illustrated above apply to every sales activity, whether it be in real estate, motor vehicles, computers or any other industry.

There are no other ways of improving personal sales productivity for any of us who are in the selling business. Why then do so many salespeople fail to use these simple measures to increase their productivity? It's because they adopt the attitude of 'This is who I am' or 'This is what I do'; they keep on doing what they are accustomed to doing and feel comfortable doing. Very few of them sit down at the start of a new year or a new period, review their performance and decide to increase their productivity by a specific amount. They tend to let it all happen to them, rather than taking charge and making their career go the way they want it to go. Their failure to increase their productivity stems from their attitude.

This book will show that it is possible to double your sales volume not by increasing your workload, but by changing your attitudes and adopting methods that will enable you to sell smarter not harder. Because of its central importance, the subject of attitude will be discussed throughout this book with specific chapters covering topics which are crucial to success like commitment, being a salesperson, the job of selling, thinking big and paying the price. Very simply, our attitude governs our selling performance. Let's look at some examples which you can refer to whenever you want a motivational lift.

Thinking big

How often do we dream of the finer things we will do? The great accomplishments? The richer life that will be ours? We know there are great opportunities waiting. We know they can be our opportunities if we will but take the first step to grasp them. If we follow through with an earnest routine of steady and effective daily work and study, then the opportunities can be ours.

Tomorrow, we say to ourselves, we will get started for sure. Tomorrow we will put that new idea to work, or tomorrow we will change our routine to enable us to do more in the hours available, to be better at prospecting, to increase our sales. Tomorrow there will be time. But tomorrow becomes today and we are still on the same old road doing the same things we always do. We are slaves on the treadmill of our habits.

We attend meetings, seminars and conventions. We hear how others have made the change, how their lives have been enriched by extra performance, and we plan. We plan to change tomorrow. Tomorrow we will start, always tomorrow. The sadness of our wasted tomorrows that never come! But this book is about today, not tomorrow — it's about what we can do *now*.

So I want you to start today, while you are reading this book. I want you to start by adopting the concept of thinking big as a way of life. A marvellous magic is generated by thinking big, by practising everlasting optimism in the midst of pessimism and doubt. Think big, plan big and act big. Remember always to think big not about problems but about positive possibilities. Think big not about obstacles but about opportunities. Be receptive to change, to new ideas, especially those changes and ideas that confront you today. Take advantage of them. Work on them. Step off the treadmill of habit. Take charge of your life. To have free choice and not exercise it is to deny opportunity. Today is your opportunity; don't miss it on the promise of tomorrow.

Start thinking big now. Set yourself the challenge of doubling your sales. You might think it can't be done. Perhaps it can't with your present methods and attitudes. But *what if*? If you changed your methods and attitudes, could you do it then? If you still have doubts, take a different approach. Ask yourself: If I want to double my sales, what will I have to do? Instead of saying it can't be done, do the exercise overleaf on page 14.

After doing the exercise, you may have decided that perhaps it *can* be done, but you are unwilling to do this or that or to give up something in order to get what you want. Now you are not talking about how to double your sales; you are talking about paying the price, which is the first obstacle to doubling your sales.

Paying the price

Paying the price for what we want in life is a key issue for those of us who want to succeed above the ordinary. Pay little, and we will get little from life. If we want little from life, the price is small. The more we want, the more it costs. Success is limited by the price we are willing to pay. The price is not paid in money. It is paid in knowledge,

Take several sheets of paper and go somewhere where you will be alone and undisturbed.

1. List all those things you would need to do in order to double your sales volume now.
Consider everything, discount nothing.

2. List all those things you would need to stop doing in order to double your sales volume now.

3. List the names of anyone who you think would be willing to help you make the changes you wish to make. If you can't think of anyone, write my name down and call me.

activity, creative thinking, innovation, identification, preparation, commitment, compromise and a willingness to change.

Unless utopia has arrived unannounced, compromise on our part will be necessary. To compromise is a fact of life. All of life is a compromise. Trading off one aspiration against another is a reflection of our willingness to pay a particular price. Everything demands a price; the trick is to pay the right price for the right thing, to know when to compromise and which compromises to make. Do you know your prices? Do you understand that you are currently paying only sufficient to get your current rate of success, and that if you want more success then you will have to raise the price? Let's consider three of the most important prices you need to pay if you want to enjoy a higher level of success.

◆ **Identification.** Do you know what you want? Do you know when you want it? Do you know how to get it? How will you know when you have it? Most important of all, have you decided what you must give in return for that which you expect to get? There are no free lunches. If we want to win, we must ask ourselves these elementary questions, yet very few people take the time to clearly identify their goals.

Have you written down your goals? Why not? Do you expect to achieve them just by doing your best? In most cases, it's not that easy. Having a clearly defined objective, a specific date for its accomplishment and a logical written plan will increase your chances enormously. The answers won't come to you on a galloping horse in a high wind on a dark night. You need to be able to identify your goals clearly so that you can visualise them constantly. Keep them uppermost in your mind, because, in some way never made clear to us, nature ensures that the events that we vividly imagine on the life screen of our minds and support with purposeful action and faith will come to pass. That's the way people achieve. That's the way it is. If you don't care where you are going, you are bound to succeed. Read Chapter 26, 'Achieving Your Goals' for the answers that will get you the success you desire.

◆ **Preparation.** Now that you know where you want to go, you are in a position to prepare for the journey. While people's needs may differ, identification and preparation are vital for everyone. How long is it since you read a book on your current job? On the job you would like to have? How long is it since you read a book on management, so that you can understand both sides of the coin? How many motivational tapes do you own? How often do you listen to them? What are your plans for improving at what you do? The list is almost endless, but it's part of the price you must pay to achieve success if that's what you want. But the fact that you are reading this book shows that within you is the essence of the success you need and want.

◆ **Commitment.** Of all the prices to pay, commitment is the most important. Without commitment it is doubtful that you will pay any other price. You will need absolute dedication of purpose to stay with your plan long enough to make it count. Very few plans run smoothly and very few worthwhile objectives are achieved easily. So when the going toughens up, it is then that you need the grim determination of absolute commitment. It has been said that success is a day-by-day, inch-by-inch struggle towards the goal ahead.

My message to you is: clearly define your goals, prepare yourself for the journey and then commit yourself to the job ahead. It will not be easy; everything has a price. But if you are willing to pay that price and commit yourself to the attainment of your goals, then you are almost certain to get there. I am no clairvoyant, I can't see into the future, but I *can* predict the consequences of certain actions with great accuracy. For instance, I can promise you that if you read this book but make no changes and continue to work as usual, then you will produce as usual and get the same result. If you don't change the cause, you won't change the result. If you do this year exactly as you did last year, then don't be surprised if you get the same result. Like begets like.

In the business of selling, most people fall into three broad groups:

◆ *Those who are new in the business.* Generally, they work hard but need to improve their prospecting and selling skills.

◆ *Those who have been in the business for some time and who are making a good income.* They generally have good prospecting and selling skills, but many don't work as hard as they could. By working hard, I mean asking more prospects to buy. Many salespeople who are doing well could ask more people to buy what they sell. If your level of income decides how hard you work, you may be missing out on the pleasure of ultimate accomplishment, which is the knowledge that you are performing at the peak of your ability.

◆ *Those who fall into the large middle group.* Although they could improve in all three areas of prospecting, selling skills and working harder, they are largely satisfied with their present level of achievement.

Whichever group you fall into, you may be pleasantly surprised at how little you need to do to increase your sales productivity and prospect your way to millions. Go for it!

CHAPTER 3

PROSPECTING YOUR WAY TO MILLIONS

Without prospects, a salesperson has no business.
The quality of our prospects decides the
level of our success.

OF ALL THE skills required by a salesperson, prospecting is the most important. No prospects, no business. You can be a master of every other skill, but unless you are a master prospector you won't make much of a living. Prospecting is the most important skill in selling, and the most neglected. Many of us have a good client base supplied by our employer, so we don't worry about finding new prospects. If we're not careful, we can fall into the habit of calling on customers and taking orders for what they want to buy. Peak performers do more than just take orders — they prospect their clients. They are always looking for ways to help their customers increase their productivity and profits. They see their customers' business as being their own business, because they know that when their customer grows, they grow. They also know that customers and prospects change, and so they are always looking for changes because change represents opportunity. When people have to change, they must open their minds; in doing so, they become open to other changes.

THE CHANGING WORKPLACE

The industrial and manufacturing society which has served us so well for over 100 years is being replaced by a new information society. You are in the right place at the right time. What you do with the opportunity will depend on you. The communications industry has spawned hundreds of occupations in which a large number of people will be employed. It will play a major role in the national economy and for that reason will become a major source of prospects to those of us who are in the business of selling. Are you ready to take advantage of the changing workplace?

The birth of the information society and the growth of the communications industry doesn't mean the death of manufacturing. Manufacturing will remain a vital part of our country's economy and products will be as important as ever, but what products? Who will make them? How will they be sold? Who will sell them? Where do you fit in? How will the new information society affect what you do? What do you need to do in terms of self-development in order to keep up with and take advantage of what's happening? All these questions are important to anyone in the business of selling, no matter what your product or service.

Let's look at some other trends in the marketplace so that you can better prepare yourself for the changes that are taking place.

◆ *The greying of society.* Can this mean business for you?

◆ *The purchasing power of the two-income family.* Are you getting your share?

◆ *The death of old industries and the birth of new ones.* Can you identify them? Where are they, and what do they want in terms of goods and services? How can you help them to get what they want and need?

◆ *The wealth created by inflation.* Who are the newly wealthy and what could they mean for you?

◆ *The opportunities in the financial services market.* How can you take advantage of them?

◆ *The easy availability of money.* Are you ready to show your clients and your prospects how to use money to get rich?

◆ *The growth of self-employed people.* Many people who are retrenched start up their own business. Are you getting your share of this growth in small business?

The opportunities are endless for salespeople who are prepared to search out new markets and new prospects. Let's now look at how to become a master prospector.

HOW TO PROSPECT YOUR WAY TO MILLIONS

If you want to win more, sell more, have more, earn more and be more, then become a master prospector. The process of finding prospects for what you sell must become a way of life: a way of thinking and of doing. The bells must always be ringing. You must see people and situations in a prospecting sense, ever alert to the possibilities and opportunities that present themselves every minute of the day. While you are reading this book, your customers and prospects are making changes that will affect your business. If you are on the ball and wide awake, most of these changes can benefit you. If you are too slow in reacting, someone else will seize the advantage in your place. Peak performance selling is just that: always being at your peak, always looking for opportunities and prospects, and being committed to improving the productivity and prospects of your customers.

Pandemonium, or crisis, prospecting, with all its problems and disadvantages, is not for us. The price — lost prospects and customers and a diminishing of our future success — is too high.

To become a master prospector you must be able to recognise a prospect when you see one or hear about one. The best way to do this is to have a superior understanding of what your product or service will do for those who buy it. Remember that your product or service will do nothing for those who don't buy it, and you can't sell to the prospects you don't have. The problem with most of us lies not in not knowing what to do, but in not doing what we know.

There are three aspects of prospecting:

1. Organising prospect and client information.
2. Analysing your sales performance.
3. Organising your daily and weekly activity.

Organising prospect and client information

Prospecting is a process and therefore needs a systematic method of controlling its functions and activities. The system should be simple and easy to manage. It will require your daily attention, or it will break down and then it's back to pandemonium again. You should make it a rule of your operation that you bring your prospecting system up to date every day, so that the paper war doesn't get on top of you.

You should divide your information files into a prospects file and a clients file.

◆ *Prospects file*. In this file you keep all the information you need on each of your prospects. It should be in alphabetical order for ease of access. A plain box system with an alphabetical index which will take 13 cm x 8 cm plain cards will work very effectively, or you may wish to put them on file in your computer. Each time you get a prospect, fill out the information card, name, address, home and work contact numbers, and any other information that may help turn the prospect into a customer. Then file the card. If you do this each day, you will always have a basic card on each of your prospects.

◆ *Clients file*. Each time one of your prospects becomes a client, move them into your clients file.

Your information system now contains all the current information on your prospects and clients, and makes access and updating easy when the need arises. Alternatively, if you have a computer, you can run your information system on that and bring it up to date as you complete each call.

If your organisation provides you with prospects via a computer printout, you will be saved the trouble of setting up a card system. Whatever your system, you need to be able to access the information you want, when you want it. Use the system that will work best for you.

Analysing your sales performance

You have your prospects and your clients in an information file, but you also need a system that allows you to see your total prospecting situation at a glance. Try this method and see if it works for you. You can see an example of how it works on pages 22–3.

◆ Get yourself a hardcover, A4-size ruled book. Open the book so that you have a double page open at a glance. Across the top of the page write the month.

◆ Rule the left-hand page into four equal columns. Number the columns. Call the first two columns 'Prospects secured this month', and call columns 3 and 4 'Prospects to see this month', as shown in the example overleaf. You can now record each new prospect (name only) obtained and plan which prospects you will see this month. The system is entirely flexible; adapt it to meet your own needs.

◆ Now turn your attention to the right-hand page and rule it into four equal columns. Number the columns as shown in the example. Call column 5 'Clients to see this month', column 6 'Prospects to close this month', column 7 'Sales made this month' and column 8 'Dollar amount of sale'. If you are a commission salesperson, then call column 8 'Dollar commission earned'.

◆ Now enter into columns 3 and 4, 'Prospects to see this month', the names of all the prospects from your information file that you intend to approach this month. As you get new prospects during the month, enter them in columns 1 and 2 under the heading 'Prospects secured this month'.

◆ In column 5, 'Clients to see this month', enter the names of all your existing clients from your clients file that you intend to see this month.

◆ In column 6, 'Prospects to close this month', write the names of all those you intend to make a presentation to with the objective of making a sale.

◆ Each time you make a sale, enter the name in column 7 and the amount in column 8.

Your entire prospecting and sales performance situation is now revealed to you at a glance every working day. If you choose to put your system on a computer, it needs to be in the same format because its effectiveness depends on seeing it all at once. There is nowhere to hide in this system. It is ruthless in exposing any of your selling weaknesses. This is its strength for peak performance salespeople, because they are always looking for improvement and their rewards come from knowing they are performing at the limits of their ability.

Follow the procedure described above and prepare double pages in your book for every month of the year. Consider each prospect. If you are satisfied that a prospect is of no value, cross their name off the list and do nothing more; the prospect will fall out of your system. If you see a prospect and he or she says, 'Come and see me in a month or three months or a couple of weeks', then simply move the prospect's name forward to the appropriate month to the 'Prospects to see this month' column. If there is a possibility of closing a prospect and you

Sales Performance at a Glance			
1	2	3	4
Prospects secured this month	Prospects secured this month	Prospects to see this month	Prospects to see this month
1 W. Mathews	7 J. Phillips	1 W. Dobson	7 L. Armitage
2 L.Williamsl	8 G. Mendolson	2 H. Gladman	8 P.Nicholls
3 D.Hadrill	9 R.Donaldson	3 V. Killan	9 D. Leven
4 J. Fallon	10 K. Palin	4 D Gollan	10 J. Lorrin
5 N. Lorigan	11 H. Zegrov	5 K. Chekovic	11 S. McDonald
6 A. Beardsly	12 C. Nolan	6 D. Buchanan	12 L.Fenton

make an appointment for later in the month, then enter their name in the 'Prospects to close this month' column.

As you call on clients listed in the 'Clients to see this month' column, take the same action. If it is a service call and nothing eventuates from it, add information about your call to the client's card and return it to the clients file. If clients become a prospect for further business, then list them under the 'Prospects to close this month' column or move their names forward to the month in which you intend to present the business. When you make a sale, enter it in the 'Sales made this month' column.

On the last day of each month, move the names of prospects you have not seen to the next month's 'Prospects to see this month' column. Do the same with prospects to close and clients to see. The next month, write all new prospects into the 'Prospects secured this month' column.

After you have brought your monthly system up to date at the end of the month, it is time to analyse your activity and sales results for the period just ended so that your next month's planning will be based on real current figures. Do this by filling in the analysis section at the bottom of columns 6, 7 and 8. Your analysis of activity and sales results should look like the diagram opposite. (The statistics in the diagram bear no relation to the records shown in the at-a-glance diagram. They have been used to make analysis possible without a calculator.)

Was it a peak performance month, or was it a disaster full of disappointments and problems? Whatever the result, you need to know why. The only way to keep on top of your selling performance is

Month of: _____			
5	**6**	**7**	**8**
Clients to see this month	**Prospects to close this month**	**Sales made this month**	**Dollar amount of sale ($)**
1 H. Mallory	1 J. Phillips	1 V. Donaldson	1567
2 F. Cahill	2 L. Mallinson	2 M. Clauson	10 496
3 C. Zylstra	3 M. Clauson	3 V. Killan	26 789
4 L. Mangelsdorf	4 K. Palin	4 K. Palin	4 987
5 F. Gleghaus	5 H. Zegrov	5 K. Chekovic	31 800
6 A. Beardsly	6 V. Donaldson	6 S. McGrath	62 197

Analysis of Activity and Sales Results

Telephone	
Number of calls made	20
Interviews obtained	4
Sales made	1
Calls to interviews ratio	5 to 1
Interviews to sales ratio	4 to 1
Calls to sales ratio	20 to 1
Face to Face	
Number of calls made	12
Interviews obtained	4
Sales made	2
Calls to interviews ratio	3 to 1
Interviews to sales ratio	2 to 1
Calls to sales ratio	6 to 1
Sale and Call Value ($)	
Total value of sales	11 400
Dollar value of each sale	3800
Dollar value of each phone call	190
Dollar value of each face-to-face call	643
Total earnings for month	

to consistently analyse your performance and develop a set of ratios that show month by month how well you are performing.

Here are some things to watch out for:

◆ How many new prospects did you secure for the month? If you need 100 a month to make the income you require and to succeed at the level you aspire to and you only secured 75, then you are running on prospecting overdraft. You will reach your limit when you exhaust your present store of prospects. When you do, you will be out of business.

◆ How many prospects did you see during the month? If your usual closing rate is 1 in 6 (that is, you see three prospects to get an interview, and you make a sale from every two interviews), then your ratio of prospects to sales is 1 in 6 and you need 20 sales a month to be successful, you will have to see 120 prospects a month. If that was your plan, did you achieve it?

Your ratio of customers seen to sales made is critical in planning for peak performance. You must establish reliable sales ratios that will make it possible for you to plan your success in advance. There may be some salespeople who believe this doesn't apply to them. WRONG — it applies to everyone who sells, without exception. You may need to deal with different information or be looking for different ratios, but ratios are essential for effective planning. Not knowing your ratios doesn't mean they don't exist; it just means you don't know them. If you are successful without knowing your ratios, think how much more you will achieve when you know precisely what is happening.

Here is a simple but powerful example of how analysis of ratios can disclose problems. Two salespeople, Mike and Richard, each achieve a sale in every 12 calls on new prospects. Mike's ratios show that it takes six calls to get an interview and two interviews to make a sale — 12 calls for one sale. Richard takes two calls to get an interview, but it takes him six interviews to make a sale — 12 calls for one sale. Both achieve the same result, but each has a different problem. Mike needs to improve his ability to get interviews, and Richard needs to improve his closing skills. There are many variations on performance to be analysed, some of which can be complex but all of which will improve your ability to double your sales, master the art of selling and reach peak performance selling on a consistent basis.

The advantage of this system is that it is a complete prospect-at-a-glance system. You can see how many prospects you are getting, the number of prospects you are seeing, the number of clients you are servicing, the number of prospects who are close to closing, and the number of sales you are making. This prospect activities system works regardless of the product or service being sold, and it will work for YOU.

Organising your daily and weekly activity

In order to keep track of the calls, interviews and sales you make each day, you need to have a planner in which to record this activity. At the end of each week or month, you can then analyse your activity records to establish current sales ratios. The following diagram of a basic activity planner shows part of a day's activity.

Daily Activity Planner				
Date:				
		Call	Interview	Sale
7.00	James West	1		
8.30	Sharon Telford		2	
9.00	Glen Hartford	1		
9.30	Sam Willings	2		
10.00	Sandra Daylesford	1	1	Yes
10.30				
11.00				
11.30				
12.00				
12.30				

West is shown as a first call: no interview or sale. Telford was a second interview: no sale. Hartford was a first call: no interview or sale. Willings was a second call: no interview or sale. Daylesford was a first call which resulted in a first interview which produced a sale.

Although this is a very simple example of sales activity, the results over a week or a month can produce information which, if used correctly, can be of enormous help in improving sales skills and planning sales activities.

You should have a method of planning your daily and weekly prospecting and selling activity so that you are always ready to prospect and sell. There are a number of highly effective daily and weekly work organisers on the market, any of which would do this part of your sales work very effectively. Preparation is one of the hallmarks of being a peak performer; crisis control is a hallmark of being a loser.

Your basic weekly sales planning will need to answer the following questions:

◆ Who do I plan to see this week?
◆ Who do I plan to sell to this week?
◆ Where will I get the prospects to replace those I see this week?
◆ What preparation must I do for next week?

The best time to prepare for next week is on the last day of this week. Say you set aside Friday afternoons as organisation time. This becomes your time for catching up with what you have to do to finish off the current week and for planning what you will do next week. This basic decision about preparation and planning is one of the most critical decisions you will make in your selling career, for it is here that you must choose whether you will let events run you or whether you are going to take charge of your life and organise your activities so that you run the events. This is what the decision boils down to. Remember: not making a decision is a decision in itself.

Occasionally you will have to change your plans because of events over which you have no control. However, as your planning improves, you will be surprised how easy it becomes to adapt your plans to unforeseen events and to remain in the winners' circle.

Although careful preparation may seem like too much trouble, it is a way of avoiding trouble not creating it. Our habits are a key issue in our selling effectiveness, and this is what we are dealing with here. Are you willing to develop habits that will ensure your success, or are you going to succumb to habits that ensure mediocrity or failure? You must choose, because neither bad nor good habits can happen without your consent.

This system of planning is easy and proven to be highly successful. If you choose another system, be sure that it contains the principles inherent in this system, for it is the principles that are critical to success.

USE THESE GUIDELINES WHEN DOING
YOUR WEEKLY SALES PLANNING

1. Go through your prospects file and make sure all of this week's activities are complete and the system is up to date.

2. Prepare any presentations you will need for next week. Try to avoid doing them on the run as you need them, as this will take more time and decrease your selling effectiveness. If your presentations are written and contain recurring items, prepare a master copy with spaces left blank for the specific details of each prospect. Read the section on how to sell written presentations in Chapter 16, 'Making Powerful Presentations'.

3. Enter in the appropriate place in your weekly activity planner the names and times of appointments you have with prospects and clients for next week.

4. Working around your appointments, enter in your planner the times you propose to call on prospects or clients with whom you have no appointment. Get their cards from your files and attach any relevant information or questions you intend to ask.

5. Collect the cards and other materials you will need in a file for each day, so that all you have to do is pick up the file and you are on your way — not only to see your prospects and clients, but also to a very successful and prosperous career in selling.

6. After each call, make a note on the client's or prospect's card. Add the names of any prospects obtained to your planner. When you return to base, transfer them to your prospects file and mark off customers and prospects seen for the day. Done daily, this activity will save you more than an hour of Friday afternoon preparation time.

METHODS OF PROSPECTING

Now that we are organised, we can do some prospecting. There are many methods of prospecting, and most salespeople will use more than one method. The main methods are cold calling, observation prospecting, referral prospecting, centres of influence prospecting, servicing existing clients and lifestyle prospecting. We will consider each of these separately, but before we do it is important to emphasise that the first requirement in prospecting is to have total knowledge of what your product or service can do for those who buy it. Being a good prospector means looking beyond the obvious; it means having a clear picture of your prospects and a feel for what you sell that translates into creative thinking. A friend who was trying to sell a tax-advantaged investment program to a high-income earner failed on the first attempt but later sold him the same program to finance a walking trip around Scotland. Whatever type of prospecting you are considering, look beyond the obvious if you want outstanding results.

All prospecting relies on two factors: you either have a name and you hang a need on it, or you have a need and you hang a name on it. For example, you are at a function and you are introduced to Elizabeth Preston, who owns a successful public relations business. Elizabeth has a need for any product or service that will open doors to greater opportunities for her business or increase the productivity and profits of her existing business. You have her name, now all you have to do is to make the connection between what you offer and what she needs. The other alternative is to find people like Elizabeth whose needs your product or service will meet. Let's look at how you might do that.

Cold calling

While not the most popular method, cold calling works very well for some salespeople. In fact, I have known some people who get most of their business this way. Cold calling is often the first method used by new salespeople because they have not had enough experience or time to build up the other methods. Cold calling is an art in itself. It requires the ability to think on one's feet and a willingness to call on strangers. The most effective way of using this method is to have a sales presentation backed up with attention-grabbing visuals and to call on those you perceive to have the need around which your presentation has been built. In order to make cold calling effective, you need to master the art of making approaches. Some of these will be dealt with in Chapter 6, 'Be A Master At Making The Sales Approach'. Cold call prospectors rely on lists of names of individuals or organisations, or they go to locations such as shopping centres and look for those who have a need for what they sell. Usually, they start with industries that use a product or service similar to their own.

Observation prospecting

Observation prospecting is the ability to make sound prospecting judgments based on what you see. For this method to work, you need to become more than a casual observer. Looking for prospects has to become a way of life for you. Wherever you go, wherever you are, your frame of mind must be one of constantly looking for prospects. In shopping centres, look for new businesses, new employees or new products; in industrial areas look out for new factories and companies. All the time you are looking for the people behind these new activities. Don't just be a looker, be a careful observer. Look for the need and then try for the names or find the names, and then look for the need. No matter what business you are in, observation prospecting is one of the most powerful tools for finding good prospects.

Look in newspapers, periodicals, house magazines, government gazettes, trade papers and seminar attendance lists. Subscribe to newsletters and publications that feature information on trends and events that are important to your industry. Not only will you get prospects from these sources, but you will also find excellent ideas and trends that you can use with some of your customers to help increase their profits and productivity. Here is an example. I run 'Ideas' seminars for business and during the seminar I discuss 50 or more ideas for improving profit in a business. At one seminar I mentioned an idea for using benefit price signs to improve sales, based on an article I had read by Professor Patrick Kelly, K-Mart Chair of Marketing Management at Wayne State University in the US. After the seminar a young woman who said she sold to hardware stores asked for a copy of the material to give to the owners of a store with whom she had been trying to do business. She called me later to say how pleased they were to get the information and how impressed they were with her efforts on their behalf. Naturally, she was pleased to get an account which until then had not been possible. Doing business isn't always just about our products and services; on many occasions it is about unrelated things we do to show that our main interest is to help our customer or prospect succeed in their business.

Whether you are selling real estate, insurance, cars, advertising or anything else, you need to look for changes in the lives of individuals. Changes make people receptive to thinking about their situation. They can be job changes, businesses bought and sold, marriages, births, success stories, ambition stories, company registrations or debt registrations. (Those selling out are as important as those buying in.) Whenever changes occur, possibilities exist for salespeople, because those who are part of the change are open to new possibilities and so are most likely to be receptive to suggestions. When changes occur in organisations, some things are going to be done differently. New services will be needed, new products will be bought, new people will be hired. Outsourcing may occur — do you want to be considered? If you do, you have to be there and know what's happening. You need to be constantly alert to opportunities. Thousands of people who were previously employed as executives in all kinds of businesses are now setting up their own businesses. They need a great variety of products and services. Get a list of new business registrations and call those new owners — you may soon be doing business with a number of them.

Here is another example of observation prospecting. My book *Yes You Can* is a personal development book on mind power, time and goals, which has been very successful. I have since noticed three organisations with slogans similar to my book title. Two had adopted the slogan 'Yes You Can', the other 'Yes We Can'. I rang the senior executives involved, two of whom I knew personally. The third was unknown to me. I followed the same approach with each. Here is how all three conversations went.

SE: Good morning.

JC: Good morning. My name is Jack Collis and I am calling to congratulate you and your organisation on your slogan 'Yes You/We Can'.

SE: Do you like it?

JC: I sure do, so much so that I wrote a book on the subject. *Yes You Can* is 240 pages of how to win in life, and from your slogan I believe that's what you want your people to do.

SE: Yes, we do. Can I get a copy of the book?

JC: Yes, you can. I'll send you one today.

We had a short conversation about the slogan and I sent the book. The three bought around 800 copies between them.

Referral prospecting

Referrals are probably the most effective method of prospecting. Most salespeople don't use them as often as they should. Many salespeople find it difficult to ask for referrals and tend to wait for them to come of their own accord. No matter what product or service you sell, at the conclusion of every sale you should ask for referred leads. If you have done your job well and your customer likes you and your service, they will consider it a compliment to be asked and most will respond by giving good names because they would really like to help them as well as you.

Although popular opinion seems to be that you should ask for referred leads only from clients, it is my view that you should end every presentation by asking for referrals whether you make the sale or not. Many of those to whom you make your presentation will be very impressed with the way you went about your business, and even if they are unable to buy they will be willing to give you other prospects because they believe you are the type of person people like to do business with. Research indicates that referral selling is the most powerful method of prospecting. The success of referrals lies in the recommendation given by the third party. The introduction says to their friend or associate that it is okay for them to do business with you. Referral prospecting is twice as effective as any other method, yet many people don't use it because they fear rejection or don't want to be seen as being pushy.

One method of asking for referrals, called 'Who do you know?', is designed to ask for referred leads from anyone you approach. They don't have to be a client, although those who are satisfied with a purchase are usually not only willing to help by giving referrals but anxious to do so. The 'Who do you know?' presentation is based on the principle that most of those we ask for referred leads will think of some names but decide that those people won't want our product or service. As a result, they often reply: 'I don't know anyone.' The way around this is to ask 'Who do you know?' and then describe the type of person you believe would buy your product or service. Here is an example.

You sell CD-ROM kits for computers. They are an add-on kit for those who have a computer but not the CD-ROM facility. You have

32 The Great Sales Book

just finished delivering and installing a kit for Bruce Jamison who runs his direct marketing business from home. You are now on first-name terms and you want referrals, so you say:

'Bruce, thank you for your business. It's been a pleasure dealing with you. No doubt you realise that most of my business is done with people like yourself who are operating their own businesses from home, or perhaps a business location, and have a computer and now realise they need a CD-ROM facility. Bruce, who do you know who is in their own business who fits this description, and if you were me who would you see first?'

By directing Bruce's attention to specific types of people, it becomes easier for him to identify those he knows who fit your description. However, Bruce is not only thinking of names but also about whether they might want a CD-ROM facility and whether they will want to buy one now. Now is the time to add:

'Bruce, I don't expect you to decide whether or not they want to buy now, because many of them will not know themselves until the opportunity to buy arises. What I would like is for you to withhold judgment on whether they'll buy and I'll ask them. That way we can be sure of not making a mistake. Okay?'

Now wait while Bruce thinks. He will probably respond with:

'Jack, I was telling my friend Gordon that I was getting a CD-ROM and he said he would have a look at it when it was working, so I think Gordon would be interested.'

Write Gordon's name and contact details on your prospect list and then wait for more names. If necessary, keep prompting with 'Who do you know' questions. Lead him to give you more names as though giving names were an everyday occurence.

Say, 'Bruce, I only want the opportunity to show them the kit. Whether they are in the market to buy now is not important. When they are ready they will come to me if I show them now, and you can rely on me absolutely to look after their interests as I have yours. That's fair enough, isn't it?'

When you have the names, say: 'Bruce, would you mind giving Gordon a call and telling him I can see him in about an hour? You might tell him about your system at the same time. OK?'

When it is time to leave, it is also time to thank Bruce again for his business and for helping with referrals.

When you are asking for leads, describe the people you have in mind by their age, occupation, income, locality, sex or other relevant characteristic. If you make it a habit of asking for referred leads, you will be highly rewarded by the number you get. Remember: those who cannot ask, cannot live; and those who don't ask, don't receive.

Centres of influence prospecting

Centres of influence prospecting, also called networking, is a highly successful method based on people's tendency to help those who help them. Centres of influence don't necessarily have to be satisfied customers. For the same reasons that people who don't buy from you will still give you referrals, they can become your best centres of influence. Not everyone can buy and not everyone is willing to help, but if you identify a network of people who you think could help you by referring prospects to you, then it is up to you to go about developing them as a centre of influence.

Here is a real example. My territory was in the country in south-west New South Wales. I serviced several towns other than the one I lived in. One town and its surrounding districts was a key part of my territory and I was there most weeks. After about six months, the father of one of my new clients said to me: 'If it would help you, you are welcome to use one of my spare offices when you are in town.' He was in the general insurance business and not only gave me the use of an office but also referred many of his general clients to me for their life business. He became a major centre of influence for me in that town.

One of the easiest ways is to simply ask for people's help. If they are unable to help at that time, don't forget them but list them in your system and keep in touch. The golden rule for centres of influence and referred lead prospecting is always to report back on the prospects people have given you. Set up a schedule of visits to your centres of influence. Don't always rely on telephone contact. Pay them the compliment of taking them to lunch occasionally. Above all, don't go too long without seeing them face to face. In almost every walk of life there are those who stand out as people of influence. These are the people you need to cultivate, and you should always do your best to return the compliment. When you are talking with your centres of influence, use the 'Who do you know?' technique. It works, if you work it.

Your centres of influence people need to be educated about and kept aware of all the products and services you offer. When new brochures come out, make sure they get one. When a special deal is on offer, make sure they know about it. When a new product is launched, take the time to go and tell them about it.

Servicing existing clients

Many salespeople neglect those who have become customers. They tend to treat them as if they own them. They take them for granted, which is a sure-fire way of losing them. Constantly review your client's needs and wants. However well we know people, it is often difficult to understand exactly what it is they want. Have a wants presentation for your clients and go through it regularly to make sure you aren't missing out on anything they want.

Use your prospecting organisation system to ensure that you see them face to face on a regular basis. If that's not possible, call them on the phone or write to them and thank them for doing business with you.

Many books have been written on how to develop your customers so that they stay with you. Remember the three Ds: they die, they desert, they depart. You can't do much about the first D, but you can do a lot about the second. Research shows that they desert because they believe they are not treated as someone of value. In one survey 68 per cent gave as the reason for leaving a business, 'They didn't care about me'. It doesn't matter that you value them and are in touch often. The only reality is their perception. If they feel they aren't valued, then they aren't valued. The critical issue is staying in touch. Send newsletters, involve them in surveys, send them thank-you notes. Stay in constant touch and show them you care. Most of your opposition won't take this trouble.

Keep your customers on a database and send them offers of other products and services. Run customer campaigns with give-aways for responding. Send your clients customers for their business, and do reciprocal business with them wherever possible. It is six times as easy to maintain an existing customer as to find a new one. It is much easier to sell to an existing customer than to a new prospect. You have done the hard work in selling to them in the first place, so make sure you harvest the benefits of the relationship you have developed.

Lifestyle prospecting

Lifestyle prospecting is about using modern technology to do some of our lead generation for us. Most businesses today use computers to produce mailing lists, letters, etc. Direct mail is an excellent way to get to large numbers of people with an offer which generates leads for us now. For instance, we can get lists of people based on their occupation, age or income. We can get lists of people who play different sports, or who are interested in art, music or books. The types of lists are almost endless.

If you don't have your own list, then rent one until you build your own. List sellers stay in business because they produce lists which produce business. The trick is to understand your product, or service very well and to match it to lists of people who you think would be interested in it. You can then prepare a first-class direct mail campaign which will produce a number of leads generated by interest in your offer.

When planning for direct mail or seminar selling, consider using lists of people with the same occupation but different recreational pastimes and interests, or with different occupations and incomes but a similar lifestyle. Lifestyle is a highly emotive factor, so an offer made by way of mail or a seminar that is linked to lifestyle will generate more interest.

Set out overleaf are the eight steps to writing a successful direct mail letter taken from Murray Raphel, a world-renowned direct marketing consultant who lives in the United States and visits Australia on a regular basis.

Make your letter look good. After all, it is speaking for you and your business. Get involved in direct mail as a lead generation method. Feature station WIIFM (What's In It For Me?) in your letters. Talk about them, their wants and in their terms, rather than about yourself. The method works if you work it. All of this activity is aimed at getting good-quality prospects with whom you can do business.

Activity is very important in prospecting, and you need to start close to home. For instance, go through all the information you and your family have on people to whom you should be offering your product or service. Go through your own telephone numbers, the lists of people you know, and lists of schools, service organisations, churches and social groups. Look in your own street: find out your neighbours' occupations and lines of business.

EIGHT STEPS TO WRITING A SUCCESSFUL DIRECT MAIL LETTER

1. Promise a benefit.
2. Enlarge on the benefit.
3. Be specific.
4. Give proof.
5. What happens if they don't act?
6. Repeat the offer.
7. Ask for the order.
8. Summarise the offer.

Remember that in terms of prospecting, if you can get access to one large commercial office building, then technically you can have upwards of 1000 prospects located in one spot where you can develop centres of influence and use the referral method to go from one to the other. It is almost like having a small town to yourself. I have known many successful salespeople who employ this method as the basis of their prospecting.

Using the same technique, you can work within one occupation. You might decide to become an expert in one segment of the market and understand everything about it. I have known many salespeople selling all types of products and services who have become experts in one or two occupations and have increased their business dramatically by understanding those occupations better than their competitors. Refer to my interview with Bob Miller in Chapter 8, 'Why People Buy' for further discussion of this critical issue.

Segment your markets and become a specialist in at least one of those segments. Look for new enterprise developments, such as the Melbourne Grand Prix. Who is making money out of these new ventures? Where are the new businesses that have developed to support them?

Once you have built your own list, consider making an offer by way of running a seminar. For instance, you could prepare a list by occupation and then organise a seminar on a product or a service that you believe would be of interest to those people. From the seminar you will get some highly qualified prospects, as well as some sales because a number who attend will be ready to buy now.

The inventory method of valuing prospects

The inventory system values each name as you get it by sale value. Break the names down into categories that are meaningful to you. The following example could apply to any business and the figures used were chosen to make the calculations easy. It might just as well be real estate and be based on property values, motor vehicles and based on vehicle value, or computers and based on model values.

We will divide our prospects, into the following categories:

$500–1000
$1000–3000
$3000–5000
$5000–10 000
$10 000 +

Now write a value alongside each prospect in your system. If you take the average value of each prospect, the worth of your current list will be:

Five at $10 000–20 000 = average $75 000
10 at $5000–10 000 = average $75 000
20 at $3000–5000 = average $80 000
65 at $1000–3000 = average $100 000
100 at $500–1000 = average $75 000
TOTAL: 200 prospects = $405 000 total average value

Based on your inventory, who would you plan to see next week?

◆ The five prospects who could bring you $75 000 in sales value?
◆ The 10 prospects who could bring you $75 000?
◆ The 15 prospects in both groups who could bring you $150 000?
◆ The 100 prospects who could bring you $75 000?

Common sense says you should invest your time in your best-quality prospects, but if you don't assign them a value when you write them into your system you may be working on the wrong group. When you assign a value you are also improving your skills and you will be surprised how accurate your assessments become.

The moment you get a new prospect, automatically assign them a value. Do it without thinking. It's surprising how often you will be right. The real benefit lies in getting that value into your prospect system so that you can make choices based on your best prospects. After a while you will generate a statistic which will tell you how many dollars you will sell out of each $100 you put up for sale. This does wonders for your motivation! If you sell $1 in every $4, then you need to put $4 million up for sale to generate $1 million in sales income or $1 million to get $250 000 in sales value. How much do you currently have on your books? How much do you plan to put up for sale next week? next month? You can't sell what you don't put up for sale, and it's hard to put $1 million up for sale if you only have $100 000 worth of prospects in your system.

This inventory system method will revolutionise your potential. Use it to value your current prospect file and you will then know the real potential of your prospects. Whatever business you are in, or product or service you sell, the inventory method will work for you. Be sure to read Chapter 20, 'Concepts', because it will give you more creative ideas that will sharpen your skills and increase your productivity.

PREPARING A PROSPECTING PLAN

The goal of a prospecting plan is to increase your sales productivity. How much can you get from improving your prospecting by 10 per cent? 20 per cent? 50 per cent? or even 100 per cent? The following simple but effective prospecting plan will give you a prospecting goal to aim at.

Breaking down the process makes it easier to follow. Prospecting isn't a matter of luck; it's a matter of applying specific skills, of putting your knowledge and understanding into action. If you aren't prepared to work through the process to make your task easier and more productive, you will never fully reap the benefits. If you complete this exercise, you will be in a position to carry out your plan and achieve your goal. You will know how many new prospects you must find, how much business will come from existing clients, what markets your business will come from and, above all, where you intend to find your prospects. You will be prospecting successfully and preparing yourself for a year of outstanding sales results.

WRITE DOWN ANSWERS TO THE FOLLOWING QUESTIONS

1. How much sales volume do you want to sell in the next 12 months?
2. How much did you sell last year over the same period?
3. How many sales did you make last year, or in whatever shorter period you have been in your current position?
4. In what markets did you make the sales?
5. What was the average sales value per sale in each market?
6. How many sales will come from existing clients?
7. How many sales do you need to make in each market to reach your objective?
8. How much will come from your current clients?
9. How many new clients do you have to find?
10. How many interviews are needed to make the sales, including those to your clients?
11. How many calls are required to get the interviews? This is the number of prospects.
12. How many new prospects must you find each week?
13. How many new prospects must you find each day?
14. Where and how do you propose to find them?

BEATING YOUR OWN BEST PERFORMANCE

Whatever you do in life, it is likely that you will eventually have to do better. That's the nature of life. In sales, no matter how well we do, as we progress we need to do better. That's the nature of the job. So commit yourself to performing at a high level, because performance is our number one sales obligation and we must meet that obligation. Meet it now, today, tomorrow, continually. This is the abiding challenge that sales has to offer. It is a challenge that strengthens all who embrace it and weakens those who fight it. Let it strengthen and reward you by setting yourself the task *now* of beating your best year's, month's or week's performance. Do it now!

Beating your own best performance is a worthwhile goal because it is about creating a better you. It is not being done for the business, or the boss or someone else. It is being done because by nature you need to be self-fulfilled. It is being done because we can only move forward or backward, and for us it must always be forward. If you embrace the concept of beating your own best performance then you will have increased the benefit of the past and guaranteed the rewards of the future.

The concept is one thing; the opportunity it creates is another. The outcome will depend entirely on you as the salesperson, as it is your personal choice whether to reach the highest possible standards or to stay as you are. If you can respond to this challenge and are willing to commit yourself to this goal, then the motivation and inspiration it promotes will significantly increase your chances of being a peak performer. To deny yourself the opportunity for improvement is to deny existence, for without growth we perish.

If you want to earn more, own more, be more, see more, have more or do more, then go for it! Commit yourself to these goals and enjoy yourself. Tell someone about them, so that you have someone keeping track of your progress, and then go out and make it happen for you. If *you* don't care enough to make your dreams come true, then it is unlikely that anyone else will.

Having or not having goals is a dilemma for many people. However, there's really no choice — we either have a goal to achieve or we have a goal not to achieve. Not choosing our goal just means that we self-impose a goal of 'I just hope I get lucky'. This way of thinking is usually a result of being fettered by the past instead of allowing ourselves to be freed by the future. We all need to be free to dream, to achieve in our own way. One of the best ways of doing this is to take up the challenge of beating our own best performances. Go for it!

CHAPTER 4

INTRODUCTION TO THE SALES PROCESS

*Results are the outcome of process. Focus on the
result, for it is the only purpose of process.*
ANON.

THE SALES PROCESS is the sequence in which the separate parts of the total sales presentation are carried out. Each part builds on the preceding part in a logical problem-solving sequence. While the sales process has acquired a number of different names and descriptions over the years (the 'Needs Satisfaction Method' is one example), the sequence of parts has always been pretty much the same. The focus in this book is on the activities that need to be carried out to take a sale from preparation to after-sale follow-up and ongoing service.

Changes in the marketplace have brought a new focus to the meaning of each step in the sales process. This book recognises and examines these emerging new attitudes and emphasis, but continues to describe the steps in the sales process by their traditional titles, since that is what most people will be familiar with. For example, the goal of the modern salesperson is to 'reach agreement' rather than 'overcome objections'.

These activities are traditionally described as:

◆ Preparation
◆ The approach
◆ Presentation
◆ Dealing with doubts and objections
◆ Closing the sale
◆ Follow-up

The following diagram shows both the traditional and emerging descriptive titles of each step. The chapter headings in this book are a combination of the two.

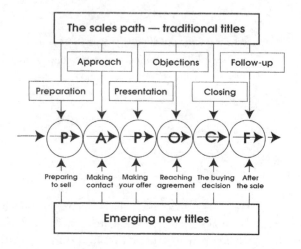

No attempt is made in this chapter to describe each step in the sales process in detail. The purpose of the following brief summary is to acquaint you with the general principles of each step.

◆ *Preparation or . . . Preparing to sell.* Your willingness to spend time on preparing for a prospective sale is a measurement of your commitment to building success, as well as a declaration that you accept that selling is not so easy as to be taken lightly. Preparation is the good work done in advance to make the selling function easier. The road to success is littered with failures caused by inadequate preparation.

◆ *The approach or . . . Making contact.* Making contact is about making the right impression so that you will have the opportunity to make an offer to a prospect. As most lost sales are lost within the first minute, it is important that you prepare well for this first contact. The chapter on this subject will teach you some very effective opening approaches.

◆ *The presentation, or . . . Making your offer.* This is the creative part of the sales process that requires not only good descriptive powers but also the support of great visual aids. The offer itself needs to add value to whatever you are selling, because today adding value and focusing on the welfare of your buyer is a sure way to increase the effectiveness of your offer.

◆ *Dealing with doubts and objections or . . . Reaching agreement.* The term 'reaching agreement' is preferable to the traditional 'overcoming objections' because today the salesperson is working for a win/win solution based on problem solving and mutual gain, rather than focusing on overcoming objections to win a sale. Overcoming objections has an element of hard sell in it, while today adding value, reaching agreement and using a soft-sell approach are more effective.

◆ *Closing the sale or . . . The buying decision.* The answer to any offer is going to be either 'Yes' or 'No', depending on the value of your offer and how well you have presented it. It is often a problem for salespeople to ask for the order and complete the sale, so this book focuses on having the buyer make the decision, which saves the salesperson from having to ask for the order. You can do this by being expert in identifying buying signals and using the 'Not if, but which' technique to get the order.

◆ *Follow-up or . . . After-sale service.* There is a need to follow through and see that what has been promised is done. An after-sale follow-up service procedure should be put into effect to ensure that all the hard work done to get the business doesn't fall by the wayside because of poor follow-up.

By mastering each of the above steps, you will become a peak performer.

Although the sales process has only six main stages, each part has a number of other subsidiary activities which are essential to effective performance. For example, making powerful presentations is a major part of the sales process, but without a sales story, benefit selling, and negotiating, communicating, questioning and listening skills, the presentation would at best be ineffective and at worst a total disaster. These and other essential skills are discussed at some length in later chapters.

CHAPTER 5

MAKING APPOINTMENTS BY TELEPHONE

The telephone is either a great communicator or a great time waster. You must choose.

ANON.

IN TERMS OF selling skills, the sale you want to make from a call to a prospect is not your product or service, but the idea that they should give you an appointment. This chapter looks at the need to be properly prepared when making calls, and at some useful telephone tactics. Then, at the interview, you present your offer to the prospect.

BE PREPARED

Preparation is the key to success in making appointments by phone. The main areas in which you need to be prepared are:

◆ Know the name and position of the person you should call.
◆ Know when to call.
◆ Know why you are calling — that is, the reason why your prospect should give you an interview.

◆ Be rehearsed — know what to say and how to say it.
◆ Be prepared for doubts and objections.
◆ Have an approach to secretaries.
◆ Be prepared to use different approaches to get an appointment.

Know who to call

It sounds elementary, but knowing who to call is the process of matching your offer to a name or position which sparks off the feeling of, 'This is someone who could benefit from my offer, because it will be of value for a number of reasons'. Once you are satisfied that there is a genuine reason for making the call, you only have to confirm the name of your prospect and, if necessary, their title or position in their organisation.

Know when to call

You will be successful more often if you call at the right time. For example, it is not much use calling a doctor during surgery hours, or a school teacher during classes. Do some research into the best time to approach prospects in particular industries or occupations. If your sales activities are confined to a narrow section of business activity, then you will be familiar with the times your prospects are most likely to be available. If you are in any doubt, make an exploratory call and ask when is the best time to call the person concerned. More often than not, you will be given a time to call back, however you should always be prepared to make your call immediately in case the person is available to take your call.

If you are asked if someone else could help you, you need to have an answer ready. If you sound hesitant or unsure, the listener may become suspicious of your motives. Truthful answers and upfront behaviour have a power that guile cannot match. If you are asked, 'Can I help you?', say:

> 'Thank you very much for the offer, but you already have helped by telling me when I am likely to be able to contact [say] Mr Peterson. Would you give him the message that [give your name] will call him at 9 am tomorrow?'

When you call again, the prospect will be expecting your call or at least be aware that you have already been in touch. You are now not a complete stranger.

Know why you are calling

You need to be able to write a 30-second commercial describing your reason for calling. It should describe in approximately 70 words (most people speak at a rate of 140 words per minute) the benefits that will flow to the person you are calling as a result of a meeting with you. Your message needs to have excellent content, and the words should paint a picture that will lead to you getting an interview. Don Mehlig, who runs his own financial services business, has one of the best approaches I have come across. For example, he thanks the prospect for taking his call, introduces himself and says:

> '[Mr Peterson], my purpose in calling you is to arrange a time suitable to you so I can show you how you can benefit from those things your corporation can do for you more effectively than you can do them for yourself, taking account of current tax laws. I am sure you would like to know what other successful people in businesses similar to yours are doing to increase their spendable income and after-tax profits. Mr Peterson, are you interested in increasing your after-tax profits and having more money to spend? It will take just 20 minutes to show you how.'

Don says that most of his prospects say yes. He has also spent a lot of time matching his approach call to his market. There are no approaches that work all of the time, but the more you test and adapt your presentation to the wants, needs and desires of your market, the better your results will be.

Know what to say and how to say it

We have discussed building a presentation that will have enough appeal to your prospects to influence them to give you an appointment so that you can make a presentation. Now that you have the story, you need to practise it until you are word perfect so that you can focus on how to say what you have to say. People learn by repetition. Champion golfers practise until their swing becomes an automatic response to the need to hit the ball. They depend on their mind reproducing that swing every time they hit the ball, irrespective of the club they are using. Salespeople need to do the same practice on their presentations so that they can reproduce their story perfectly every time. This is especially the case in phone approaches. There is nothing as painful to a listener as a salesperson who sounds unsure, indecisive or dull. The response to this kind of approach is nearly always negative. To avoid this problem it is necessary to practise not only the words but also how you say them.

Be prepared for doubts and objections

You also need to be prepared to answer the doubts and objections given as reasons for not agreeing to your request for an interview. Write down the four most obvious reasons or objections a prospect is likely to make, write an answer to each and then learn them by heart. This is no time for adlibbing, which is for amateurs. Be prepared. Read Chapter 11 on dealing with doubts and objections and prepare yourself so that you can respond in a way that will get you the appointment.

Secretaries — friend or foe?

Every salesperson makes calls that must go through a secretary, and much of the sales training on getting interviews deals with this as a problem to be overcome. In my view, it should simply be another process. Secretaries have to decide which calls should go through, based usually on criteria decided with their employers. We should assume that the objective of the secretary is to make sure we don't get to her employer unless we meet those criteria, as well as to be as helpful as possible to those who call. Our objective should be to help her do her work, not create problems for her. After all, if our approach is not considered of sufficient value or interest, that is hardly her fault. If you want better treatment, start by giving better treatment.

Be warm, friendly and truthful and treat her as a person in her own right. When a secretary answers your call, she will usually state the name of the business and give her first name. Start your conversation by asking her how she is. She will generally reply in a positive way, such as 'I'm well, thank you', which gives you the opportunity to make a further friendly comment, such as: 'Do you mind if I call you [Helen]?' I have never had a secretary say no when asked this. Then ask 'May I speak with Mr Peterson, please?' When the secretary asks, 'May I ask what it is you want to speak to Mr Peterson about?', reply by saying:

> 'Yes, you can, and I have no objection to telling you what it is.
> If you can do for me what I need Mr Peterson to do, you will
> have saved both him and me some valuable time.'

This is the key issue, because now you must state what you want to talk with Mr Peterson about. It must be something the secretary cannot answer for him. If the secretary cannot solve the problem, she will either put you through if the prospect is available or will undertake to have him call you back if he is not. Now you must choose: a call back to you, or another call by you? Always choose to call back. Say,

> 'Thank you for your kind offer, but I am moving around and when he calls me I won't be available. Then I'll call him back, he'll be busy, and we'll just end up making the phone company rich! When is the best time for me to call Mr Peterson so that we can be sure of getting together?'

The secretary will give you a time, say 8.30 the next morning, to which you can reply:

> 'Helen, if I call at 8.30 tomorrow morning, will I be able to talk with Mr Peterson?' Ideally, she will reply: 'Yes, you will. I'll make sure he is available.' Now you are getting help, not resistance. When you treat secretaries with respect and courtesy and acknowledge their help, they will in most cases respond in a like manner. Always be open about what you want. Truth has a power invention cannot match.

Try an alternative approach

Here is a different approach that not only seeks an appointment but also provides an excellent technique for dealing with a 'No, thank you' response. The technique belongs to a colleague called Laurie. I consider it to be one of the best I've heard.

The method contains three parts:

1. The call for an interview.
2. The response if the answer is 'No, thank you'.
3. Getting the interview.

If you do use Laurie's technique, you could substitute Don Mehlig's approach to calling for an interview (part 1), as it will be more effective in getting an interview on the first call. However, if you fail to get an appointment, parts 2 and 3 of Laurie's method are the only way I know of consistently turning 'No, thank you' into 'Yes, please'.

When I interviewed Laurie about his method, he told me his objective was to deal only with people who knew him. Here's the method:

1. Laurie rings a prospect — in this example, Mr Peterson. After thanking him for taking the call and introducing himself, he says:

    'Mr Peterson, my purpose in calling you is to arrange an appointment to discuss with you some ideas I have which could be very beneficial to you.'

    If, after some discussion, Mr Peterson, like many prospects, says 'No, thank you' or 'I'm not really interested', Laurie isn't concerned. He never tries to influence someone to change their mind, because his system is designed for 'No, thank you' responses.

2. As he thanks Mr Peterson for his courtesy in taking the call, he says:

    'Before I go, Mr Peterson, would you mind if I put you on my provisional client list?'

    Most people, Laurie says, ask what a provisional client list is. Laurie replies:

    'Mr Peterson, my provisional client list is a list of those prospects who I would like as clients but who have currently said no to an appointment. I mail these people every month with my newsletter on how to decrease their tax and increase their spendable income. Mr Peterson, are you interested in paying less tax and having more money to spend? If you are, this newsletter will tell you how. There is no charge for it. May I send it to you?'

    Eighty per cent of Laurie's phone contacts say yes.

3. Laurie mails his newsletter to the prospects who said 'No'. He mails them each month for six months and then contacts them by phone. When he says 'This is Laurie calling. I think it's about time we met', 80 per cent say 'You're right' and agree to an appointment. Those he doesn't phone he calls on in person at their place of business. He asks the receptionist to give his card to the prospect, saying: 'Please tell him that Laurie says it's time he met you'. The success rate of this approach is 100 per cent, with interviews arranged either then or for a later time. Sixty per cent of all the interviews, by phone or in person, resulted in business.

Here is the genius of this method. Once the initial six months of mailing is done, Laurie keeps on mailing and from then on he never has to deal with a prospect who doesn't know him. Every month after the first six months he has a fresh batch of new prospects.

You can adapt this system to suit your particular needs. It is the most effective method I have come across for obtaining an interview over the phone without the hassle of having to get a 'yes' response on the initial call.

TELEPHONE TACTICS

Here are some useful tactics when making contact by telephone:

◆ When arranging interviews, use odd time frames to gain attention. For example:

> 'Mr Peterson, it will take just 21 minutes for me to show you how you can achieve this goal. Would morning or afternoon suit you better?'
>
> 'Afternoon would be best.'
>
> 'How about 9 past 2 tomorrow? That way we will be finished at 2.30 pm.'

◆ Using an odd number, instead of the traditional hour or half-hour, you set yourself apart from the mob. Once the prospect is ready to see you, and after pleasantries are exchanged, confirm your promise to take only 21 minutes of his time by saying:

> 'Thank you for your time. When I have had my 21 minutes I will tell you, and then I am finished unless you ask me to stay. Is that OK?'
>
> When your 21 minutes is up, say:
>
> 'My time is up unless you want to continue.' If the prospect believes what you have said is important, they will ask you to continue. If not, leave; you can always come back if you have kept your word. On the way out, thank the secretary or receptionist for the help she has given. You may want to come back.

◆ Stand to make your calls. You will be more alert, feel more authoritative and, as a result, sound more positive and dynamic.

◆ Try and identify the personality type of your prospect before you make the call and match your presentation to that type. During the call, check if you have made the correct match.

◆ Relax and focus on a mental picture of your prospect and talk to that picture rather than a phone.

◆ Never work while making your call. Only have on your desk the information you need to make the call.

◆ Smile during your call. It will make you sound more friendly than if you choose to be detached and impersonal.

◆ Make your phone presentation simple but effective. Be precise. In these days of rush, hurry and complexity, a short, powerful, but simple message is most effective. Remember that most TV and radio advertisements are no longer than 30 seconds or 70 words.

◆ It is always good practice to ask, 'Is this a good time to speak with you for a few minutes, or would you prefer me to call you back?'

◆ If your call is a cold call, be as brief as possible. People are usually busy, and the longer your call takes the more certain it will be to cause problems.

◆ At every stage of your call be polite, even if your prospect is irrational and irritating. Never display annoyance.

◆ Use words that lead you easily into your presentation. For example: 'My purpose in calling is . . .', 'My reason for calling is . . .', 'I am calling you because . . .'.

◆ People usually recall best what they hear first and last. If you are giving options for consideration, always give your preferred option last.

Do not take the telephone for granted. It is not just a piece of modern communication technology; it is a vehicle for first-class communications which, if used properly, can greatly increase your sales effectiveness. The phone will do its work well, but it is the user who breathes life into it. The more skilled you are in its use, the better your results will be.

CHAPTER 6

BE A MASTER
AT MAKING
THE SALES
APPROACH

*Being prepared and having an interesting offer are
the critical issues in making the sales contact.*

RESEARCH INDICATES THAT 75 per cent of lost sales
are lost during the first 45 seconds of the initial contact, because that
is how quickly a prospect makes a decision about you. Sales are not
always lost on the merits of the offer. Frequently they are lost because
the prospect didn't like you: it may have been your manner, your
speech, your dress, or the way you presented your offer. Buyers first
decide on you, then on your ideas and, finally, on the product or
service you are offering. If they buy you, they are more likely to buy
what you sell. Peak performers know this, so they do everything they
can to be prepared for every contact they make. The objective of
whatever type of approach you make is to gain the prospect's attention
and to create interest in your offer so that your prospect will be willing
to listen and discuss the merits of your offer.

The first part of any sales contact is to open the prospect's mind.
Until that happens, nothing is possible. In order to do that you need

to have an interesting sales story, a visual aid that supports the story, and the ability to use power phrases and to paint word pictures. You want to make an approach, not just any old approach, but one that will get you maximum results. But first you must decide if the contact is to be:

◆ by letter,
◆ by telephone, or
◆ face to face,

and if it is to:

◆ secure a lead,
◆ obtain an interview, or
◆ make a presentation.

Each sales contact will be a combination of these factors. It might be a letter followed by a phone call, resulting in a face-to-face meeting which might be a fact-finding mission or a selling interview. Or it might be a cold call, front-up, face-to-face selling presentation without an appointment.

To win more often, you need to master each type of approach, decide in advance which one you are going to make and decide your objective in specific terms. Preparation is critical, and peak performers are always prepared to sell. It is a sad fact of selling that the prospect or customer is often better prepared to resist the sales approach than the person making it is prepared to sell. Most sales success occurs when preparation meets opportunity. Peak performers are happy to get the breaks, but they don't count on getting them. Unprepared salespeople count on getting them, often with disastrous results. Mary Key Ash has some invaluable advice for salespeople: 'Pretend that every single person you meet has a sign around his or her neck that says, "Make me feel important". Not only will you succeed in sales, you will succeed in life.'

THE LETTER APPROACH

Your letter needs to be simple, short and to the point and contain only the relevant information. It can be standard, personalised or adapted to the occasion, but it must have a specific benefit for the receiver. Remember: Radio WIIFM (What's In It For Me?) is the station they listen to, so tell them what's in it for them. Load your letter with benefits. Your letter can be interesting, different, clever or catchy — *you* have to decide what technique you use to get your prospect's attention.

The following letter takes the creative approach. It is about a specific problem and was sent to prospects who had the problem. A five-cent piece was attached to the top left-hand corner. I have changed the wording to avoid identification.

Dear Mr Prospect

You and businesspeople like you are losing a fortune every year to this problem. You can see from the enclosed article that the cost is approximately $4 million per day.

Becoming a permanent contributor to these losses can be a very real financial problem. You have two basic choices.

1. Keep on incurring your share of the losses and pay the price in real dollars; or

2. Give me 15 minutes of your time to show you how you can solve the problem for good and put the dollars you are losing in your own pocket at the cost equivalent of five cents in the dollar of your current losses.

I will call you in the next four days to arrange an interview to show you the most cost-effective solution available in this country today. It's new, exciting, great value for money and will pay for itself with a fraction of what you are now losing.

All you can lose is the 15 minutes. You could gain thousands!

Kind regards

[Your name and signature]

You need to match your words to the market you are approaching. If you are dealing with people who are freethinkers and open to a creative approach, then a letter like the one above will be appropriate. If the market is more conservative, then a more conservative approach may be better, though it is always dangerous to make up your mind without testing. I saw a letter sent to the legal profession by someone seeking an interview to sell a product. The letter had an imported sweet pinned to the top left-hand corner. The letter was quite conservative, but the P.S. said: 'Here is a sweet for you to chew while you are chewing over my offer.' The writer had outstanding results from this approach. At a recent workshop I was running for small businesspeople, one of the people present said he had received a similar letter with a tea bag attached. The P.S. said: 'Perhaps we can share some tea while we talk?' I asked his reaction to the letter and tea bag. He said he had been keen to meet the sender because of the creative approach taken, but that the sender never turned up. All that good work and he or she did not follow through!

There is no one way. There is no easy way. But there is a way that will get you better than average results. You need to spend the time to write winning letters and test their effectiveness. Discard those that don't work and constantly improve those that do. The better they are matched to the needs and wants of your prospects, the more effective they will be. If you find it difficult to write approach letters, borrow from someone else or pay a professional writer to do the job for you.

THE TELEPHONE APPROACH

Do your homework as best you can. Call at the best time and be considerate. You need to sound good and to speak clearly. Speak confidently rather than softly. Use simple, easy-to-understand words. Your objective is not to impress with your vocabulary; it is to get the interview.

Write down your approach and read it until you know it word perfect. It is better to read it than wing it. There is nothing more frustrating than listening to someone who is not prepared for a call. Reading your approach in a positive, clear voice is better than using a hesitant approach due to a poor memory. When you are preparing your approach, limit it to 70 words, which on average will take 30 seconds. Why 30 seconds? Because that's the average person's attention span when listening to someone. Then it's their turn to talk. Most commercials on radio and television last no more than 30 seconds for this reason. Anything longer than that becomes entertainment and should be told in story form.

Rehearse your answers to expected objections until you are word perfect. Write them down and remember to stay close to 30 seconds.

Shorter is better, providing you can get through the information you need to impart.

Sound confident, sound equal. If you come across as too smart, the listener will resent you; too dumb and they won't respect you. You will be judged as an equal if you sound as good at your work as they are at theirs. At this time you can only make one genuine offer: you will trade your ideas for their time. Ask, 'Can I trade you 20 minutes of your time for 20 minutes of my ideas?' That's the question you must ask.

An easy way to say why you called is, 'Mr Prospect, my purpose in calling is. . .' From then on, it's about how attractive the listener finds your reason for the call. For example:

> 'Mr Nolan, my purpose in calling is to arrange an interview with you so that I can show you how our new fast loader can benefit you by saving you time and money. It will take just 20 minutes to show you how. Can I trade you 20 minutes of your time for 20 minutes of my ideas? I promise you will profit from this trade. Mr Nolan, can we trade?'

If you get objections, soften your reply with: 'I can understand why you feel that way.' Don't argue, and don't use the word 'but'. *But* is a rebuttal, a hard word; soft words win more often. Make your offer non-threatening so that a logical, reasonable person would accept it, and then treat them as a logical, reasonable person. Here is an example of a first-class phone approach used by Don Mehlig, one of the world's great salespeople and a real peak performer:

> 'Mr Nolan, my purpose in calling you is to arrange a time suitable to you so I can show you how you can benefit from those things your corporation can do for you more effectively than you can do them for yourself, taking account of current tax laws. I am sure you would like to know what other successful people in businesses similar to yours are doing to increase their spendable income and after-tax profits. Mr Nolan, are you interested in increasing your after-tax profits and having more money to spend? It will take just 20 minutes to show you how.'

When you call to make an appointment, you will usually be put through to a secretary. Be warm, friendly, equal, truthful, and treat them as an important person. If the prospect is unavailable and the secretary offers to arrange a call back, thank her for helping but decline, because you will be away from your office on occasions and then you will be on the telephone roundabout. Say you will call again, and ask when would be a suitable time. You will get the best time and all the help your approach deserves. You have to earn the help of others, and you can best do that by being courteous and helpful. Most people have ordinary lives; treat them extraordinarily well and they will be willing to help you get your interview.

Practise the approach card method on every call you make. On a plain 13 cm x 8 cm card, write on one side 'Mr Prospect, my purpose in calling is . . .' and write down your purpose. On the other side, write down the four most likely objections you will get to your approach and the answers you propose to give. If you don't know the answers word perfect, you're not ready to call. Remember: prospects have as much practice in objecting as you do in answering them.

THE FACE-TO-FACE APPROACH

Whether or not you have an appointment with your prospect will depend mostly on what you sell. For example, if you sell products or services that apply to the home, such as repairs and renovations, or gardening services, it is possible to cold call in a specific area and take your chances of finding someone at home who can make a decision or who will arrange a call-back interview for you.

This type of cold calling can be extended to businesses if you want to take your chances of getting time with the decision-maker on terms that are favourable to you. This can be a very effective approach, as you can call on a large number of prospects in a short space of time. So let's look at an approach without an appointment.

Making an approach without an appointment

To achieve success with this method, it is necessary to be well prepared.

◆ Have an opening approach story of not more than 70 words (remember the 30-second ads) that is interesting and will get the attention and arouse the interest of your prospect.

◆ Use visual aids to get and hold the attention of your prospect. It may be the product itself, an illustration of the product or service, or something that will demonstrate why your prospect should be interested in your offer.

◆ Prepare answers to the four most likely objections your prospect may raise after listening to what you have to say. Remember: the initial objective is always to open the prospect's mind.

Here is an example of an actual approach made to a menswear retailer, James Reid, in a country town. He was busy rearranging one of the in-store displays when a young man (let's call him Stephen Mathews) came into the store and approached him. The conversation went like this:

SM: Good morning, is it possible for me to speak with James Reid please?

JR: I am James Reid, how can I help you?

SM: James, my name is Stephen Mathews and I represent the sales division of WIFM broadcasters [a country radio station in the area]. I would like to discuss a special radio advertising program that we believe will interest and reward you by increasing your sales and profits. May I have 15 minutes of your time to discuss this program with you?

JR: Stephen, you can, as long as it takes no more than 15 minutes. I want to finish this display.

He placed a small recorder on the store counter, switched it on and played a 30-second commercial jingle. It was terrific. The music was great, and the words were very descriptive of the retailer's business. It had his name in the jingle. When it was finished, he turned the recorder off and said:

SM: It's great isn't it? Do you like it?

JR: Yes, I do. It's very good.

SM: Then let me tell you how your program will work for you.

He then went on to give details of price, frequency of advertisements and so on, and the retailer signed up for the program. It ran very successfully for two years.

This case is a classic example of superb preparation. The sale was made when they prepared the jingle with the retailer's name in it and when the words matched his store image. He only had to approve it. It was so easy, yet so many salespeople would have tried to sell the program on the basis of value and price and the benefits of a commercial jingle, with the promise that they would find the retailer a great jingle and he could approve it. Preparation is always critical in any sale. The better the preparation, the better your chances.

Making an approach with an appointment

Your preparation should include the same steps as for an approach without an appointment — that is, a first-class sales approach story and a visual aid that will create a desire to hear your story. Practise the approach card method. On a plain card, write on one side your purpose for calling, exactly as you intend to say it. On the other side, list the four most likely objections you may receive and the answers you propose to give.

Here are the basic steps to follow when making your approach:

◆ Greet your prospect.
◆ Identify yourself.
◆ State who you represent and what you do.
◆ State your purpose in arranging an interview.
◆ Ask an involvement question, or use whatever approach method you decided on during your preparation. Remember: your approach objectives are to gain the prospect's attention and interest and to open their mind so that you can proceed with making your offer.

Here are some examples of involvement questions, ranging from simple to more detailed questions:

◆ 'How are you today?'
◆ 'My purpose in calling is to show you how to increase your profits without additional expenditure. That would be of interest to you, wouldn't it?'
◆ 'My purpose in calling is to show you how you can cut your stock holding in printing by 50 per cent by using our multi-purpose product. You don't really want to hold all that stock, do you?'
◆ If you are in the financial services market, what better involvement question is there than a variation of Don Mehlig's great approach: 'Mr Prospect, my purpose in calling is to show you how you can benefit from those things your corporation can do for you more effectively than you can do them for yourself, taking account of current tax laws. I am sure you would like to know what other successful people are doing to increase their spendable income and after-tax profits. You would be interested in making larger profits and having more money to spend, wouldn't you?'

Your questions need to be asked in such a way that you are almost certain to get agreement. This gives you permission to proceed and show how you can arrange what you said and, as a result, benefit your prospect as you promised.

You may prefer to ask your prospect an involvement question like, 'Mrs Prospect, what is the most important thing my service should do for you?' This question has the advantage of seeking information that will help you focus on your prospect's perceived need. Or perhaps it is possible for you to use a demonstration approach that involves your prospect. Here is an example of a demonstration approach used by a salesperson (let's call him Peter) who represented a shirt manufacturer. He called on one of his regular clients, and the conversation went like this:

P: Great day, Sam. How's business?

S: OK, nothing startling. But I don't need shirts.

P: That's OK, I'm not calling about shirts. I want to show you some fantastic ties.

S: Peter, I have more ties than you have. If you want some, I'll sell them to you at a discount.

P: Sam, you haven't got ties like these.

He opened a box of a dozen great-looking ties.

P: The price is right, but more importantly they won't crush or stain. Do you have a dish or a bucket of water I can use?

S: Sure, but why do you want the water?

P: Bring me some and I'll show you.

Sam got some water and Peter tossed the ties in, sloshed them around until they were absolutely soaked, wrung them out and gave them to Sam, saying:

P: Would you mind hanging them up where they'll dry? I'll be back in a couple of hours, OK?

S: Yes, that's OK. But remember *you* wet them.

Peter left and Sam hung the ties up to dry. Two hours later, Peter returned and asked for the ties. They were bone-dry and as perfect as when they were in the box.

P: Sam, how many do you want?

S: Two dozen, please, until I see how people like the designs and how they react to being able to wash them.

Those ties became bestsellers. Peter's demonstration method of selling was superb: he let the ties do the selling.

This example proves again the benefits of being fully prepared to make the sale. Selling isn't difficult as long as you make it easy for your prospect to say yes. Peter could have done what most salespeople with a similar product do: relied on telling Sam about the benefits of non-staining, wrinkle-resistant, fully washable ties and left him to visualise the benefits. Instead he used a dramatic demonstration that literally had Sam begging to buy.

Be prepared and confident

When you are preparing to make an approach, whether you have an appointment or not, focus on the answers to these questions:

- ◆ Do I know enough about my prospect to create a 70-word approach story that will grab their attention and create enough interest so they will listen to me?
- ◆ If the answer is no, who can provide me with information, or how can I find what I need to know?
- ◆ Do I have all the material I need to support my story or offer? If not, what else do I need?
- ◆ Is my material organised in a way that will allow me to demonstrate my offer effectively?
- ◆ Am I confident and ready to sell?

Confidence is essential for achieving success in any form of selling. It is an outward reflection of your inward belief that you are a person of value who can contribute to the welfare of your prospects, while building success for the enterprise for which you work and a career for yourself in your chosen occupation. Confidence is a reflection of past successes, and, in its own way, it builds confidence to buy in your prospects' minds. Most people want to do business with successful people and enterprises. No-one has ever said to me, 'Prove you are a failure and I will do business with you'. Bravado is not confidence. It is a very poor substitute and, subconsciously, most prospects will detect it and resist it. The success on which you build your confidence doesn't have to come from selling. If you are new to selling, your past successes in life should give you confidence that you can become successful in selling. That confidence will build for you the selling success you desire.

Selling is not difficult. Developing the discipline to do what needs to be done to learn and apply the necessary attitudes, habits and skills is the difficult part. Remember, 'Hard work is the yeast that raises the dough' (Anon.). Once you develop the attitudes, build the habits and apply the skills, selling is a breeze. Go for it!

CHAPTER 7

THE SALES
STORY

Man does not live by words alone,
despite the fact that sometimes
he has to eat them.
BRODERICK CRAWFORD

YOU NEED A sales story because selling is difficult
enough without the burden of not being organised to sell. Adlibbing
is for amateurs; professionals practise before they make their
presentation — that's why it sounds so natural. Know your sales story
word perfect, make it about life not product, and tell it with
conviction. Talk about wants not needs: uncovering wants is so much
more productive than getting acceptance of needs. Base your sales
techniques on finding out what your prospects want and then give it
to them. Focus on solutions, not on problems. As Henry Ford said:
'Don't find fault, find a remedy' — it's good advice. Problems and
faults are of the past; the future is about solutions, and that's where
your success and the success of your prospects is going to come from.

Sales stories, if they are structured properly and presented correctly,
do work. Why do stories work so well in selling? They work because
life is a story. The story of the human race is one of the greatest stories
ever told, and it has entertained and inspired billions of people over

thousands of years. Stories work because we were brought up on stories. Our parents told us stories which even today impact on our life. At school we were taught by listening to and writing stories. We read stories, and watch films and plays almost every day on TV. We listen to people tell us stories, and we tell stories to others. Stories are a powerful way of communicating with each other.

Selling by using a sales story is the most natural and effective way to sell, as long as we structure our story to reflect the reasons why stories appeal so much to people. This means your story needs to have an emotional appeal that triggers emotional responses from your prospect. Your story needs to be interesting so that it is worth listening to. The more emotion the story has, the more impact it will have and the more success you will enjoy.

It is necessary at this time to comment on structured sales stories, or as they are often described, sales tracks. The myth of the salesperson who does not have an organised sales story still persists. I have yet to find one. I guarantee you that all salespeople fall into a set pattern of presentation for a particular product or service they are selling. They may not realise it, but they do. I have listened to them and they have a pattern. The real question isn't whether they have a set story, it is: How good is the story they are using?

The second myth about organised sales stories is that everyone is different and the salesperson needs a different sales presentation for every prospect. In fact, there are only four basic personality types, and we each have one of those personalities as a dominant factor in our makeup. We also have traits of the other personality types in varying degrees. To be effective, we only have to understand the characteristics of each type so that we can get in harmony with their thinking. (The four types are discussed in some detail in the next chapter.) No matter what personality type your prospect is, you are selling to the same need and want and you are offering the same products and services as the solution.

Another objection to organised sales stories is that they can sound as if they are being delivered in parrot fashion. I agree that sounding like a parrot would be counterproductive, but you *do* want to sound like a professional. Peak performers practise until they are perfect — that's why they sound natural.

Once you have mastered your sales story, you are then able to depart from it to answer questions, or deal with doubts and objections, and then return to your sales track and continue your presentation without missing out any critical parts. By keeping on track with a story that is matched to your prospect's thinking, you are in charge. The alternative is to lose your way, become entangled in a contest or, worse still, be led by an aggressive prospect who takes charge so that you are left floundering along behind him. If you do not currently have a first-class story, then get one. Master it and it will improve your selling results dramatically.

Selling is the art of persuading your prospects to buy your solutions to their problems and wants. You cannot force them to buy. Persuading means that your work is done in your prospect's mind. Because that is where you do your work, you should try as best you can to understand how your sales story matches the way your prospect's mind functions. That's why sales stories that have a sound psychological makeup work so well. They are in harmony with the prospect's thinking process, and since their thought process follows a predictable problem-solving sequence you can match your presentation to their thinking, thus making it much more effective.

There are two very effective sales story structures in general use today. The elements are in harmony with thought processes. Remember that the human brain works in a problem-solving sequence. Which of the two structures you use will depend on the product or service you are selling. If you want to create desire, you use the AIDA track. If you want to highlight loss, you use the RDRC track. Here are the two structures.

The AIDA structure has four elements:

◆ Attention
◆ Interest
◆ Desire
◆ Action

The objectives of this format are to gain attention, create interest, promote desire and cause action, in that sequence. The sequence is the critical issue.

This format works well for motor vehicles, real estate, the hospitality industry, investment products, superannuation, tax benefit plans, and many more of the hundreds of products and services on the market today. The key issue is desire for a benefit: money, power, beauty, safety, ego recognition, prestige, or any other benefit. When the desire for ownership is high, then prospects buy.

The RDRC structure also has four elements:

- ◆ **R**elax
- ◆ **D**isturb
- ◆ **R**elieve
- ◆ **C**lose

The critical factor in this format is to disturb. The objectives are to relax defences, disturb the prospect, relieve with solutions, and promote action to close the sale.

This format works well for home and business security, medical and health products, insurance protection plans, and any other product or service where a loss may occur. The key point is 'Disturb'. When fear of loss is high, then prospects buy. Fear of loss could refer to the security of the prospect's family, their home and possessions, their status, independence or health.

The heart of every sales story is composed of two elements: logic and emotion. Logic supports the concepts that make up the story, and the emotive issues personalise the presentation and promote action.

Logic is the sound, practical, common-sense reasons which appeal to most people, such as:

- ◆ It fits the need or want.
- ◆ The price is right.
- ◆ You can have it now.
- ◆ It represents value for money.
- ◆ It's the right shape, colour, size, etc.

Emotive issues which affect most of us and are the main factor in most sales are:

- ◆ Desire for wealth and success.
- ◆ Fear and happiness.
- ◆ Ego recognition.
- ◆ Security of family.
- ◆ Love of family.
- ◆ Pride in self and one's achievements.
- ◆ If I wait, it will cost more.
- ◆ Personal independence.
- ◆ Price.

Some concepts that have excellent logic and a strong emotional appeal are:

◆ The magic of 72.
◆ A man or woman at work, or a dollar at work.
◆ The four options for funding any purchase.
◆ You'll earn a fortune.
◆ The live, die or quit theme.

You can study all of these in Chapter 20, 'Concepts'.

ADAPTING THE STORY TO THE MARKET

You need a sales story for each of your markets. The structure can remain the same, but the words should differ to reflect the special needs of your prospect. You should know it word perfect and have a first-class visual aid to support the story. Being word perfect and understanding the story's structure enables you to answer questions, deal with objections and return to your sales track without losing your way. That's staying in charge. The alternative is to match your wits against your prospect, which doesn't work well. Matching wits becomes a contest, and in contests someone has to lose — too often it will be the salesperson. If you want to win more often, avoid contests, find out what the prospect wants and then give it to them. This way, you both win.

Be a peak performer, be prepared and then make a perfect presentation. Structure it to match your prospect's thinking process. Make it strong in logic and high in emotional appeal. Make it about life. Sell real-life issues and fund your ideas with your products or service. That's real selling, that's a winning sales story.

To bring your sales story alive and make your presentation more powerful, master the art of using word pictures and then build them into your story for maximum impact. Word pictures are important because both you and your prospects see in pictures. Your prospects don't *hear* what you say, they *see* what you say. For example, what picture do you see when you read the word 'security'? When I use this example in my seminars, people generally say they see home, money, banks, safes, iron bars, their work, their family and so on. The pictures are what is important to them, so it is important to check the responses your words are creating so that you will know you are on the right track. You can do this by asking a question. For example, if you used the word 'security' in your presentation, you can check by asking: 'Security is important to you, isn't it?' If the answer is no, ask: 'Why isn't it important?' Then ask: 'What is important to you?'

Sales success depends on our ability to understand dominant thinking. People follow their dominant thought by the second, minute, hour, day or their lifetime. Until something becomes our dominant thought, not only will it *not* be done, it *can't* be done. So until you make what you want to sell the dominant thought in the mind of your prospects, not only will they not buy, they cannot buy. You need to make what you sell real to those you are selling to, and you do that by word power which generates the right pictures in the mind of your prospect.

USING PICTURES AND POWER PHRASES

Sell on the lifeline to create pictures in the mind of your prospect. Don't sell products or services — sell life, and how your product or service relates to and impacts on the life of your prospects. This way you can create meaningful pictures — pictures that work on the emotions and attitudes of the prospective buyer. Will your product or service make your prospect's life easier or more profitable, or raise her status in the eyes of her employer, or will it enhance her career chances? The opportunities to tie your product to life and make it more meaningful are endless.

The following example shows how a word picture can be used in a presentation about children's education funds:

> 'All education costs. The only question is, who will pay: you for providing it, or your child for not getting it? Remember: when she knocks, will you be ready? When she arrives books in hand to enter school, you must be there cheque in hand to pay or they won't let her in. Education costs; the price must be paid. The price of education is paid in dollars; the price of not being educated is paid in lost opportunities.'

Paint pictures with your words so that your prospects can better understand the full implications of your offer. If you are selling retirement real estate, then show some pictures of your seaside estate and paint pictures of how the prospect will feel living in this locality. For example: 'When you wake each morning you can watch the day break over the sea. You will experience the peace and quiet of this beautiful place, and the sound of the waves will be the music of your day.'

Word pictures are even more effective when they are backed up by first-class visual aids and power phrases. Word pictures and power phrases are linked by a common objective, which is to create descriptive pictures in the mind of those with whom we are communicating.

A power phrase is a word wallop to the heart of the subject. It is a short, concise statement that says what you want to say with maximum power and brevity. The great Ben Feldman, who was a master of the power phrase, told me that it sometimes took him weeks to develop a power phrase that would work the way he wanted. He told me that using words starting with the same letter 'produces power'.

POWER PHRASES

- People power
- Master magician
- Spending spree
- 'Big bang' theory
- Political power
- Powerful presentations

WORDS WITH BUILT-IN EXPRESSIVE POWER

- unlimited
- universal
- potential
- master
- magic
- enormous
- fantastic
- mind power
- love
- caring
- home
- mother
- fear
- pain
- worry
- hurt

Here are some examples of how power phrases can be used effectively:

- This car has safety power built in. When you are overtaking, you will spend less time on the wrong side of the road.
- Health insurance isn't the cost; it's the illness that costs.
- Retirement doesn't cost; it's the living that costs. How much living do you want to do?
- Life is all we have.
- That's fair enough, isn't it?
- Words are the children of our thinking.
- I borrowed a dream from a glass of old wine.
- A page that ached for a word.
- A man's home is his castle.
- The difference between an elderly gentleman and an old man is generally money.
- Next time you see a funeral, remember it's not a dress rehearsal.
- The sound of the waves will be the music of your day.

Words are salespeople's tools of trade. Understanding their power and using their potential to increase selling success is a constant challenge, so practise perfection. Make it easy for your prospects to see the right pictures by creating a sales story that sells the benefits of your product or service. Back up your words with the power of a first-class visual that illustrates the message you want to convey. The words you use create different responses in different people. You need to be aware of the way certain groups respond to what is said. People largely fall into three groups:

- Those who tend to *see* things.
- Those who tend to *hear* things.
- Those who tend to *feel* things.

It is estimated that each of these three groups makes up approximately one-third of the total, and each group is identified by the way it responds to information. For example, prospects who respond best to seeing things will make comments like 'I see what you mean' or 'I just can't see it', 'Can't you see what I mean?' or 'It's easy to see, isn't it?'. When you hear these or similar phrases, you should immediately show them what you mean and how it will work by using a visual aid. Draw them simple diagrams or show them pictures, because they are telling you that is what they want. They want to see it. They prefer books to audio tapes. They like to watch films or videos.

Prospects who function best by hearing will make comments like 'that sounds good', 'I hear what you say' or 'You don't seem to be hearing what I'm saying'. They won't take much interest in your visual presentation. They are telling you by their actions and words that they understand best what they hear, not what they see. This type of person would rather listen to tapes than read a book. I often have people say to me, 'Do you have tapes? I don't like reading. I would much rather listen.'

The third group are those people who go by their feelings. They express themselves by saying, 'It feels good', 'I can't help feeling . . . ', 'How do you feel about that?' or 'How would you feel if I . . . ?' These people go by gut feelings; they follow their intuition. When you sell to them, use feeling words. They like to make decisions based on their feelings.

The key issue is to look for verbal clues that will tell you which of the three categories your prospects favour. Like all attempts to place people in specific groups, nothing is 100 per cent certain and neither is this one. Each group will have a dominant characteristic, but they will also have elements of the other groups in their makeup, so use your normal presentation and slant it towards their dominant characteristic.

Remember: your objective is to double your sales productivity. If you sell a philosophy that can be funded by your product or service, you will increase your chances enormously. Selling a philosophy is the easiest, most practical and most effective way to ensure your success in today's marketplace.

Philosophies are a soft sell. They are about how people feel and what they want from life. They are about what people believe is good, and what indicates success in life. If our prospects can improve their chances in life by using some of our philosophy, they will buy from us.

Selling philosophies is about understanding the three-part nature of the sales presentation.

THE SALES PRESENTATION

Sell the idea

The important thing is to sell the idea first. If the prospect buys the idea, you have made a sale. The idea is the emotive part, but you can't sell the idea before you know what the prospect wants or what problem they want solved. Once you know this, you can put forward your idea and see if they like it. The idea is the basis of why you think your product or service will benefit your prospects. If you have no ideas, you have nothing to sell.

Sell yourself

You need to sell the idea in a way that sells you at the same time. The more creative, exciting and emotive your idea, the more certain it is that the prospect will buy you and your idea, providing it solves their problem or fits their want. By making your idea exciting and presenting it in an enthusiastic manner, you are selling yourself.

This is your opportunity to show your prospect that you are an original thinker and that your main concern is to add value to the solution of their problem or want. Everything you do and say should demonstrate that you are willing to put in the time and effort to add value for your prospect. What you do is more important than what you say.

Funding

Funding is the logical part of your sales story. It needs to stand up and be competitive. Funding is your product or service. For example, if you sell cars or trucks, you are selling transport. With cars it is personal transport, and you probably sell speed, comfort, safety, silence, prestige, etc., depending on your prospect. The car is the solution to a desired state of personal transport; it is the funding of your idea and their wants regarding personal transport. Funding makes your idea about personal transport possible. If you sell trucks, you are probably selling capacity, convenience and ease of loading, speed, reliability and cost-effectiveness per tonne of freight moved. You are selling these ideas as a solution to the problem or want of transport of goods, and your truck is the funding that makes it possible. If you are selling real estate, then you sell position, design and layout, views, etc., all of which are your ideas on how to meet the wants of your prospect. The house you offer is your funding which makes your ideas work. If you sell insurance, you are selling security, safety, income, retirement lifestyle, school fees, etc., which are your ideas for meeting the wants of your prospect. The contract is the funding that makes the rest possible by providing the money. You may be selling an investment program, and the shares are the funding that make the program work. You could be selling a home entertainment program, and it is the products that fund your ideas and make the program work by providing the sound and picture. Perhaps it is home security, or any one of a thousand different ideas on how to make life easier, more enjoyable, safer and more profitable. But whatever the idea, it needs a product or a service to make it work. The product or service is the funding.

While this idea of funding may seem a little obscure to you to begin with, it is an important concept in that it separates your product or service from the ideas that solve the prospect's problem and it focuses your efforts on selling in the right sequence. First, the clearly-defined problem or want; second, your idea that will solve the problem; and third, your product or service which funds your idea and makes it all possible. Funding is the solution to wants. Those who sell product first, limit their chances because they sell solutions first.

Remember: your prospects and customers must identify their own problems and want to solve them before they will buy any solution. Spend 80 per cent of your time on the problem and 20 per cent on the solution — once the prospect accepts the problem, the sale is made; the solution is only completing the process. If you don't have a solution, the prospect can get it somewhere else.

You can have the world's best solutions, but if you have no problems the solution is useless. There is nothing as frustrating to salespeople as having a perfect solution to a problem that doesn't exist. It is almost as bad as having a problem to which there is no solution.

Your sales story is the organised discussion you go through to complete the process that makes the sale. The better your story, the better your chances. You will find some great stories in Chapter 20.

CHAPTER 8

WHY PEOPLE BUY

*Satisfied customers are those
who have bought good feelings
and solutions to problems.*

BUYING CAN BE a pleasant and enjoyable experience, or it can be a frustrating ordeal. It can be a welcome diversion from the everyday routine of making a living or running a household, or it can be a seemingly endless, ongoing chore. It is a full-time task for some and a part-time task for the rest of us. For salespeople, those who are doing the buying can be seen as an obstacle to be overcome or an opportunity to turn dreams into reality. Whatever our perception, we must face one simple truth: our responsibility as salespeople to motivate people to buy. In order to do that, we need to understand buyer motivation and to act on what we understand. As Will Rogers explains: 'Even if you are on the right track, you will get run over if you just sit there.'

UNDERSTANDING BUYER MOTIVATION

If we understand what motivates people to buy, we will be better able to meet their expectations and create pleasant and enjoyable experiences for them. If we don't understand the reasons people buy, then it is likely that we will create many of the frustrations that seem to dominate their buying experiences.

Almost everyone wants to be a buyer, but few want to be sold. The skill is in understanding people's motivation and meeting their expectations. People buy for only two reasons:

1.   To make themselves feel good.
2.   To solve a problem.

No matter what reasons people give for buying, they fall into one or other of these two categories. If there is no problem or no need, they don't buy. If they don't want or need to make themselves feel good, they don't buy.

Selling and buying is a communication process which takes place in the minds of those who sell and buy. Sales don't take place in shops, factories, offices, cars or homes; they take place in the minds of those who are selling and those who are buying. People think in a problem-solving sequence, and we should match our presentations to their thought processes so that understanding will take place. Selling and buying is an emotional issue. It has been tested and proved a hundred times that emotion will sell more than logic. People buy mostly for emotional reasons.

In every sales process, the elements of both logic and emotion are present and if we are to succeed in understanding why people buy we should take account of each of them.

The importance of logic

Logic needs to be present in each sales presentation because unless our prospects and customers can defend their purchase on the basis of sound logic, they usually won't buy. None of them wants to be seen as being gullible, so they defend their self-image. Almost every purchase has to be defended in these terms. No one wants to be told, 'They saw you coming' or 'Why did you pay that much when you could have got it from their opposition for 20 per cent less?' These are all ways of saying, 'You weren't very smart'. Advertising is constantly working on this factor and conditions us to be careful when we buy. Add one or two unsatisfactory buying experiences to all of this and it's no wonder people are anxious to defend their self-image. That's why our offer must first make sense, be credible and stand up to the test of logic. If the logic is not good enough to support their self-image, they won't buy. Even if the logic is sound, it doesn't mean they will buy today — maybe tomorrow, or some other time, or perhaps from someone else. Logic on its own does not guarantee that you will get the sale.

The importance of emotion

The second and most important element is emotion. Emotion must be strong in your sales presentation so that prospects and customers will buy now, today and from you. Desire is an emotive issue. People with a strong desire want to have, touch, own, smell or do whatever it is that arouses their desire and they want it *now*. If you want your customers to buy now, then emotion which creates desire is the way.

If you are an outside salesperson calling on prospects and customers and you are getting more than your share of call-backs, you can be certain your presentation contains either too much logic or not enough emotion. If you are selling anything and decisions to buy are being put off, it is likely there isn't enough strong emotion in your presentation. This applies to everyone, no matter what their business is, or where or when they are selling. If your sales to interview ratio is too low, then increase the emotion in your presentation. Remember: emotion is about your customers, about how they feel and what they want. It is created by soft questions, or by statements that create an emotional picture on their life screen. Without it, your presentation could apply to anyone. By the use of emotion, you personalise your presentation and focus on the elements that create the motivation that causes people to buy.

The diagram following shows a product or service emotion exercise. The line represents the division between logic and emotion. Above the line are the logical reasons for buying a particular car. Below the line are the emotional reasons for buying the same car. Some reasons can be both logical and emotional.

When I ask attendees at my seminars or workshops to do this exercise on one of their favourite products or services, they almost always end up with a long list of logical reasons but few emotional ones, yet we know it is emotion that sells. To ensure that you don't develop the tendency to rely only on logic, do this exercise for each product or service you sell and carry the results with you as visual aids to ensure you don't overlook any benefit that will help you to build the emotional part of your presentation.

Product: new car

Logic

- Size is right
- Value for money
- Fuel consumption low
- Good trade-in value
- Dealer service excellent
- Dealership close to home

Emotion

- Colour is right — Makes me feel good
- Model looks good — Makes me feel good
- Car has prestige — Good image
- V8 motor — Power gives control
- Dual airbags — Safe
- ABS braking — Safe
- 3-year 100 000 km warranty— Safe
- Value for money — Good decision

OVERCOMING CONCERNS OF COST, FEAR AND RISK

Most people have three basic concerns when making decisions, including buying decisions:

1. Cost.
2. Fear.
3. Risk.

To overcome their concerns, it is necessary to outweigh them with benefits, support and assurance. This is shown in the diagram opposite.

Cost versus benefits

When the concern is one of cost, it means the customer doesn't want to pay too much. They also worry about paying too little. If it seems cheap, maybe the quality isn't good. What they want is value for

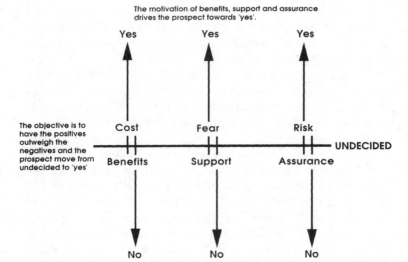

The motivation of benefits, support and assurance drives the prospect towards 'yes'.

Yes   Yes   Yes

The objective is to have the positives outweigh the negatives and the prospect move from undecided to 'yes'

Cost   Fear   Risk   UNDECIDED

Benefits   Support   Assurance

No   No   No

The motivation of cost, fear and risk drives the prospect towards 'no'.

money and the knowledge that they have made a wise decision. The key to overcoming the concern of cost is to focus your prospect's attention on the benefits they will get from paying the price. When the perceived benefits of buying outweigh their fear of paying too much or too little, they will buy. If they don't perceive the benefits as being greater, then they won't. Unless your prospects can see themselves enjoying the benefits of the service or product and that enjoyment outweighs their concerns about cost, they won't buy.

Cost is not always seen in terms of money. For example, you may be trying to convince a person to be president of your local youth football club, and their main concern may be about time. 'If I take on this position, I will have to give up something else. I don't have the time to do both.' Or the cost may be in terms of self-image or ego. Unless the perceived benefits outweigh the perceived cost, few people will pay the price. Most of us are constantly tuned into Radio WIIFM: What's In It For Me?

Fear versus support

This is largely a concern about making a wise decision and about the possibility of losing something of value as a result of making this decision. The fear is expressed by thoughts such as 'I could lose my job' or 'If this goes wrong it will cost me heaps'. Or it might be: 'If I get it wrong and lose this money, I don't have time to make it up before I retire.' The fear may be as simple as: 'I will look an idiot if this goes wrong' or: 'How can I be certain they won't bring out a new model in six months' time?' Or: 'I like this outfit, but does it suit me?'

The way to overcome fear is to support your prospect's desire to make the decision. This can best be done using simple logic, such as 'No decision guarantees success in advance; however, what you are considering is weighted in your favour. It's great value for money and the guarantees are excellent', which supports the customer's desire to have the benefits that will flow from making the decision.

Each time the customer voices a fear, focus on the benefits and then support making the decision with logic. This is not sales stuff, this is basic effective communication. In most cases, your support can and may have to take the form of a guarantee: 'I understand your concern; however, you have our guarantee. If this product doesn't perform to our description, bring it back and we will refund your purchase price or replace it with an alternative of your choice. That's fair enough, isn't it?'

Today the customer is taking less and less of the risk, and that's how it should be. Your support can range from testimonials of satisfied users, through your own experience of the product, to the ultimate of specific guarantees. While I was writing this paragraph, the doorbell rang. (I was writing in my studio at home.) When I answered the door, a young man said:

YM: Good afternoon, I am from Optus cable television. My purpose in calling is to explain to you why there will be a lot of our people working in your area over the next few weeks. Are you familiar with Optus and what it does?
JC: Yes, I am.
He then explained that crews would be installing connections to cable television for those people who had accepted their free offer.
YM: Could I show you the offer?

The answer, of course, was 'Yes'. The offer was simple:

YM: We will connect you to our cable network free of charge. You can use the service for one month free of charge. If you like it, you keep it. If you don't want it at the end of the month, we will take you off the service at no cost to you. Mr Collis, can we connect you?

JC: Yes.

The whole offer was a perfect example of removing the cost, fear and risk factors.

Risk versus assurance

Many customers worry about taking risks.

'Perhaps the venture will fail.'

'If I change our organisational structure, I will risk losing good people.'

'If I buy this new skirt, it might not be warm enough.'

'If I buy this new car at this dealership for a bigger trade-in value, I might lose when it comes to service.'

The truth of life is that everything we do has an element of risk and rarely can we enter into total risk-free decisions. What we need to do to help our customers make a decision is to outweigh the perceived risk by focusing their thinking on the benefits of making the decision and offsetting their fears with our assurance that they are making a wise decision. Only when people's concerns about cost, fear and risk are outweighed by your benefits, support and assurances will they be confident enough to make decisions and take action.

While you can give advice and suggest courses of action, this willingness to do as we suggest will be greatly influenced by whether:

◆ *You make them feel good.* People like to do business with those who are pleasant, helpful and courteous, and who treat them as a person of value.

◆ *They make the decisions.* Most people want to buy, but very few want to be sold. Help them to buy. Identify their personality style (see later in this chapter) and adapt your style to suit theirs. If your prospect wants to get involved in a discussion, respond in a warm, friendly way. No matter what their style, show concern for satisfying their needs and solving their problem. Use a problem-solving approach. Remember that their tastes may be entirely different from yours. Respect the differences and do your best to understand why your prospect chooses those differences.

◆ *You are a good listener.* The only way to find out what prospects want is to listen to them and understand what they say. When you listen, you pay them the compliment of treating them as a person of value; you are putting the power of silence to work for you. When a customer has a problem, simply ask: 'What do you see as being the best solution?' and listen to the answer. If you believe there are other solutions, don't say: 'Here is a better solution.' Very few people like to be told they have got it wrong. A better technique would be to say: 'That's a good idea. Have you considered . . .?' and then give your option.

◆ *You ask them back again.* When your customer has completed his business, pay him the compliment of asking him to come back again. If he has made a purchase, reassure him that he has made a good decision and say: 'Thank you for doing business with us. Please come back again.' If you can't satisfy your customer this time, suggest where, or how he may be able to get what he wants, and say: 'I am sorry we have not been able to do what you want this time. Please come back again and give us another chance.' People like doing business where they feel good. Do all you can, whenever you can, to make them feel good about you.

BUYING AND SELLING

Retail or wholesale shop-floor selling and buying differs very little from any other form of selling. All selling is about someone being interested in buying something, or someone being interested in selling something, whether it is an idea, a product or a service. No matter what is being sold, or by whom it is being sold, whether the sale is being made door to door, between a salesperson and a prospect in a retail store, or between a salesperson and a customer, or whether it is being made in the office of an accountant or a solicitor who is selling his client, in a surgery with a doctor or dentist and a patient, in a courtroom, or on a rural property with a farmer and a stock and station agent, the process of selling is practically the same. The products or services being sold may be different, but the process is the same. The relationship may be different, but the process is the same. The client may be buying, or being sold, an idea, a product or a service, but the process is the same. The process may be hard sell or soft sell — only the emphasis is different.

The process, no matter where or when, is the same. It is one of communication between two or more people, and the purpose of the communication is essentially to ensure that the prospect or client receives satisfaction in terms of the want or need they wish to satisfy. The factors which motivate different people are essentially the same. They want to solve a problem or make themselves feel good, or both. To some degree they will all be affected in their decision-making by cost, fear and risk. The person doing the selling will therefore need to counter with benefits, support and assurance.

Unless you accept this point of view, you could easily be deceived into thinking that you are not involved in selling yourself, your services and your products. We all sell ourselves every day of our life. The only question is how well we do the selling.

Success in communicating your ideas, in getting others to follow your suggestions, and in selling yourself, your products and your services depends on your ability to understand, accept and apply basic psychology to your dealings with your prospects and customers.

Vroom's expectancy theory

This theory is based on the belief that two factors combine in a multiplying effect to motivate a person. The factors are:

1. The belief that a particular action will satisfy a need.
2. The strength of the need itself.

For example, if a prospect believes that if she buys your solution it will solve her problem and she really wants to solve the problem, then the multiplying effect of a good solution to a strongly perceived need will raise her motivation to the buying level. This is illustrated by the diagram over the page.

Here is an example of how the theory works in practice. If the strength of belief that an action will solve a need is, on a scale of 1 to 10, rated 8 but the strength of the need on the same scale is rated at only 1, the motivation to buy would only be 8 out of a possible 100, which would mean the prospect would not buy. If, on the other hand, belief and strength of need were both rated at 8, the motivation to buy would be 64, which would mean the prospect would probably buy. It would seem that to be successful in a sale, both factors need to be rated

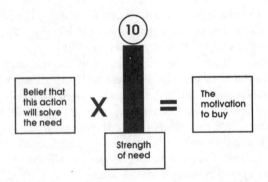

high. The best course of action is to rate every sale you make on these two factors until you have a reliable body of evidence on which to construct your own 'will buy' score.

How shop-floor selling is different

The basic difference between outside sales situations, where the salesperson calls on prospects and customers, and inside shop-floor selling where the customer visits the business, is the method of approaching the customer or prospect. In shop-floor selling, the salesperson usually approaches the customer and says either: 'May I help you?' or 'How can I help you?' Customers who know exactly what they want to buy, and are ready to buy, generally respond by telling the salesperson what they want. No problem.

But what do customers and prospects say if they haven't made up their mind, are still exploring options and don't want to be sold just now? Nearly always, the answer is: 'No, thank you. I'm just looking.' The result of this approach is that the salesperson has been refused, is sent away and has to wait and see if the customer comes back to them. It is difficult for the salesperson to come back to the customer without being seen as pushy and hard sell. For this reason, many salespeople are not effective in making sales. The customer looks and leaves without ever getting into a discussion with the salesperson, and the opportunity of taking part in the buying process is lost to the salesperson.

The opportunity is lost because of the method of approach. Research on lost sales indicates that 75 per cent of lost sales are lost in the approach, no matter when the decision not to buy is made. So, our approach must be first class. What can we do to make our approach more effective? First, in shop-floor selling we should never use 'May I help you?' as an approach. Instead, we can adopt the following approach technique. When customers come into your business, you should immediately recognise them by making eye contact and saying, 'Thank you for coming in. Can I leave you to browse for a few minutes, and then I will be back to help you. Is that OK?'

The choice is now with the customers. If they know what they want and want it now, they only have to say so. If they want to look around, they only have to say OK. No pressure, no hard sell. They haven't been ignored, or left waiting, but more importantly you haven't been sent away and you can come back. The customer is now expecting you to come back.

Here is a real example of how to use this method. Recently I was in the David Jones store at Chatswood with my wife, Valerie, while she did some shopping. I was looking at some silk ties. I am always in the market for silk ties. There was a rack of new ties, several of which I had set aside because I liked them. A young man of around 20 came up and said, 'Good morning. Beautiful ties, aren't they?' Naturally, I said yes. He replied, 'I'll leave you to look while I serve this customer. I'll be back in a few minutes. However, if you need me sooner, please call me. I will be at the counter.' He showed me where he would be and then left.

I could see he was watching my progress and, always being interested in how people sell, I wondered what would happen next. About three minutes later, he came by again (clothing in his hand) and said, 'Are you making progress? Have you seen these?' He showed me more silk ties. 'They look beautiful, don't they?' I agreed and continued selecting. He returned to the counter.

By this time I had around six ties that I was considering buying. I started to put some back on the rack. Within moments he was with me and said, 'It looks like decision time.' I agreed, and then he said: 'I would like to help you make a selection that will really make you feel good. Tell me, do you wear ties often in your work?' (I was in jeans and a sports shirt.) I answered, 'Always'.

'What colour suit do you generally wear?'

I replied, 'Blue, or very dark grey, white pinstripe'.

'What kind of work do you do?'

I told him, 'Professional speaker. Generally at conventions.'

'That's interesting,' he said. 'May I ask your name and what subjects you speak on.' I told him.

'Mr Collis,' he said. 'It sounds to me as if how you look to your audience is very important to you. Would you tell me how you want to look to your audience?' I told him, and he said: 'Would you mind bringing your ties with you and coming with me? I have more ties in a different department and I want you to see them. They have all the power and prestige you want, they look great and will be easily seen by most of your audience, and they are excellent value?'.

I thought, 'This young man is a genius. Twenty years of age and he sells like this. Every word is right. Plenty of benefits, value for money but not cheap, power, prestige and the audience will see them.' I bought two ties that he had suggested and one of my own choice. I have never met a better in-store salesperson. At no time did he ask, 'May I help you?' At no time did he put himself in a position where he could be rejected, or sent away. At no time was he pushy. At all times he was in charge. What a pity all in-store salespeople aren't as skilled as he is. You can improve your in-store sales dramatically if you sell this way, by never again using: 'May I help you?'

Anyone can learn from this example. Whatever your occupation, these principles apply to you. Superior selling is good two-way communication based on an understanding of why people buy, which results in their satisfaction. Knowing what motivates them to buy is critical to being able to communicate effectively with them in a way that will not only help you to satisfy their wants and needs, but will also enable you to build long-term, high-quality relationships with them.

Another critical issue in being able to communicate effectively with your prospects and customers is personality differences. Identifying and understanding the differences between your prospects, customers and yourself is critical to your ability to successfully communicate with them. Every time you communicate with a customer or prospect you have an opportunity, and: 'No business opportunity is ever lost. If you fumble it, your competitor will find it.'

PERSONALITY STYLES

There are four basic personality styles which go under a variety of names. All of us fall into one of these categories. Some may be easily identified because they strongly exhibit the characteristics of that type. Others may not be as easy to identify because most of us have more than one style present in our personality makeup, but we have one style that is dominant. It is the dominant one you need to focus on. Once you have successfully typed your prospect, you are in a position to influence him or her by using emotional techniques aimed at that personality style. Our definitions below have been reduced to the simplest possible terms.

- *Type 1*. This is a person of action who is motivated towards results and tends to be uncomfortable with anyone who isn't. Wants to make decisions now. Appreciates help in making decisions. Is today-oriented. Is open to a direct style of approach with a minimum of small talk.
- *Type 2*. An emotional person. Warm and friendly. Likes to build relationships. Tends to be happy and fun-loving by nature. Is tuned to others and their emotional problems. Emotion is critical with this personality.
- *Type 3*. An innovator. Keen on ideas, and very creative in his or her approach to problem solving. Tends to be theoretical. Dislikes chaos and much prefers a tidy and organised approach. Looks to the future. Prepared to make decisions and plans on a longer-term basis. Open to both logic and emotion.
- *Type 4*. Methodical and systematic. Willing to consider ideas. Likes order and structure. Likes to analyse problems and tends towards a problem-solving approach. Calm, cool and objective. Appreciates logical solutions.

It is important to recognise that there are differences in customers' personality styles and that we also fall into one or more of the four styles. Very few people are totally one style. Most have a dominantstyle and traces of the other styles in differing proportions in their makeup.

It is one thing to recognise dominant styles, and another to do something about them. Our responsibility is to adapt to the prospect's style. It is easy to see that if you are one dominant style and your prospect is a totally different style, the differences may make communication difficult. If you don't adapt your style to accommodate the customer's style, it may prove impossible because of the increased risk of a personality clash. Because of these potential differences, it is important that you become flexible enough to modify your behaviour for each sales interaction if necessary.

People are driven by different emotions, motives, needs and wants, and are almost totally focused on their own self-interests. They listen to Radio WIIFM: What's In It For Me? Your objective should be to make sure they know what's in it for them. With a sound understanding of why customers buy and an ability to recognise their dominant personality style, you are in a position to satisfy their wants and needs to their satisfaction and to build yourself a wonderful career in selling.

Creating satisfied customers is your purpose for being in the selling business. Everything you do should aim at achieving that purpose. Customers are not an option, they are a necessity.

HIDDEN BUYER MOTIVATORS

No explanation of buyer motivation would be complete without reference to the built-in motivators that cause people to respond favourably when confronted with one of these motivators. Expert sales and marketing people have been using these motivators to positively influence their sales results ever since selling and marketing became organised functions of society. People have been using them to get favourable responses for thousands of years. They are reliable, powerful tools of communication and influence.

Most successful salespeople are first-class networkers. They get to know the 'right' people according to their requirements, and as a result of this networking they build relationships which have a positive influence not only on their business life but on their life in general. Often they use these built-in motivators without actually making a decision to use them. They automatically take an action to solve a problem or meet a need, which calls up a favourable response because it seems to be the way to get help. By the same token, they are often called on to help someone else in the network and they respond accordingly.

Here are four hidden buyer motivators.

1. The obligation factor

The first of these built-in motivators is the 'I help you and you help me', or obligation, factor. For centuries, people have been setting up obligations by giving help to others which is returned when they want something. What you do to earn this reciprocity may be as simple as showing interest in what someone is doing. It may be as little as being seen at a function to honour or reward someone or going to someone's wedding. You may have received an invitation as a payback for a perceived action on your part, and the invitation is seen by the person sending it as a payback. Whatever and however you cause obligations to arise, there is always a desire — perhaps not even at a conscious level — to pay back by the person who receives something they see as favourable to them. This is a powerful influence and you should not underrate its importance to your sales success.

In the marketing and sales field, the free gift or 14 days' free trial exploit the payback rule by creating an obligation within the mind of the prospect. So powerful is this obligation factor that most people will do everything they can to pay back when the opportunity arises. Whenever you go the 'extra mile' by way of a service or a gift, you automatically embrace the power of the obligation factor. That's why salespeople who focus on improving the business or life of their prospects and customers are so successful. That's why networking creates influences that pay off in pay back. That's why building relationships is so productive.

2. Testimonials

Because most people are followers or imitators and only a very small percentage of the population are innovators, it makes sense to add testimonials to your sales presentation. If the great majority are motivated more by what others do than by the proof of what you say about your product or service, then you should use that motivator by showing testimonials and endorsements of how others are profiting by using your product or service.

We see this motivator being used in commercials when a well-known person endorses a product. We see it being used in the marketing of books when a critic says 'Buy this book' or when it makes the bestseller list. We are influenced by critics to buy paintings or attend restaurants that have just won an award. We see a film because it has received rave reviews. The proof that products and services are socially acceptable is a powerful motivator. If others are doing it, then it's OK for me to follow, is how this motivator works. I have shown in Chapter 6, 'Be A Master At Making The Sales Approach', how Don Mehlig uses this principle to get appointments. As part of his approach sales story, he says: 'I would like to show you what other successful people in positions similar to yours are doing to increase after-tax profits and spendable income.' Do you have strong, powerful testimonials in your sales kit and do you use them? If not, it's time to increase your sales success. If you want proof that they work, remember that successful salespeople have been using testimonials since selling was invented.

3. The friendship principle

Successful salespeople have always used this buyer motivator to influence prospects. It is the most successful prospecting method and is called 'referred lead prospecting'. Yet, despite its success, it is the least used of all the prospecting methods. This is probably because it entails asking for a direct favour. However, by using this method of buyer motivation in conjunction with the obligation principle, the 'asking for a favour' problem disappears because once you have established a payback obligation, no matter how small, the natural desire of the person you are asking to help with referrals is to do all they can to help you, which fulfils their desire to pay you back. This payback obligation may arise because you have gone to a lot of trouble to make an outstanding presentation during which you have made offers to help solve their problem. If they have just purchased from you, the 'obligation' now exists. If you are given referrals, you now have an obligation to them which you pay back by reporting back the results of your approach to their referral, and saying thank you and showing appreciation for their help.

4. The referral method

This method is effective because when you approach a prospect and use the name of your referrer, you are giving an endorsement of you and your product or service. It uses the motivation of 'Jim bought it, so it must be OK for me' element of social acceptability. A friend has said it's OK to deal with you. It also embraces the result of many research projects, which is: they buy *you* first, then your *idea* for solving the problem, then your *product or service* to *fund* the idea and make it work. The friendship referral eliminates much of the need for you to sell yourself; the referral is doing that for you.

SEMINAR SELLING

Seminar selling is such a powerful means of influencing people and tapping into these hidden motivators, because most of the psychology of influence is present at the meeting.

◆ *A number of people are at the meeting,* which says it's OK to be here and this is a desirable topic to be considering.
◆ *The presenter has credibility* because of his or her position as an authority on the topic, so it's OK to take this suggested course of action.
◆ During the meeting, *testimonials are given* by persons who attended a previous seminar, bought the offer and now say this is how it has helped me. So it's OK for you to buy.
◆ When an individual sales approach is made to a prospect after the close of the seminar, *the payback principle is operating.* The seminar was free, it was good, and it was put on for me and others. Now it's my turn to show my appreciation and pay the presenter back.

Nothing works all the time and with all people, but these hidden motivators are powerful and ever present. Not only are they used *by* us, but just as often they are used *on* us. They form a very powerful group of buyer motivators which lurk just below the level of conscious awareness waiting for someone to trigger them off. We are largely powerless against them unless we have done a great deal of work in recognising and understanding them and then preparing techniques to combat them.

THE PRINCIPLE OF TAKING AWAY

It seems that people are more motivated when confronted with loss than when they have an opportunity of making a gain. In Chapter 10, 'The Visual Way To Sales Success', I explain that taking away a perceived benefit is very powerful and I describe a technique for using a graph in a way that takes away the benefit. It is possible that much of the success we attribute to the benefits gained from the purchase of a product or service is more a result of the loss people will suffer if they don't buy. Do people buy shares because of the profits they might make, or is the real motivator the lifestyle, prestige and status they will lose if they don't buy them? Are the profits simply a way of avoiding a loss? While this may sound confusing, current research indicates that the fear of loss is more powerful as a motivator than the prospect of a gain.

A key factor in some very successful advertising campaigns is scarcity. The promotion will run for three days — after that, you'll miss out. The three tenors will be appearing for three performances and never again in this country. Once 200 of these plates are made, the moulds will be destroyed and they will never be offered again. This is the last appearance in this country of this speaker. Scarcity is what makes an antique valuable. Land becomes a good investment because this is all there is. Rare stamps and vintage motor cars become valuable because of scarcity. Scarcity is another powerful buyer motivator, but everything that is sold is not scarce. However, the principle behind scarcity, which is loss of whatever is now available, can be generated by focusing on the loss of the value of the benefits if the prospect doesn't buy. No matter how available the product or service is, they have lost the benefits if they say no. The way to generate that feeling of loss is by identifying a benefit and then focusing on the loss incurred by not buying. Taking away creates a powerful buyer motivation, and its use at the right time can increase your selling performance dramatically.

CONCLUSION

I can think of no better way to conclude this chapter than by having Bob Miller, Marketing Manager for Toyota Australia, give you his views on buyer motivation. In 1993, the Australian Marketing Institute recognised his outstanding contribution by awarding him its prestigious Sir Charles McGrath Award for marketing. Bob has just been voted by his peers the marketer of the decade, which means the best in this country for the last 10 years. Bob is the man who, in marketing terms, has made Toyota the force it is. His successes in his field are legendary and inspirational.

◆

JC: Bob, I have said that it is important for salespeople to understand marketing as well as selling. Do you agree, and if so in what way?

BM: Jack, I do agree. To be successful, salespeople must discipline themselves to understand the role of marketing in the overall process in which they are involved. The task of a professional marketing group is to create the optimum environment in which sales can occur. The marketing people's job is not to sell the product or service; it is to sell the idea of the product, but more importantly the idea behind the brand on that product. If they do their job successfully, then the salesperson's job of negotiating a deal at a price that satisfies both parties is much easier than it might otherwise have been.

For example, in Toyota's case my role as a marketer is to convince Australia of the values of the Toyota brand: reliability, good value for money, high quality at a reasonable although slightly premium price, excellent customer service from dealers and the factory, and reliable parts and service availability anywhere in this vast continent. Not only does our success in achieving these objectives simplify the selling process for our dealers and fleet departments, it makes the franchise itself more easily saleable to new investors as we need to change or expand the dealer network.

JC: What are the key issues for sales success in today's markets?

BM: An Olympic-standard focus on prospecting, record keeping, and relentless follow-up before and long after the sale is made.

Personal discipline in conducting one's sales business at, or above, 'World's Best Practice' with regard to the basics that all of us know, but that so many of us, through lack of personal discipline, ignore.

A broad excellent knowledge of one's particular field of endeavour, complemented by a highly focused specialisation in one particular segment of that field so that the salesperson is unchallengeable on that defined area, regardless of whether he or she is dealing with other specialists in that segment, or lawyers, or accountants, or representatives of government bodies such as the ACCC or the ATO. This kind of expertise builds confidence, advances one's reputation publicly and, through word of mouth, enhances a thousandfold one's chances of building a referral business and guarantees renewal business. When the practitioner combines these skills with the talents of others in either formal or casual partnership, one is able to provide highly reputable, sound advice, and be rewarded as a recognised top-level professional.

Superb product knowledge and a complete understanding of the benefits associated with even the tiniest feature.

Being totally familiar with the features, advantages and benefits of one's product or service range. One must be able to demonstrate clearly the solutions these offer to a prospective customer's problems.

JC: Bob, what else do you think salespeople should embrace to ensure their success?

BM: I believe it is important for all salespeople to have a strong problem-solving attitude and a genuine desire, easily identified by prospects, to empathise with their problems and provide advice on how to solve them, using the products you represent.

The ability to shut up and listen. Read, and preferably memorise, Hugh Mackay's most recent book on Australian consumers, *Why Don't People Listen*.

A professional or, at very least, self-trained memory combined with disciplined and routinely developed powers of observation.

Professional training in speed reading so that one can absorb completely and memorise the avalanche of data and information one is required to absorb and memorise on a daily basis.

They also need reasonable typing skills and the ability to use a computer at a level equal to or slightly above those with whom they are dealing.

Outstanding time-management skills and the personal discipline to apply them. A comprehensive under-standing of the telephone as a selling tool and the ability to teach others who use it on your behalf.

A professional understanding of direct mail and of how to write letters that get a response.

The ability to develop press advertisements that pull responses on a basis other than price slashing.

A recognition that, as the type of personality that revels in the sales process, the thrill of the chase, the elation of gaining the order with money, and the personal intercourse that comes from meeting new people and helping them to achieve their own goals, and solving their own problems using your skills, products and services, you may not be the kind of personality that makes the world's best manager. Recognise your own shortcomings and hire someone who is outstanding in management competence so that you can get on with focusing on what you do best: selling.

Be a great communicator. Be able to make your point succinctly, and these days preferably graphically, in a way that builds confidence in the prospect and encourages him or her to recommend you to others as a no-nonsense, non-mystery presenter of worthwhile information. In these days of consumer protection and the obscurity of legal hocus-pocus, clear graphic communication makes a refreshing change and provides you with an edge over your competitors.

JC: Bob, what do buyers value from the purchases they make?

BM: Jack, all the research tells us that the buyer's highest priority is to see value for money. This may not be the cheapest, but it will make them feel that they are getting a good deal and are happy to talk about it to friends and colleagues, thus providing salespeople with referral business. A satisfied customer will always feel that his or her specific personal problem has been solved through investing in whatever the salesperson has delivered.

We can define value as being a function of the overall quality and brand qualities of the product divided by its price, multiplied by the amount of time it takes to acquire that product, further multiplied by the amount of stress that is involved in finding, testing, financing and acquiring that product, and then using it for a reasonable (warrantable) period of time without it failing to meet the owner's expectations.

Thanks for asking me to be part of your book. I wish your readers good selling.

◆ — ◆ — ◆

There you have it. Great advice from the marketer of the decade. I am sure that if we follow that advice, we will enjoy in our career the success Bob has achieved in his.

CHAPTER 9

SELLING BUYER BENEFITS

Don't sell me products or services . . .
Sell me ideas, a better self-image, freedom
from fear and want, and a philosophy
that will help me achieve my potential
as a human being.

THE CRITICAL FACTOR in all selling is the benefit your prospect or customer will get from dealing with you and buying what you sell. Your prospect's main interest is self-interest, just as yours is. There is a big difference between self-interest and being selfishly interested. All of us are self-interested. Self-interest is a natural human function — it can save your life. If you are not interested in your own welfare, it is unlikely that many other people will be.

People are usually tuned into one radio station — WIIFM: What's In It For Me? Whenever you are asked to do something, to comment on something or to think about something, the subconscious question you always ask yourself is: What's in it for me? When the perceived benefit is seen to outweigh the perceived disadvantages, you are moved to respond in a positive way. When all you can see are the disadvantages, you respond in a negative way. You are constantly working towards your own self-interest. In selling relationships, the same process is at work. It is in your prospect's interest to want the best result they can get in return for their time and money. It is in a business's best interest to see that customers get what they want, and that they return again and again to buy. It is in your best interest in dealing with prospects and customers to ensure that both they and your employer get the result they want. Whenever this occurs, all three win and everyone feels better. The customers get what they want. The business retains the customers. You enhance your career prospects, increase your job satisfaction and do what you are paid to do. Focusing on 'What's in it for me?' is a fact of life.

People are interested in products and services that fulfil their wants and needs. Products that make them feel good, products that taste good, products that are real value for money. People don't buy products for what they are; they buy them for what they do for them. Last year, hardware stores sold thousands of 13 mm drills. No one wanted a drill; what they wanted was a 13 mm hole. In that same year, thousands of up-market cars were bought by people who wanted not only transport but also prestige, ego recognition, superior comfort and safety. Who isn't interested in what will make life easier and more enjoyable for them? People buy what the product or service will do for them. They are more interested in the sizzle than the steak; in how it tastes, not what it is. How they *feel* is the critical issue.

When making your sales presentation, remember that research into why people buy shows that 75 per cent of all purchases are made mainly for emotional reasons. People buy because of how they feel. The other 25 per cent buy largely based on logic. Emotion and logic are contained in every sale, but emotion dominates in 75 per cent of cases and logic dominates in 25 per cent.

People who buy mostly on grounds of logic need good reasons to reinforce their feelings of wanting to buy. They don't want to be seen as gullible. They don't like being pressured, and they don't want to feel guilty about what they have bought, so make sure that you give some sound, logical reasons why they have made a good decision. Explain why it is a good buy: It does its work better than similar products. It will last a long time and is good value for money. It is very reliable and the guarantees are excellent.

No matter what product or service your prospect buys, he or she wants to feel justified in their purchase. They want you to reassure them and to remove any doubts they may have about the wisdom of their purchase. Any time you spend with them that is aimed at overcoming their fear of making a mistake will be well spent.

Benefit selling is the most under-used skill in selling. Most of us would substantially increase our sales results if we concentrated on selling benefits. 'Sell the sizzle, not the steak' is the key to benefit selling. Yet, despite this adage being bandied around the marketplace for scores of years, most of us fail to implement the message. People don't buy products or services for what they are; they buy what products and services will do for them. This is the ultimate truth of buyer motivation and benefit selling, yet in most cases we are still focusing on what products and services are, instead of on what they do.

THE DIFFERENCE BETWEEN FEATURES AND BENEFITS

Here is the main reason why we find it difficult to sell benefits. Very few salespeople really understand the fundamental differences between features and benefits, so they mistakenly sell features as benefits. A feature is a fact about a product or service. If it is not an absolute and undeniable fact, it is not a feature. For example, to say that a feature of your company's service is that it is the best in the business is not a fact, it is an opinion and therefore cannot be a feature. If a business makes deliveries to its customers seven days a week and the salesperson says, 'A feature of our service is we deliver seven days a week', then that's a feature. It is true that the delivery service operates seven days a week. It is very easy to fall into the habit of describing opinions as features, which results in prospects either openly disagreeing or, worse still, turning the statement of features into a hidden objection. When a true feature is described as a feature, the truth of the statement is obvious to the prospect and there is no disagreement. It is accepted as a fact. Here is a simple and very effective method of separating features from benefits and then describing both in a way that is easy for your prospect to understand and which closes the sale at the same time. It is in four parts:

1. The feature.
2. The words that connect the benefit to the feature.
3. The benefit.
4. The commitment question.

Four-part Benefit Selling Model

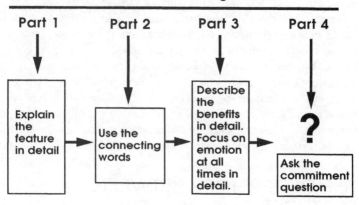

These parts are shown in the diagram above.

Here is an example of how to use this structure to make feature and benefit selling easy. In this example, your prospect is Mr Williams who is interested in a new car which you are demonstrating. You are describing the features and benefits of the car.

> 'Mr Williams, a feature of this car is that it has six cylinders and generates 220 horsepower. [*The six cylinders and 220 horsepower are true, undeniable facts. The description of the feature is part 1 of the structure.*] Which means [*these are the connecting words, which is part 2 of the structure and connect benefits to features*] you will always have reserves of power when you have to overtake and pass another vehicle. You and your family will be safer in this car, because you will spend less time on the wrong side of the road. Overtaking uphill will be a breeze. Passing semitrailers will be no problem. In an emergency you will have the power to keep you and your family safe. [*This is benefit selling, which is part 3 of the structure and keeps the benefits separate from the feature.*] Safety is important to you, isn't it?' [*This is the commitment question, which is part 4 of the structure.*]

You may wish to continue selling the safety features and benefits of the car. If so, simply repeat the procedure by saying:

> 'Another very important safety feature of this car is that it has twin airbags in the front. It has both passenger and driver

protection. Which means that your front-seat passenger will have the same protection from injuries as yourself. You would want your family to have this protection, wouldn't you?'

The important point about this structure is that it separates features from benefits and forces the salesperson using it to actually describe benefits as well as features. Many salespeople describe features and leave the prospect to turn the features into benefits, but prospects can't always see the benefits. Many sales are lost because the salesperson has only gone halfway in their explanation. If you leave out benefits, or do not describe them properly, you are leaving out the part that produces 75 per cent of sales: the emotional part.

To ensure that you don't overlook the potential of this structure, do the following exercise on your major product or service.

1. Draw a line across a blank page. Remember: this is the line that separates logic from emotion.

2. Identify all the logical reasons for buying and write them above the line.

3. Identify all the emotional reasons why a prospect should buy your product or service and write them below the line.

4. Now see if there are any features in your logic list. If there are, list them as features and add the rest of the features to this list.

5. Write all your remaining logical and emotional reasons for buying as a benefits list.

6. Take each benefit and write it as a graphical and emotional statement that fully describes the benefit.

When you have completed this exercise, you will be in a position to describe each feature separately. Then use the connecting words and select the appropriate benefits for the feature and build them into a concise description of the benefits your prospect will enjoy as a result of the feature. Close your statement with a strong commitment question, and you now possess the most powerful tool in your selling presentation. Mastering this technique will improve your sales results dramatically. When I have done this exercise at my sales seminars or workshops and had the participants role-play the prospect and salesperson, and then describe how they felt about the exercise, the answers were always the same:

◆ The 'salespeople' said it was easy to do once they had mastered the structure and they felt more in charge.
◆ The 'prospects' said it was very easy to understand.

Easy to do and easy to understand, yet most of the participants had no structured way of dealing with benefit selling, and most were selling features not benefits. Whatever you do, be sure to complete this exercise, practise it until you can do it perfectly and then use it. Here's some good advice on practice from Peter B. Gosper, consultant and speaker:

> *Practising till you get it right gives you a chance to win.*
> *Practising till you can't get it wrong ensures that you will.*

MORE ABOUT FEATURES AND BENEFITS

A feature is generally derived from the way a product is manufactured or from its design. It could be colour, size, shape, power, safety, economy, weight, balance, durability, or any other undeniable fact about the product. It could be about the service that goes with the product, guarantees, delivery, payments, exchanges, replacements, support, advertising, discounts, etc., as long as they are undeniable facts.

In the following example you are selling Mr Shepherd the idea that he should stock your new product in his retail store.

'Mr Shepherd, a feature of our advertising support for this product is that it is nationwide both in newspapers and on TV. All the major papers carry an advertisement at least twice a week, and the product will be featured before and after the evening news on the national TV station. [*This is part 1. The advertising campaign format is an undeniable fact.*] Which means [*this is part 2, the connecting words between features and benefits*] this advertising is going to be seen by millions each day for at least the first month. The campaign will generate store traffic that will build your turnover and raise your profits. [*This is*

part 3, the benefits that will flow to Mr Shepherd.] That would be
helpful, wouldn't it?' *[This is part 4, the commitment question.]*

You then go on to outline other features and benefits that come with
this new product. If a product or service has multiple benefits, you can
keep them in this format.

'Mr Shepherd, this new product has four major features, which
are performance, safety, ease of handling and maintenance.
The safety feature is. . . '

Describe the safety features then deal with the other features in order of
importance. The technique is to describe each feature separately, using
the features and benefits structure. There are no short cuts if you want
maximum results.

While products have been used in these examples, the technique
applies equally to services. The services could be provided by a law firm
or a home maintenance service. There is no difference in how the features
and benefits are described. The only difference is in the service itself.

Connecting words

The words you use to connect benefits to features can vary with the
product or service, as long as they flow easily and describe accurately.
Here are some alternatives:

◆ Which means . . .
◆ And demonstrates . . .
◆ You will find that . . .
◆ In other words . . .
◆ Because of these . . .

Commitment questions

You can ask any question at the end of your description of benefits,
providing it generates agreement and leads the prospect towards a
positive acceptance of your presentation. Here are some alternatives:

◆ That would be important to you, wouldn't it?
◆ That would be helpful, wouldn't it?
◆ You could use these in your business, couldn't you?
◆ This will be of value, don't you think?
◆ That's a first-class solution, isn't it?

Now that you have a structure to support your benefit selling, you need
to practise the technique until it becomes a habit. Practice makes perfect

sales sense. Adlibbing is for amateurs. Peak performers do not practise on prospects or customers. They practise before they call. They prepare before they call, and then they fall into a routine that makes selling easy.

Don't take it for granted that your customers and prospects know the difference between features and benefits. Some do, most don't, and many sales are lost simply because you have not motivated them to buy, because you have not focused on the benefits and described them in emotional terms. It is your responsibility to motivate them to buy, and I guarantee that if you become expert in the art of selling benefits your sales results will rise significantly. Your customers will buy more often. You will create satisfied clients who recommend you and your organisation to their families, friends and associates.

When designing a product or service, most designers focus on the features not the benefits. The brochures reflect this; it is assumed that explaining the features is sufficient. In some cases it is, but rarely is explaining features as effective as describing benefits. To increase your effectiveness, make sure that you know your products and services. Know the features, turn the features into benefits, and, when dealing with your prospects and customers, focus your efforts on the benefits.

Benefit selling is a key to outstanding results in the field of human communications. Selling is simply a matter of communicating ideas and solutions that will benefit your prospect or customer.

Attitude is another important key to unlocking your sales potential. How you feel about selling decides how you go about selling. How you see yourself as a salesperson decides your success. Some salespeople tend to see themselves as servers rather than sellers. They always leave the initiative with the buyer. If the buyer buys, a sale is made; if the buyer doesn't buy, a sale is lost. The server waits for the decision.

Most people want help in making up their mind about a purchase. They want assurances that they are making a wise decision. They want to feel they are getting value for money. Selling is not a high-pressure activity; it is a communication exercise in which one person helps another to get what they want. Treating your prospects and customers in a thoughtful and considerate way is a simple exercise in good manners. Making them feel good is an investment in your career. Selling benefits is the best way to help them buy.

If prospects and customers could express how they would like to be treated when they are buying, I am sure they would say something like this:

◆ 'Don't sell me an investment program. Show me how to get rich.'
◆ 'Don't sell me a holiday. Show me how to enjoy myself.'
◆ 'Don't sell me self-improvement products. Show me how to develop my career.'
◆ 'Don't sell me cosmetics. Show me how to look beautiful.'
◆ 'Don't sell me furniture and carpets. Make my home more attractive and nice to be in.'
◆ 'Don't just sell me a car. Make me feel more important and safer.'
◆ 'Don't sell me products or services. Sell me ideas, a better self-image, freedom from fear and want, and a philosophy on life that will enable me to grow and reach my potential as a human being.'

How much better to sell benefits rather than price. How much better to sell solutions than products, wants rather than needs. How much better to sell yourself as a person of value whose main objective is to help your prospects and customers grow their businesses and grow as people. How much better to have them say to others, 'if you want good advice and service, call. . .' and then, to recommend you. How much better to have a career than just work.

People buy to feel good, and every time you sell the benefits of your product or service you are making them feel good. Your business is your customer, and selling them benefits instead of things will make them feel good about you and your business and will help you to build effective and enduring relationships that will turn your employer's business into a customer satisfaction organisation that will produce and prosper. They win. You win. Your employer wins.

CONCLUSION

You now have the opportunity to hear suggestions on benefit selling from Imelda Roche who, with her husband Bill, is one of Australia's greatest business success stories. They launched Nutri-Metics in Australia in 1968 and later established operations in seven countries in the Asia-Pacific region. In 1991 they acquired Nutri-Metics' worldwide interests, and the head office is now in Sydney. Imelda's achievements are too numerous to mention. Among them is the Officer in the Award Order of Australia (AO) General Division. In 1993, Imelda was appointed Chairperson of the World Federation of Direct Selling Associations for a term of three years, the first woman and Australian to hold that position.

◆

JC: Imelda, in your opinion, what is the key to selling buyer benefits?

IR: I believe the key to successfully selling buyer benefits is first to establish a need (and a desire), then to introduce the product(s) that will best meet those needs, highlighting the quality, value and the features before focusing on the benefits. A critical step in this process is to have effectively convinced the customer that she is buying more than a product, she is buying quality, value and performance, and, more importantly, she is buying a personalised ongoing service. Service and relationships have become critical in creating and maintaining customer loyalties. I believe it is clearly recognised today that it is far more costly to have to continuously find new customers than to maintain existing ones, and the key to maintaining existing customers is to have established a valued relationship.

JC: Imelda, because of the great success you have had in your particular business, I am sure all those reading this book would be anxious to know whether the buyer benefits and the views you expressed had much, if anything, to do with your success.

IR: Jack, the answer is most positively yes. The thoughts I just shared with you in identifying customer needs and effectively meeting those needs through high- lighting all the buyer benefits of quality, value, performance and service, was and is the foundation of Nutri-Metics' continuing success. We recognised very early that relationships are critical to establish- ing and preserving customer loyalty and that Nutri- Metics should always focus on building quality relationships and this of course starts with the people who choose to represent us as consultants and in the training of those people. It has always been of critical importance to have our consultants recog- nise that their personal success is in large measure dependent upon the quality of the service they provide to their customers ... and ... if their personal goal is to build an expanding and sustainable business, the quality of the relationships they in turn build with others they invite to join them as Nutri-Metics consultants will play a major role in that success. So yes, that principle has been absolutely key to the growth of Nutri-Metics. We have constantly focused on the buyer benefits our consultants and their customers enjoy through their association with Nutri-Metics.

Jack, I believe that Nutri-Metics has enjoyed a much higher than average loyalty to both company and product because of the fact that we are recognised as having a caring concern both in our approach to people and to business, which is a widely-acknowledged buyer benefit, both for our consultants and their customers. In training our consultants we place great emphasis on the benefit of creating an environment in which customers want to buy rather than feel they are being sold. The ability to create an environment where people truly want to buy establishes you as a salesperson who believes in the value and benefit of the product or service you are offering. This will come through to the client, because they will see that you are focused on their benefits rather than on how the sale will benefit you, the salesperson. When you are seeking to build long-term customer–supplier relationships, there must be genuine sincerity.

Meeting customer needs through a sincere desire to provide a valued service is as important in professional practice today as it is in business and trade. At the core of economic progress in any community or society is the ability to convince others that they will benefit from buying what you have to offer or can produce. This clearly identifies salesmanship (interpersonal skills and the ability to relate well to others) as one of the most valuable skills we can develop — it is the accomplished seller of ideas, products or both — the tangibles and the intangibles — that keeps the wheels of industry turning and economies growing. The well-worn cliche: 'Very little happens until a sale is made' is a truism. There is great value and dignity in sincere salesmanship.

In Nutri-Metics, quality, value and recognisable buyer benefits is key to everything we do. To our consultants we promote the benefits of an enhanced lifestyle through achieving the rewards available to be earned by anyone who cares to make the commitment to do so. 'Earned' is a key word in the Nutri-Metics corporate culture. We believe that earning promotes a sense of achievement which enhances self-esteem, and when people are encouraged to develop a high level of self-esteem they have a better chance of achieving their true potential in life. When people know they have genuinely earned, it does great things for their self-esteem.

Finally a little personal philosophy. It is my strong belief that success in life should not be measured by the accumulation of wealth and material possessions. True success is being in a position to make the choice to do with your life something you truly enjoy and feel good about doing, and preferably that something should allow you to care for and provide well for your loved ones and for others who may be dependent on you. For me that means being financially self-reliant and being in a position to influence others to achieve financial self-reliance.

When you can choose a career or a path through life that gives you a high degree of personal satisfaction and maintains healthy self-esteem, that in my view is true success.

◆ — ◆ — ◆

What an inspirational message! If you follow the examples and suggestions given by Imelda, you will surely be on the way to building a successful career in selling.

CHAPTER 10

THE VISUAL
WAY TO
SALES SUCCESS

A picture is worth a thousand words.
ANON.

SELLING IS A creative business, and much of what you
sell is ideas. If the product you sell is a tangible item and small enough
to carry with you, or if your client will come to where your product is,
then you can use your product as a visual aid.

Most of us don't have that luxury, however. We aren't able to show
our product or to demonstrate our service. We have to rely on words.
That's why it is so important to speak simply, clearly, and concisely.
But you can enhance your words, by using a visual aid, especially if
what you sell is intangible. The saying 'a picture is worth a thousand
words' says it all, yet many salespeople continue to rely on words only
and, as a consequence, they are less effective than they could be if they
supported what they sell with an effective visual aid.

If you can't show your prospects your product or service, you can
show them what it does and how it works and you can make it real
with a visual aid. This is especially important when presenting
complex and detailed information. Visuals can simplify the most
complex message.

The challenge is to present your product or service in a new and exciting way that will grab your prospect's attention. There must be a better way than just talking about what it is you want to sell, and there is. It's the visual way.

ADVANTAGES OF USING VISUALS

Here are five good reasons for using visuals in your presentation:

1. It keeps you on track and enables you to tell your story quickly and effectively.
2. It helps your prospect to understand more clearly what you are proposing.
3. It helps you to overcome objections.
4. It raises your status in the eyes of your prospect.
5. It increases your chances of making a sale.

Too many sales are lost because of poor presentation. If you're not ready to sell, your prospects won't be ready to buy.

Visual aids can be a picture, a sheet of paper with some figures on it, a photograph, the product itself, a video, a chart, overhead transparencies or slides. They can be of commercial quality, handwritten or typed. There is no end to the variety of good visual aids that will help you in your presentation. The key issue with visual aids at all times is how graphically and clearly they express to the viewer what you are trying to convey in words.

Now let's look at these five reasons for using visuals.

It keeps you on track and enables you to tell your story quickly and effectively

Your visual should be keyed to your sales presentation and should demonstrate the important issues that you want to convey to your prospect. When you have a good visual aid that is keyed to your sales track and you have to stop and give information or answer an objection, then your visual makes it easier for you to go back to your presentation and continue where you left off. There is nothing as damaging to a presentation as a salesperson who has lost his or her way because of poor preparation, whether it is because of the lack of a visual or of presentation skills. Continuity of ideas and word sequence is essential if you want to keep in harmony with the problem-solving sequence of human thinking. Being relaxed and positive during your presentation is possible only when you are confident that your support material and its preparation is first class. When you are using visual aids that have worked well for you in previous presentations, your confidence level will be high and you can relax knowing that you are in complete control of the current situation. These qualities influence your prospects in a very positive way.

It helps your prospect to understand more clearly what you are proposing

This really is an important issue, because it is difficult to explain a product when you don't have the product to show. It is so much more difficult to explain abstract ideas and creative thinking just with words. The objective is to have a creative visual aid that highlights the idea you are proposing. The key issue is whether the visual explains in dramatic terms what it is that you want to convey to your prospect. There are no short cuts to success in this phase of selling. As products and services become more complex, the need for simplification grows. The simpler you make it for your prospect to understand you, the greater your chances of making the sale. There is no more graphic way of conveying the message about driving safely than by placing wreaths on a road where someone has died in a car accident.

It helps you to overcome objections

If your presentation is soundly organised and you understand your market, then you will be in the position of knowing what objections you are likely to receive during your presentation. This enables you to prepare a visual to counter each objection you are likely to get and to have them available so that if objections do arise during your presentation you only have to move to your objections visual, answer the objection and then resume your sales presentation. Again, the key issue is how clearly, concisely and dramatically the visual conveys what it is you want to say in order to overcome the objection.

It raises your status in the eyes of your prospect

In too many cases, salespeople simply don't take the trouble to be a step ahead of the opposition. Many don't seem to understand how important it is to be different. Perception is the reality of human experience. If your prospects perceive you to be no different from the other salespeople they deal with, then you aren't. It doesn't matter what *you* think, it only matters what *they* think. In order to ensure that they perceive you as being different, you must work hard at adding value to what you do. Using dramatic visual aids is one way to create the perception of being different. You can be certain that most of your opposition won't go to the trouble. Above all, if you want to raise your status in the eyes of your prospects, then you need to convince them that you know what you're talking about, that you understand what is important to them, and you can do this by presenting your ideas clearly with a good visual aid.

It increases your chances of making a sale

This is surely the best reason for using a visual aid. If it's not important to make the sale, there's no point in going. Whether you sell advertising, cleaning services, cars, real estate or anything else, the need is the same: creative ideas reduced to clear copy which is easily understood visually. The problem is that salespeople generally are slow to respond to the need to show, not just tell, potential clients what they propose. The reason why showing is so much better than telling is that the prospect's ability to absorb information and their willingness to understand is increased dramatically by using their eyes as well as their ears.

Here is an example. Because financial services is an abstract product, it needs to be made real by the power of visual aids. Most financial services presentations involve pages and pages of words and figures, which are better than hours and hours of talking, but inferior to clear, concise, easily understood graphics. Graphs can easily be prepared on a computer. Graphs for financial prospects can be used much more effectively than pages of figures. One good graph can tell the story almost at a glance, and this reduces the prospect's need to wade through columns of figures trying to unearth the idea or understand a difference. Graphs are good for any product or service situation which has comparative figures, or in leasing or running costs, or if your offer contains different options.

A visual aid can be a letter with the product attached or enclosed in the envelope. One very creative approach letter I saw recently, and which I mentioned in an earlier chapter, had a wrapped sweet pinned to the top left-hand corner of the letter saying, 'Here is a sweet for you to chew while you are chewing over my offer.' The letter was conservative, but the sweet was a friendly way of attracting attention, increasing the chances that the prospect would read the rest of the letter and decide that the writer was worth an interview. Creativity mostly pays off.

USING VISUALS EFFECTIVELY

Having a good visual aid is one thing, using it effectively is another. The example below shows some of the key elements of using a visual aid to its best advantage. You are presenting Andrew Philips, a printer, with solutions to his printing needs. If your visual is a complete written sales presentation and has been designed to do the selling, then follow the suggestions contained in Chapter 16, 'Making Powerful Presentations'. If your visual is to support a verbal sales presentation, then here's how to use it most effectively. (If your visual is a computer, you may need to make some slight alterations to these suggestions.)

◆ Position yourself so that you can show your visual aid to its best advantage. That means sitting alongside Andrew. If that isn't possible, position yourself as close to him as you can.

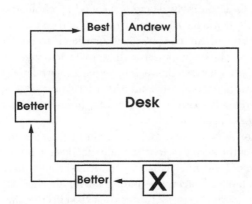

◆ Always give Andrew a clear view of the visual. If one of you must view it side on or upside down, let it be you. If you are sitting alongside Andrew, sit on his right side so that when you point to a part of the visual your arm doesn't get in the way of his view.

◆ Use your pen as a pointer to highlight critical aspects of the idea your visual contains.

◆ Take your time and guide Andrew with your eyes, which are your primary pointer, and your pen, which is the secondary pointer. Keep your eyes on the aid when you want him to read it and your pen on the *specific* part you want him to read. Lift your eyes and your pen when you want his attention. If he doesn't respond when you lift your eyes and pen, stop talking until eye contact is achieved. When you want him to resume looking at your visual, guide him back to it with your eyes and pen. Very quickly, he will get the message that he is to follow your eyes and pen.

◆ Control of Andrew's attention is critical to your success, so don't confuse him by constantly changing his attention from the visual to you and back again. Remember: the purpose of the visual is to reduce confusion; don't undo your good work by bad technique.

◆ When you have made an important point with your visual, wait for a response. Do you need to do more? Does Andrew understand it? If you want to know, ask: 'Have I made myself clear?' Remember: silence is your most potent weapon if you use it properly, so don't speak if it isn't necessary.

◆ If your presentation has more than one idea or option as a possible solution, then give your preferred option last and arrange your visual aids accordingly. There is a sound psychological reason for doing this. If you have a series of options and you are in the process of examining them, the one given first tends to be blotted out by the others. The common-sense thing to do is to give your preferred idea or option last, so that it is uppermost in Andrew's mind.

◆ Keep control of your visual aid. Don't let Andrew take it over. Use it in such a way that you can remove it from your presentation just as easily as include it.

◆ If you are using a graph as a visual aid in your presentation, then remember the need to sell on the line that demonstrates the benefits the prospect will receive. It may be a cost-benefit analysis showing the accumulated savings at intervals over the life of, say in this example, a printing press. In this case, the effective life is expected to be 10 years and the benefits are shown at two-yearly intervals. Focus on each two-year period and describe in emotive terms the benefits received, and then suggest ways of using the savings that will add even more value to the savings your graph will demonstrate.

◆ When you are using a graph as described above, use the technique of covering up that part of the visual that doesn't apply to the period you are demonstrating. For example, if you are demonstrating the second year of benefits, use a piece of paper to cover all the graph except that part showing the second year. If you then move on to year four, move the paper a little to the right and reveal all the graph that applies to that year. That way, you keep Andrew's mind on the point you are trying to make. If you reveal the complete graph, he will tend to look past where you are describing because he can think faster than you can talk, so it is important to anchor his mind at the spot that you are discussing by removing the option of looking ahead.

Another technique in using graphs is to cover, or take away, the benefits, while explaining, 'This will be the situation if you don't take this course of action.' Then describe as emotively as possible what life will be like without those benefits. Taking benefits away is often more effective than just describing the benefits Andrew will enjoy, but don't take them away until you know he wants them.

Using a visual aid is mostly sound common sense, and your biggest problem will be to pace yourself in your presentation so that you don't get ahead of the ideas you are proposing. If you are too eager or anxious to give your prospect the good news and hammer home the points of your presentation that you think are important, you may lose impact. Don't move too fast.

Good visual aids take time to prepare, but they are the key to improving your selling success without improving your knowledge. The essential ingredient, however, is better communications between you and your prospect. This results in understanding, which produces more sales for you.

CHAPTER 11

REACHING AGREEMENT BY RESOLVING DOUBTS AND OBJECTIONS

*Nothing is ever gained by winning an argument
and losing a prospect or customer.*
C. F. NORTON

PROSPECTS AND CUSTOMERS will raise objections, and be glad that they do, otherwise you would never know what they are thinking or how much progress you are making. Objections, or doubts, are natural; they are the signposts that show you the way to create a satisfied prospect.

To deal effectively with objections, it is essential that you don't fear them. Welcome the prospect's involvement and use that involvement to make sure the prospect gets what they want.

The first principle of dealing with objections is to listen and learn. Listen carefully and with interest to what your prospect is saying, and you will reduce objections to a process rather than a confrontation. In a confrontation, you can easily win the fight but lose the war.

There are no smart, sure-fire answers to objections; there are no answers that work all the time. But most of them will be effective if they are used at the right time and with the right person, especially if they are used to answer the concerns of the prospect rather than simply to fight to get a sale at any cost. Most sales discussions produce some doubts or objections. Even in a successful sale, there will be something the prospect doesn't like or want or that they are concerned about. These objections are a valuable part of the sales process. They tell you what progress you are making and what your prospect is really thinking, and that is the purpose of the whole sales dialogue.

The only way to ensure there are no objections is to have absolute power over your prospects during the discussion, so that they must buy what you offer. The truth is, your prospects have the only absolute power. They can turn off, say nothing, not listen, or terminate the discussion at any time they wish. They can go somewhere else and buy what they want. They can cease being your prospect anytime they want, and many will do so unless you meet, or exceed, their expectations. The objective at all times is to satisfy the needs and wants of your prospects.

You don't have to answer all objections. Some you can ignore. However, if an objection comes up twice, be sure you answer it immediately. If you choose to ignore an objection, be sure you are right in doing so or you will be seen as hard sell. Try to answer as many objections as you can by anticipating them in your discussion. The more objections you answer before they come up, the better your image will be. You will be seen as straightforward, honest and helpful, and that surely is how you want to be seen. If you must put off giving an immediate answer, let your prospect know when to expect it.

REASONS FOR OBJECTIONS

Generally, there are only three reasons objections are raised. They are:

1. There is something the prospect doesn't understand.
2. There is something they don't believe.
3. There is something they are trying to hide.

Your prospects may not understand how a product or service works, why it costs so much, why they must wait for delivery or why you can't do what they want. When something isn't understood, find out exactly what the problem is and then provide in simple language the information the prospect needs in order to understand. You can do that by asking questions. Never say, 'Do you understand?', because that infers the prospect is stupid. Always ask, 'Have I made myself clear?' and take responsibility for ensuring that understanding takes place.

If the prospect doesn't believe what has been said, you should use the same technique to ensure understanding, but you also need to back up what is not believed with specific information which will confirm what has been said. If your prospect is trying to hide something, don't embarrass them by digging too far into their reasons. Ways of dealing with this situation are discussed below.

TYPES OF OBJECTIONS

There are only two kinds of objections: those that are genuine and those that are false. It is only possible to answer those that are genuine. There is no answer to a false objection. When prospects raise genuine objections, they will discuss them and will stand by them stubbornly if they aren't answered satisfactorily, because to them they are real reasons for concern.

False objections can't be answered. The only hope is to uncover the real reason, and this is not always easy to do. They are a put-off to hide the real reason, which might be embarrassment or humiliation. Perhaps the price is more than they can afford, but they don't want to admit they can't afford it so they raise a false objection. False objections are usually indicated by reactions such as avoiding eye contact, displaying anger or attempting to change the subject. When you are reasonably sure you are dealing with a false objection, accept the prospect's reason, offer an alternative if possible but then let the matter rest if the prospect persists with the objection.

The key issue is always to preserve the relationship. The prospect may not buy today, but if you keep their confidence in you they may very well buy next week. You are in business for the long term, and to survive long term you need prospects who become customers.

Objections fall into four categories:

1. No desire.
2. No need.
3. No money.
4. No time.

No desire

The prospect doesn't want what you are suggesting, which is an emotional reaction. Your only chance of changing the situation is by creating a stronger emotional desire within the mind of your prospect for your offer. They may not desire what you are offering more than their present alternative, which is not to buy. You create desire in your prospect's mind by highlighting the benefits in a way that will appeal to them. More than 70 per cent of all sales are made on emotional issues, and unless the prospect becomes emotionally involved with the product or service, they are unlikely to buy.

No need

The prospect may truthfully believe there is no need, or that other products or services will suit the situation better. It could be that they are dealing with a competitor. If it's a case of 'No, not *now*', you have a better chance. You can show your prospect what will be lost in terms of money or security, or the hardship they will experience by not buying now. You can light some emotional fires. If it really is a case of no need for your suggestion, don't waste your time and energy and risk losing the prospect's goodwill by being seen to be hard sell and pushy.

No money

This generally falls into one of two categories. The prospect definitely doesn't have the money and can't find it no matter how much they want what you are offering. In this case, gracefully cease selling and plan for the future. Six months from now it may be different.

In the second case, there is no money from disposable income, but the prospect could find some if their desire for your offer forced them to reassess their current priority list so as to include your offer. Only when the desire for what you have suggested is stronger than for something that is a current priority, will the prospect buy.

No time

Again, it's a priority list of wants. Unless you strengthen the desire for what you have suggested, you can't win. Show the cost of waiting. Express it in WIIFM terms. Unless benefits are increased and the prospect gets emotionally involved to the point where possession is more important than time, they are unlikely to act.

TECHNIQUES FOR ANSWERING DOUBTS OR OBJECTIONS

The 'I understand, however' technique

When an objection is raised, answer: 'I understand how you feel. However, . . . ' and then state your point of view. This technique is perhaps the most widely used for answering doubts or objections. The 'I understand, however' method is a soft, tactful way of denying the objection without offending the prospect. No one likes to be told they are wrong. Don't use the 'Yes, but' technique; it is a rebuttal, no matter how it is used. It is better to use expressions like 'I understand how you feel' or 'However', or 'It can seem that way; however, have you considered. . .' and then give the benefits. You may wish to use expressions such as 'I understand how you feel', then pause and say: 'Would you consider. . .' and then express an alternative to or variation on what you have been discussing. These techniques are soft and non-offensive. They show your prospect that you are listening and that you are concerned about their feelings.

The third party referral technique

A further often-used technique is the third party referral method, where you supply information on how other prospects have used this

---

BASIC STRATEGY FOR HANDLING DOUBTS OR OBJECTIONS

- Listen actively. Show you are listening. Nod to show you have heard.

- Hear them out. Listen patiently to everything the prospect has to say. Don't interrupt.

- Feed it back. Ask your prospect to confirm that you have understood by restating in your own words what has been said.

- Think before answering. When you are sure you understand the objection, give your solution.

- Answer calmly and convincingly. Don't become emotional and defensive. Your objective is to help the prospect, not to impose your opinion on them. Confirm the answer and move on.

particular product or service to their advantage. This is a very valid and powerful way of answering a doubt or objection. It is often used when prospects indicate that they don't believe something that has been said. Think how often you have wanted to buy a particular product or service and have asked your friends if any of them have made this particular purchase lately. When you have found someone who has, and they have recommended you go to the same place to buy, you have done exactly that. Why did you go to where your friend had bought? Was it because you always follow what your friends do, or was it because their good experience overcame your fears of making this purchase and you were reassured enough to go to the same place? The answer is nearly always the latter. If you feel reassured by another's experience, why not use the same technique to help your prospects overcome their fears and doubts?

Most people require some assurances when making decisions, and if you always have some third party referrals available to help them you will find they will respond in a positive way.

The feel, felt, found, technique

This technique is taken from Ron Willingham's book *The Best Seller*. When a prospect raises an objection, answer calmly and convincingly: 'I understand how you *feel*, and I *felt* that way until I *found* out how much more value there was in this product over the one I was previously using.' Or: 'I understand how you *feel* and many of my prospects have told me they *felt* the same way until they *found* out how reliable this new machine is. Now they use nothing else.' Then go on to describe more of the benefits the prospect will get from using the product you have recommended.

This is a very powerful and effective method of answering doubts and objections and can be used on almost every kind of objection. It also has the advantage of being a very soft and friendly way of answering objections. Not only does it encompass a third party referral technique, but the framework of the technique is in a logical sequence and is easily understood. This is the way of the peak performer who is always looking for not only the most effective way, but also one that will help to build the relationship.

Answering objections effectively is one of the key skills of communicating with your prospect. There will be objections, and how well you deal with them will decide whether you win or lose. More importantly, it will decide whether you build your relationship with your prospects in a way that will not only keep them coming back, but will also have them asking for you.

SPECIFIC OBJECTIONS

Now that we have explored the basics of why objections are raised, and you have mastered basic techniques for dealing with them, let's look at some specific objections and how you might deal with them.

Price objections (no money)

The following quotation will help you to understand that in the end you generally get what you pay for: 'There is hardly anything in this world that some man cannot make a little worse and sell a little cheaper, and people who consider only price are this man's lawful prey.'

Price is important because it is nearly always a consideration, even if only to judge value. For those in a very price-conscious industry, it is the only consideration because meeting the price without consideration of quality or service may be a matter of survival for them. Happily, such people are in the minority and, unless you are supplying that industry, they are probably not on your list of prospects. But price will still be a consideration in terms of assessing value, and value for money is critical to most people. Current research says that value for money is the biggest single issue for the majority of people in most purchases today. Value is a perception, not a reality. If the consumer says your product or service is value for money, then it is. If they say it isn't, it isn't. So your prospect's perception is critical when you are selling. If you want to avoid price objections, build value for money perception at every opportunity. Don't wait for price to become an objection.

Many salespeople who are continually meeting price objections find it easier to seek price reductions in order to meet the competition and win the sales rather than develop an effective answer to the objection. Before you seek reductions, you should understand that no matter how low the price, you won't get all the market — not even a large share. You won't win every quote, and you won't make every sale. Your competitors, who may be under your price, don't, so why should you? Remember, competition is important — it keeps us on our toes and helps us to grow. In the words of Hamilton Mabic: 'Don't be afraid of opposition. Remember, a kite rises against, not with, the wind.'

SPECIFIC PRICE OBJECTIONS

- 'Your price is too high.'
- 'I can do better from your competitors.'
- 'Your price is too high for our needs.'
- 'Your discounts are too low.'
- 'It looks great, but it's more than I can afford.'

Market leaders are rarely the cheapest. Why? Because other issues are involved and some of these are more important to many consumers. Style, service, exclusivity, fashion, durability and a host of other considerations all play a part in the assessment of value for money. It may be more effective to raise the value for money perception of your product or service by adding benefits rather than lowering your price.

As a salesperson, you must accept that if price is to be the only consideration in determining sales success, then you don't count and aren't needed. Your place can be taken by the lowest-paid member of staff who can understand a price list and fill out an order form. If you are to count, then you have to be the difference. The only question is, how are you going to be the difference? The answer is by building value in the perception of your prospect's mind, and that is done by selling the features and benefits of your offer until it is perceived as real value.

Here is another quotation which I have used successfully and taught others to use just as effectively. I first saw it on the door of an upmarket manufacturer of high-quality furniture. It sums up the price issue very clearly: 'Our competitors sell their products cheaper than we do. Our competitors are smart people, they know what their products are worth.'

One way of handling price objections is to try to control how and when the issue of price is raised during your presentation. You might decide to talk price early in your presentation. This gives you control and the opportunity to give supporting positive evidence of the value for money of your offer. Because you raised the issue of price yourself, you might feel and appear less defensive than if you waited for your prospect to raise the issue. *You* have to choose; it's *your* presentation. If you decide to let the prospect raise the issue and they do so early in the presentation, you might choose to ignore it and press on. If you do this, get your prospect's approval and let them know when you will answer. This is a common course of action; however, you run the risk of being seen as not wanting to deal with the price and this may cause your prospect to become unduly suspicious of you and your offer and decide not to do business with you.

Before you answer a price objection, find out exactly what the prospect is objecting to. Do they want more information? Is their objection based on fact or misconceptions? Is it really about the price of the product or service, or is it more about your terms and conditions? When you know what aspect of your price is the problem, you are better able to respond effectively.

The most effective way of dealing with price objections is to focus on building value with features and benefits, so that you reduce price to a minor and manageable issue. Here are some issues to take into account when a price objection is raised.

◆ *Performance.* Part of the price of products is their quality and standard of performance. Usually, higher prices mean better performance in terms of reliability, lower maintenance costs, greater speed, which means savings in time, and greater efficiency and effectiveness, all of which save money and improve the service or quality of whatever the product is being used for.

◆ *Quality.* If your product has a longer life because of built-in quality, it is better value over the term of its effective life than a cheaper product. Always stress the trouble-free nature of better products. Downtime through product failure is an expensive issue for anyone in today's fast-paced world, so you need to paint pictures of the inconvenience and problems that it causes so that these issues are clear in the mind of your prospects.

◆ *Satisfaction.* Saving a few dollars on the day of a purchase is soon forgotten when problems in performance arise. Pride of ownership of a superior or prestigious product or service is a tangible matter. If the only benefit of ownership is to constantly remind oneself that it was cheap, then it is likely there will be little joy.

◆ *Profit on savings.* Now you are talking the price buyer's language, so your message should be welcome and of interest. Your message is price, but it's about paying a little more now in order to reap much more over the life of the product or service. Value for money means delayed profits and saving but instant satisfaction, pride of ownership and superior performance. Your task as a salesperson is to sell the benefits of making that trade.

Reducing price to small amounts by dividing the total price into months, years, days, and in some cases hours, is always productive. A prestige car may cost $100 000, but it can be leased for about $7 a day which makes it available to a far greater number of buyers. While leases avoid the initial lump-sum payout, reducing the initial price in the mind of your prospect to smaller units has a distinct advantage. If you do the same unit comparison over the difference in price between your offer and your competitor's price, it is even more effective because the difference may be so little it should be easy to build your advantages so that they outweigh the savings.

Once you have reduced the price to units, it is time to emphasise what your prospect will lose in order to save a few dollars a week. In this exercise of demonstrating loss of features and benefits, be sure to focus on the unit price of the difference, because this is the real issue. Emphasising the difference is critical, because the prospective buyer may see the *total* price as being the problem.

If you dramatically emphasise loss, it can bring home to the prospect the value of the features and benefits of your offer more effectively than building value. However it is counterproductive to talk loss before you have built value unless you are selling a product or service that has been designed to overcome loss, such as insurance products, health services, etc.

Here are some sample answers to specific price objections.

Your prospect is Mrs Fenton, who is proposing to buy a new video recorder. She has just said:

> MRS F: I like this recorder, *but the price is more than I want to pay.* Your competitor has a very good model which I liked and it is several hundred dollars cheaper.
>
> YOU: Mrs Fenton, I appreciate you don't want to spend more than is necessary and you want the best value you can get for your money. I am sure you will find this model is far better value for money, especially when you take into account actual recording costs.
>
> MRS F: The cost of recording? Surely that is the same on both models?
>
> YOU: Not really. Remember the long-playing and recording feature I spoke of that is an exclusive feature of this model?
>
> MRS F: I'm sorry, I must have missed it. What is it?

YOU: Mrs Fenton, it means that your ordinary three- and four-hour tapes can record for six or eight hours on this machine. By selecting long play, you effectively cut your tape costs in half. You said earlier that one of your main reasons for buying a new machine was to record entertainment information for your children. You will soon save the difference in price, and you will have the added convenience of not having to change tapes as often — and a superior machine into the bargain.

MRS F: And I won't have to store as many tapes?

YOU: That's right. You only need half the storage space, and after a while you will be making money.

MRS F: OK, I'll pay the difference. When can I get delivery?

Your prospect is Chris Williams, a buyer from a small construction company.

CW: Your price is too high. *I can buy it cheaper from your competitor.*'

YOU: I appreciate you don't want to pay more than you need to. However, profit isn't only about price, is it?

CW: What do you mean?

YOU: I mean there are all types of costs other than the initial price — for instance, delivery and storage costs. We offer a seven-day, 24-hour delivery on this purchase with minimum initial quantities. That will cut your inventory holding costs by at least 25 per cent and that means real savings, doesn't it? There is no risk of supply if you run short at weekends. Just call us and we'll deliver.

CW: Can you guarantee what you promise?

YOU: We not only guarantee our service, but if you don't receive supply as promised, your order is free. Now that's a real guarantee, isn't it?

CW: You're on. I'd like the first delivery tomorrow before 9 am.

Your prospects are Mr and Mrs Fitzpatrick, and you have just presented a program to pay school fees for their two-year-old daughter, Dianne.

MR F: The program is OK, *but it costs too much.*

YOU: I appreciate how you feel, and I can understand why you think education costs too much. However, I can't change the school fee structure, and that's what it costs. The savings program isn't the cost; it's the school fees that cost and, no matter what you do, someone has to pay, don't they?

MRS F: I don't understand when you say someone has to pay.

YOU: Mrs Fitzpatrick, your decision is more about *who* pays, rather than *how much*. If *you* don't pay the fees, then it is probable Dianne will pay in terms of lost opportunities and a poorer quality of education. Someone will pay, because when Dianne arrives at the school with books in hand, you must be there cheque in hand or they won't let her in. Is that not true?

MRS F: Yes, that's true. But it's so expensive.

YOU: I agree. However, it's the *education* that is expensive. The program makes profit which will go towards paying the fees. I believe that this program will mean you can reduce your outlays to yearly contributions to Dianne's future while at the same time guaranteeing that if Mr Fitzpatrick should die during the period of the program, your contributions will cease and the proceeds of the plan will be available for Dianne's school fees. That's a better option than trusting to luck, don't you think?

MRS F: Yes, I do. How soon can it be done?

I could go on giving examples of how to meet price objections forever, but no matter what the objection the principles will be the same. Once you have mastered the principles, you will be in a position to develop creative solutions that will answer the objection and increase your chances of making the sale. I have spent considerable time on price because it causes more problems than any other objection, for two broad reasons:

1. Many prospects have learned that the easiest way to get rid of salespeople is to raise objections as soon as possible in the discussion. Is it not true of most of us that when we are confronted by a salesperson, we immediately go into protection mode? Few people like to be sold; most of us like to buy — in our own time and from someone we have chosen.

2. Many salespeople, especially those in industrial selling, get so many price objections that price becomes a barrier to performance instead of a continuing opportunity to learn. With all the practice salespeople have on price, they should be expert on how to deal effectively with this objection. It is difficult to understand why so

few creative solutions are developed in the field of price. If price is a problem for you, why not come up with some creative answers and practise them until you are perfect?

The no time objection

This objection is usually raised during the approach rather than as a reason for not buying. When raised in a presentation, it is usually not the real objection but simply a way of avoiding having to make a decision, and that is generally because you haven't created enough interest in or desire for your offer. Often it will be expressed as: 'Sorry, I don't have time and I'm not really interested anyway', which is more a statement of 'If I was interested I could find the time'. Thus, the real issue is to create interest. No time now is an invitation to set another time. So do that as a first step and then you will generally get the real objection once time has become a non-factor.

The no need objection

This objection is often given when the desire for your offer is weak. Some people will genuinely believe they don't need it. If they don't want what you are offering, you have a chance of converting them by showing them benefits they may not have considered or uses that your offer could fulfil that they are not aware of. More than anything else, this objection is telling you that your preparation was inadequate because peak performance prospectors don't sell to people who don't have a *need* for what they sell. They may, however, approach and present to people who don't *want* what they sell, and they are willing to exchange their time for an opportunity to develop desire so that wanting will arise. They know it's their responsibility to create the desire.

Here is a creative solution to a 'no need, don't want, no desire' situation. I have given this demonstration hundreds of times during open forum in my sales seminars, and it always works. It is based on the real-life problem of a group of agents who were constantly getting the 'don't want, no desire, no time, no need' objections, which were expressed like this:

◆ 'Life insurance? I'm not interested.'
◆ 'If this is life insurance, I've got all I need.'
◆ 'I've got no time to talk insurance and I don't want any. I'm not interested.'

The agents had no effective answer to these objections. If they used the 'No, but' answer, it only made their prospects more determined to resist. The agents gave me the problem to solve and I spent the weekend looking for the solution. Here is the solution in dialogue form, which faithfully follows the actual discussion that took place on the Monday after learning this technique, when they met their first objections.

> JW: Good morning, my name is Jim Williams from the ABC Insurance Company. I would like to show you a new and exciting insurance plan. It will take 20 minutes to show you how it works.
> PROSPECT: Sorry, I'm not interested in insurance. I've got all I need.
> JW: You know it's only insurance until you change it, don't you?

If you were the prospect, what would you say now? You're right, that's exactly what they said:

> P: What do you mean? I don't understand.
> JW: Let me show you how you change insurance. First, you can only change insurance to one thing, money. You buy insurance, but you get paid in money. Insurance is only a system of risk management that pays off in money, and there are only three ways to turn it into money.

The agents then opened their visual aid and proceeded to take the prospect through the 'Live, Die or Quit' concept, which is one of the most powerful concepts ever devised to explain the outcome of any choice you make no matter what the product or service. (For a full explanation of 'Live, Die or Quit', see Chapter 20, 'Concepts'.) In explaining the concept, the agents tied their own offer into the explanation, and when they had completed the presentation the prospect had changed from not interested to total interest and in most cases bought the offer.

Did they buy because the offer was so good they couldn't resist it? Not really. Like so many people when they are approached by a salesperson, they resisted, didn't want to listen, didn't want to be sold, their mind is closed. All the statement did was awaken their natural curiosity and open their mind to discussion, and once that is achieved the offer stands or falls on its merits.

This simple illustration of a creative answer to a problem objection shows how easy it is to solve selling problems if you are willing to spend time working on the problem. This answer worked so well that the agents were out every day looking for prospects who weren't interested in insurance and didn't want to hear what they had to say.

The no desire objection

This objection generally forms part of every other objection you get which is not based on the performance or physical aspects of your product or service. The prospect may like everything about your offer except they genuinely believe it won't do the job because it is too big, too small, too powerful or not powerful enough — there are too many possible reasons to discuss each of them in detail. They may genuinely like the product, but in their opinion it isn't suitable. If you are confident the product will do the job and they aren't, then you are really talking about risk. If you have faith and want the business, then as a demonstration of faith you should take the risk of a 30-day trial. That way, even if it doesn't meet the test and you get it back, you have probably started a relationship that will pay off with other business. If you persist and make the sale, and the customer takes the risk and it doesn't work, you will have no real future with them. They will also tell others of their experience and you may lose a lot of future business with other prospects. Building value and developing relationships is critical in today's changing marketplace, and one way to do that is to take the risk.

No desire is generally evidenced by a lack of real involvement of the prospect in the discussion, by non-committal answers, a lot of questions and a general uneasiness in their demeanour. This is a time for some soft, open-ended questions that cannot be answered with a 'yes' or 'no.' Ask questions that reveal something about how the prospect feels about your offer, what he believes, what he will do and what he won't do. Ask in a non-threatening way that involves him, and you may get him participating. No participation means no sale.

Once you get participation, you can build value and develop the desire for ownership. No desire is really a prospect saying that you have more to do, that what you have done is not appealing enough. Desire can only be built by painting pictures in the mind of your prospect so that the benefits come alive and they can see themselves enjoying them. Remember that people only buy for two reasons: either to solve a problem or to make themselves feel good. The task here is to solve the problem and make them feel good about the solution.

Here is the best example I have seen of overcoming no desire. A friend of mine in the financial services industry was making a presentation to an engineer on a 10-year investment plan which had excellent tax benefits. My friend had no problems arranging an interview and made what he thought was an excellent presentation of the offer. He was very disappointed that the engineer, whilst acknowledging the benefits, declined the offer. Some days later he called to tell me that he had sold the investment plan to the engineer. I asked him why the engineer had changed his mind, and he said: 'Because I changed the reason why he should buy.'

My friend said that when he was reviewing the case, he realised that in the first part of the interview, when he was asking questions to make sure he was offering the right program, the engineer had said he was an avid walker. Every holiday and break from work he was off walking, and he listed the countries in which he had walked and expressed the desire to one day walk around Scotland.

When my friend went back to see the engineer, he was told: 'I have already told you I'm not interested in your offer.' My friend replied, 'Mr Engineer, how would you like to walk around Scotland 10 years from now and do it on tax-advantaged dollars?' He then showed the engineer several beautiful brochures on Scotland that he had selected from a travel agency and described in detail many of the wonderful places he could walk to. He said the engineer's face lit up at the thought of finally walking around Scotland. 'Now you're talking my language,' he said. 'Where do I sign?' From 'no desire' to 'yes, please' because the offer was now about what he wanted.

There are only two reasons why people buy:

1. To solve a problem.
2. To make themselves feel good.

There is no substitute for keeping an open mind on which category your current prospect fits into. When you focus on the prime current issue, your chances of sales success increase dramatically. Remember: we are all constantly tuned into station WIIFM, so play the benefit hit tune they want to hear. Play it loud and clear so that they know beyond all doubt how they benefit from your offer.

CHAPTER 12

CLOSING
THE SALE

*Nothing happens until someone
buys something. Many do not buy
because they are not asked.*

THERE IS A time to talk, a time to listen and a time to close. Waiting for the customer to buy has lost millions of sales and created as many dissatisfied customers. Why do those who sell have so much difficulty in asking for the order? Whenever I ask this question both at my seminars and during my research, I always get the same answers:

◆ Fear of rejection.
◆ Not wanting to be seen as being pushy.

Fear of rejection

No matter who is doing the selling, the feeling is the same. We fear rejection because it damages our self-image, and we will do anything to preserve our self-image. When a prospect says 'No, I don't like the product service idea, many salespeople take the rejection of their offer as a personal rejection of self. Prospects and customers are not always concerned about how *we* feel; they are more concerned about how *they* feel. They are often abrupt, sceptical and difficult to deal with, all of which requires us to be able to think clearly about what is happening.

Our best chance of avoiding overreacting to a customer's rejection of our offer is to understand precisely what is happening. The customer is saying no to our product, service or idea, not to us as a person. They are not saying that, because they are saying no to our products, services or ideas, they don't like us. They may very well be thinking, 'I like this person' or 'This is an excellent presentation' or 'How helpful you are.' They may even be thinking, 'I can't or don't want to buy now, but when I do I will come back to this person because I enjoy the way he/she relates to me.'

Not wanting to be seen as being pushy

Again, this is protection of self-image. We want to be valued and we want to be liked. These are perfectly normal feelings which our prospects and customers also have: they want to be liked and valued just as we do. Very few of us want to be sold, but almost all of us want to be a buyer. To justify buying, we need reasons to buy. This is the clue to overcoming the 'I don't want to appear pushy' syndrome. If we stop telling prospects what they *must* do and give them options instead, they will respond positively.

It's like Winston Churchill said: 'Personally I am always ready to learn, although I do not always like being taught.' Once we realise that most people need a little help in making buying decisions, we can focus our thinking on helping them to buy rather than on not appearing to be pushy.

Helping customers to buy is a way of building enduring high-quality relationships. If your help in buying is based on the satisfaction of your prospects and customers, and is given with confidence and concern for them, you will have few problems in the pushy department. Being pushy is mostly defined by customers as 'someone trying to sell me something I don't want' or 'being involved with a salesperson who won't take no for an answer'. If we focus on selling benefits that will satisfy the customer, the pushiness will disappear.

To be effective in asking for orders, you need to know the answers to the following key questions:

◆ How will you know when to ask your prospect to buy?
◆ How will you ask them to buy?

WHEN TO ASK CUSTOMERS TO BUY

You will know to ask for the order either by coming to the end of your presentation or by reading the buying signals your prospect gives you during your discussions. Your timing will be critical. If you close too soon, you will be seen as pushy. If you wait too long, they may lose interest and you will lose a sale. When you feel you have built a climate of trust and cooperation between your prospect and yourself and you believe that your prospect has received enough information on which to make a judgment, it is decision time. Now is the time to close. Watch for buying signals and act on them, because prospects are always sending signals of intention to buy or not to buy. If you are getting no buy signals, you need to raise the emotional content of your offer. If you receive buying signals, act on them.

These buying signals are divided into three groups:

1. The prospect's questions.
2. The prospect's actions.
3. The prospect's reactions.

The prospect's questions

These questions will give you a clear indication of interest or the lack of it. The questions will always be seeking information either in order to decide whether to buy, or, having made the decision to buy, in order to seek information on matters which are essentially about completing the sale. These are buying signals. Some typical buying questions, and how you should deal with them, are discussed below.

Do you take credit cards? Now is the time to close, and you ask for the order in the way you answer the question. If you answer 'yes' or 'no', you are letting the customer buy. You are not asking for the order. If you answer the question and then ask one which will lead the customer to make a decision on buying, then you are asking for the order.

This closing technique is called the 'Not if, but which' method. It is one of the most successful and easily used techniques for all types of selling. By giving your prospects a choice of options, it becomes easy for them to decide, and as its use is based on the customer's questions it is natural and non-pushy. The technique in using it is not to answer their questions with a yes or a no, but to give the answer to the question and then ask the prospect a question which prompts them to make a decision on buying. For example, your prospect asks 'Do you take credit cards?'. You answer, 'Yes, we do and you name the cards you take. Then you ask, 'Which do you prefer?'. When the prospect names a choice, you have made the sale. Proceed and close the sale by starting to prepare the card form.

We use this technique every day in our social life. When arranging to meet a friend, you might suggest Wednesday or Thursday. When they select the day, you ask: 'Morning or afternoon?', and the process goes on until you have made all the arrangements.

MORE EXAMPLES OF THE 'NOT IF, BUT WHICH' TECHNIQUE

- Time: Before or after?
- Date: Monday or Tuesday?
- Size: Small or large?
- Colour: Yellow or red?
- Payment: Cash, account or credit card?
- Method: Pick up or deliver?
- Shape: Round or square?
- Weight: 1 kg pack or 4 kg carton?
- Speed: 60 wpm or 80 wpm?
- Lunch: Today or tomorrow?

Other questions which are buying signals:

◆ **Do you deliver**? *Closing response*: 'Yes, we deliver every day. Which would you prefer: tomorrow morning or afternoon?'
◆ **Is it possible . . .** ? *Closing response*: 'Yes, it is. Would you prefer a custom or standard finish?' (Give the available options.)
◆ **Can we . . .** ? *Closing response*: 'Yes, you can. Would you prefer to collect it from the manufacturer or our warehouse? (Give the available options.)
◆ **What colours does it come in**? *Closing response*: 'It comes in red, green, blue and yellow. Which would you prefer?'
◆ **Do you have credit accounts**? *Closing response*: 'Yes, we do. Thirty, 60, 90 days or monthly repayments.' (Ask which they prefer.)

The principle is simple. Whenever a prospect or customer asks a question which indicates interest, answer the question and give the required information and then ask the customer a 'Not if, but which' question which leads them to make a decision to buy.

Getting the order is one part of our objective; keeping the customer is the other and most important part. The critical test is: did we satisfy the customer? Do they feel good about their decision? Do we feel good about their decision? On every occasion when dealing with customers, we should focus on their feelings. Everything we do or say in our discussions will affect how the customer thinks about us, our product or service, and the business itself.

It is true that you never get a second chance at a first impression, and no matter how often you see a particular customer the law of first impression still applies. Each new encounter is a first impression. The customer buys you, your ideas, and your product or service in that order, and everything the customer sees, feels, hears or smells will shape their opinion of how they feel about us, our product, our service and the business itself.

The prospect's actions

On many occasions prospects will signal by their actions an intention to buy. For example, the customer may:

◆ Look for a pen to sign.
◆ Take out a cheque book or wallet.
◆ Produce a credit card.
◆ Take possession of merchandise as if it already belongs to them.
◆ Draw a diagram of how they intend to use or install the product.
◆ Call someone by phone to tell them how the service should be used.

All of these actions are positive buying signals, and you should test them by using a trial close based on the 'Not if, but which' principle, by asking, 'Which colour do you prefer: red or black?' and then continue with a series of such questions until you have led the customer to a final decision.

Whatever the action, you need to act on it by using one of the closing methods we have discussed. Timing is always important. Too late, and you may lose them. Always act as if what is happening is normal. Leave your prospects and customers only when you believe you have done all you can for them. Leave them feeling they are valued and appreciated.

The prospect's reactions

Listen carefully and watch closely for your prospect's reactions to what you are saying. Pay particular attention to their body language. How they react is telling you how they feel. For example, you are showing an article of clothing. Watch the customer's reaction when they touch the fabric: do they show pleasure and acceptance, or displeasure and rejection? Everything the customer feels, smells, tastes or hears will shape their opinion of what is happening to them. If their reactions are positive, then continue to build on what you are doing. If their reaction is negative, then change direction. For example, you are making an offer to a buyer for a small manufacturing company. The buyer is at her desk, and you are sitting opposite. The buyer has her pen in her hand, and her order book is close by. You are part-way through your presentation when the buyer puts her pen inside the order book and pushes it to the far corner of her desk. What are her actions saying? You're right. She is telling you that you are not doing well and you should raise the level of your presentation if you want to win. Always be alert to buying signals, and when you get one, act on it. If it is negative, focus on benefits. If it is positive, make a trial close.

HOW TO ASK FOR THE ORDER

Here are more closing techniques that you will find very effective, easy to use, and non-threatening to your prospects and customers. These techniques are suitable for every type of business and work in all situations.

The direct order technique

This method is almost self-explanatory. Here are some examples:

- Could I have an order number, please?
- Do we have a deal?
- Are you going ahead?
- Can I act on this information?
- When will we deliver your order?
- Where do you want us to deliver your order?

If you have given your prospect enough information on which to make a judgment and you have sold the benefits of your suggestion, this method will often suffice. Where ongoing relationships exist and you are constantly supplying products and/or services to the customer, this direct method is the one most often used. Be sure not to take the customer for granted. Always put in the time to build the relationship and leave the customer feeling valued and appreciated.

The 'if' technique

This method is generally used when a prospect is undecided whether to proceed and says something like, 'I'll have to talk to our accountant before I can decide' or 'We're not in a hurry. Perhaps we should think about it.' The task is to get him to make a partial decision now, without pressuring him. An easy, no pressure way of doing this is to agree with how he feels, and then ask a question. 'I appreciate how you feel. Decisions are not always easy to make. However, if you do decide to proceed, which style would you prefer?' When your prospect answers with his choice, he has made a partial decision and you are back in the discussion. If you then continue to use the 'Not if, but which' technique by asking 'Would you prefer to pay cash or account?', he will often move on to making a total decision.

In many cases, indecision is simply a matter of your prospect wanting you to help them make the decision. You have nothing to lose and a lot to gain if you use the 'if' method with care and consideration for the person to whom you are selling. Building the relationship is always the key issue.

The always be closing (ABC) technique

A powerful closing method is to take consent for granted and always be closing. Peak performers always use this method even if they have to finally close using an entirely different technique. This method builds confidence in your prospect's mind and definitely improves your chances of success. You can do this without being pushy. You have a choice of how you feel about dealing with your prospect. If you feel unsure or hesitant and adopt a negative attitude, then your chances of successfully closing the sale are less than good.

It is true that the body acts out what the mind is thinking, and if you are negative in your thinking you will display it in your actions. Moods are catching and we influence others by the way we act. It is in your interests to cultivate a 'can do' attitude, a 'The answer is yes, now what's the question?' response to your prospect. The ABC technique depends on this positive, willing to solve anything, approach. It means you always use words that indicate you expect the customer to buy. For example:

◆ 'You will enjoy every minute of this new . . . '
◆ 'When you own this, your life will be easier and more pleasant.'
◆ 'When you use this . . . you will never again have to clean up a mess after you have finished.'
◆ 'This service will move the responsibility from you to us.'

Throughout your entire discussion you take consent for granted and are always closing. Don't exert pressure. Use words that come naturally to you. Speak with conviction. Sell benefits and ask soft questions to find out how your prospect is feeling.

The don't push, apply no pressure technique

If you are still finding it difficult to close, here is a simple and highly effective way to ask for the order. Your prospect is Allan McCulloch, a buyer for a large engineering company. He has stated a preference for first names. You have presented an offer which has been reasonably well received, but you are having difficulty in closing the sale. You are getting no buying signals. You have tried several closes, but you are still receiving objections. Here's where you use the 'I would like you for a customer' close. Simply say:

> 'Allan, I would like you for a customer for myself and for my company, Jaynor Hydraulics. What do I have to do to get you for a customer?'

Don't say anything more. Wait for the answer. One of two things usually happens:

1. Allan will tell you what you have to do to get the sale. Do it and the sale is yours. If you can't do it, say:

    YOU: Allan, I can do most of what you want. However, I can't alter the delivery date because our first supply isn't available to anyone until next Wednesday. The model is OK, the pricing is right, I can do the delivery on Wednesday morning and we will

finish the installation within 24 hours, which means we will work
two shifts to make certain it's ready for work on Thursday.

ALLAN: OK, but if it's not ready on Thursday morning, you take
it back.

YOU: Done.

2. Allan says, 'There is nothing you can do. I'm not interested in
changing. I'm not sold on the machine and I don't want to discuss
it further.' You can fight on against the odds and probably make
absolutely certain you never get a hearing again, or you can accept
his decision and retire gracefully. If you choose this course of
action, you have at least left the possibility of something
happening in the future.

To prepare for the future, review your conversation with Allan.
Look for something he said he would like to improve or change,
and as soon as you can find something that could be of interest to
him in that regard, drop him a note with the information
attached, saying: 'Hi, Allan. I saw this information on the
problem you raised in our recent conversation. It may be of help
to you. Kind regards.' Sign it above the name of your firm. It may
not win him, but it won't do you any harm.

Whenever you can, send him more information that might be
useful to him. When you think the time is right, call again, take
something of value with you and try to strengthen the
relationship you have been developing.

Since I put this method together, many of those who have attended
my seminars have been in touch to say that it works well for them and
I am sure it will work for you.

As always, mutual trust is the key to developing long-term, effective
relationships. All enduring relationships from schoolfriends to parents
and children, to lovers and married couples, and to work colleagues
are based on mutual trust. You can develop trust with your prospects
and customers by always doing what you say and always working hard
to make life easier and more enjoyable for them. Customers are not an
option, they are a necessity.

Here are some more closing techniques that are very effective in any
type of selling. When you become expert at selecting the right one for
a particular situation, you increase your closing effectiveness
dramatically.

The restricted supply technique

This method is used when a new product is very much in demand and production cannot always match demand. It is an easy close to have an order increased in size. Here is an example, with the prospect Michael speaking first.

> M: I want you to be sure to work on this order for me, because several times in the last three months we have had to wait and that causes us problems with our customers.
>
> YOU: Michael, I understand your concern. We are selling heaps of it. At the moment we are ahead of schedule, but I don't know how long that will last. We only need a few of our customers ordering in advance to avoid delays and our production will fall behind. Why don't you do the same and make sure you don't get caught short?
>
> M: What you suggest makes sense, but I don't want it all in the next week. I'll just have to take the chance.
>
> YOU: What if I deliver in two orders, 10 days apart — would that help?
>
> M: If you do that, I'll double the order.

It may be that the product has been replaced by another and the special run-out price is only available while stocks last.

> YOU: Michael, this special is on until it runs out. Then it's the new product. I can get you an order now because it's first-in, first-served. You will have no problems making a good profit on it even if you run it as a special. You don't want to sit by and watch your competitors get it all, do you?
>
> M: No, I don't, but they will have to make their own decisions. Do I get my usual terms and discounts?
>
> YOU: You can have everything except your discount, because that has been factored into this special price. It's a once-only value and a once-only offer because it will sell out within the week. That's why I made this special call to give you the chance to get the extra profit. You can handle double your usual order on this, can't you?
>
> M: If you can deliver by Friday, you're on.
>
> YOU: It will be here Friday.

There may be impending industrial trouble in your industry which will affect your supply and you are advising your customers to buy now to avoid the possibility of not getting supplies if they order during the period of the dispute. Now you are tapping into the fear of losing, as against obtaining, a benefit. This is not a close arising from a normal presentation; it is an offer and a close made at the same time. If your prospect resists, you will probably have to use another close and tie it into your restricted supply presentation. The close most often used in this situation is the pros and cons close, which consists of developing a list of reasons why your prospect should buy this offer. The list should have plenty of logical reasons why your prospect should buy, because the stronger the logic of doing something the more difficult it will be for them to say no. Then, with your prospect's help, build a list of reasons why he should not buy your offer. The case for buying is usually much stronger than the one for not buying. Now you have your restricted supply as a powerful incentive for your prospect to say yes.

The try it out technique

When you are trying to sell into an outlet that runs your competitor's products and doesn't want to change, you have a difficult situation. Your prospect may admit that your range is very good — in fact, it may have some benefits that appeal to him, but none strong enough to force a change. Now it is time to ask yourself some important questions.

◆ Do you really think any buyer who is happy with their present supplier is going to cease dealing with that supplier and transfer the business to you? You're right. The answer must surely be no.

◆ Do you believe the buyer has the capacity to order from you as well as from their present supplier? You're right. Not really . . . unless the initial order is small enough not to cause problems with the relationship they have with their current supplier. You've got it right. Your best chance of becoming a supplier to this organisation is on a 'try it out' basis with a small order size and perhaps even special conditions on this order so that the buyer is taking no real risk.

When you have agreement on a token order, you should focus on two issues:

1. An order big enough to make a reasonable display. If it's a retail business, you can do that by appealing to your buyer's common

sense. If the display isn't big enough to appeal to the consumer, your chances of a second order are not good.

2. You should give all the sales support you can muster. There is not much point in getting the order and leaving it to chance that someone will push the product, or even display it in a way and place that will be a fair test.

You now have a vested interest in the success of the trial, so without becoming a nuisance stay in touch and monitor progress. Now that you have supplier status, you need to give them all the attention and help you normally give your most important accounts. Perhaps with some good advice and tender loving care this trial customer may very swiftly become one of your most important customers, because at this moment he is your most important customer, unless you want to have wasted your efforts to secure this account.

The puppy dog technique

This close technique is often used when a prospect likes your product but can't make a decision because they are concerned about whether it is the right size, colour, etc. It is mostly used in retail or other situations where a comparison is the reason why a decision is not being made. Art galleries use this method very effectively. When a prospect cannot decide which painting to choose, the gallery makes the following offer: 'I can understand your difficulty in deciding which one will fit into your home or office. Why not take them both and bring back the one you don't want?'

Such an offer is hard to refuse. It builds a relationship while at the same time almost guaranteeing one sale and, possibly, two.

This is called the puppy dog close because it works on the same principle as your child bringing home a stray pup. The conversation might go something like this. Sarah arrives home with the pup.

S: Mum, look what I found in the street. Isn't it beautiful?
M: Sarah, I have told you before, no pups. Take it back now. We're not having a pup.
S: Mum, I can't just leave it in the road. It might get run over. Let's just keep it tonight. In the morning, I'll take it back.
M: In the morning, with no arguments?
S: No arguments.
M: OK, but remember he goes back tomorrow.

Round 1 to Sarah. The pup knows it has won Sarah, and so intuitively it turns its attention to mum and dad. Its soulful eyes follow their every move and whenever eye contact occurs it wags its tail to let them know it likes them. It settles down at their feet and snuggles in, and at every opportunity licks their hands and feet. This pup is a real salesperson. From soulful eyes and wagging tail to affectionate licking, mum, dad and Sarah are getting all its attention. This is a sale it must make, or it's back to the doghouse or worse.

Morning comes and it's decision time, but the contest isn't fair. In one corner, mum and dad are trying to persist with their no pup decision and in the other corner are Sarah and the pup. Sarah is tearfully reminding them the puppy faces almost certain death if they don't keep it. The puppy is being as cute as it can. Mum is feeling the pressure.

M: Surely someone will look after it?
S: There's no one but us, Mum.
M: Who owns it? Someone must own it?

The contest is nearly over. Sarah closes:

S: Why don't we keep him here? I'll look after him and if I can find the owners I'll give him back. That's fair, isn't it?

What can mum say? She has been sold by a couple of peak performers.

M: OK, but he goes when you find the owner.
S: Thanks, mum. Will you feed him, please? I'm going to be late for school.
The pup wags its tail.

If we were half as skilful as Sarah and the pup, we would increase our selling effectiveness simply by using a puppy dog close to sell the product. When the paintings go home, they are doing the selling. There is no pressure, just an appeal to the emotions of the buyer.

Great closing is usually a matter of good timing and using a closing technique that matches the psychology of the situation perfectly. You don't need to know a great number of different techniques to be super-successful. If you learn and master these techniques, you will rarely need any others.

Peak performers rarely give up trying to win a client, but they know selling is not a competition. Winning at all costs is not the objective.

Conquest is not their goal; rather it is building relationships and building value for their clients. They don't have to succeed every time to feel fulfilled, but they do have to perform at their peak to be satisfied. They know that the better the relationship, the harder it will be for someone else to sell their customers. Perhaps the reason Allan didn't want to do business was because of the relationship he has with a current representative. Here is an example of the payoff you can get when you build outstanding relationships.

I was presenting a workshop to around 20 key people from a paint manufacturing and wholesale business. During the presentation, we were discussing sales and relationships and how the prospect's need to get approval from someone else often holds up the decision-making process. The sales manager mentioned what had happened to one of his salespeople recently. He had been trying to get a first order from a retailer and was talking with the partner with whom he had spoken on the two previous occasions. This third call was progressing well and he felt sure he was finally going to get the order when his prospect said:

> I think we can do business, but I have to speak with Bob first. Is that OK?'
>
> He replied, 'Certainly. Is Bob your partner?'
>
> He was speechless when his prospect replied:
>
> 'No, he's not my partner. Bob is the man who sells us paint. [*He named the firm, a major competitor.*] If he says it's OK, we'll do it.'

Now that's how to build relationships. He didn't get the order, but he learned a valuable lesson about building relationships.

If your close has been successful, you now need to do the follow-up to ensure that the promises you have made are kept. Check who is going to do what and when. If there is anything out of the ordinary to be done to keep your promises, make sure you let the right people know what has to be done, and then check to see it is done.

CHAPTER 13

THE
GENTLE ART
OF
COMMUNICATING

*If we all speak the same language,
how come we don't understand
each other?*
ANON.

A BUSINESS COMMUNICATES with its prospects and customers in many ways, such as face to face, by telephone, in writing, through advertising, window displays and in-store displays, and by its actions. All are important in building satisfied prospects. All provide a wonderful opportunity for us to communicate effectively with our customers and prospects and to build enduring and profitable relationships with them. It is when a business is communicating with its customers and prospects that it is building possibilities for its salespeople. If the messages it sends are strong positive messages of the benefits of dealing with this business, then the reception received by salespeople will be equally positive and will make their work more rewarding and productive.

ADVERTISING

Salespeople must take an active interest in the advertising that impacts on their work. If you want to get the best results, then let your organisation know what you think about what is being done because it does affect you. In terms of communicating with the advertising department, your silence may be taken as your agreement with what is being done. While advertising may be outside your responsibility, the results are not. You owe it to yourself and your organisation to do all you can to see that the advertising messages are positive and helpful to your cause. The only reason for advertising is to increase sales and build a business.

In order to understand how these messages affect your prospects and customers, you need to be aware that many people are under stress. Customs and values are changing more quickly than most people can cope with. The two-income family is now a necessity if the family wants to maintain its lifestyle and enjoy the benefits of a today-oriented society. If children don't do well at school and secure a good education, then in the age of the knowledge worker they will pay a penalty. In the workplace, people are expected to achieve positive results most of the time or face the possible loss of their job.

All around us the pressures are growing. When prospects and customers are under pressure, they become suspicious and defensive. They begin to look for confirmation that life is tough and the system is unfair. 'Nobody cares anymore. Salespeople aren't interested in me, they just want my money. They couldn't care less' becomes part of their belief system and they look for confirmation that they are right in believing that nobody cares about them. The moment your customer or prospect decides that you do care about them, you are in a position of trust and will continue to earn that trust for as long as the prospect believes you care. The reverse is also true: the moment they decide that you or your organisation don't care, your chances of long-term success with them are diminished, so you owe it to yourself to ensure that the way your organisation communicates with your prospects and customers is favourable to your sales activities.

Every business that wants to build strong, effective and profitable relationships with its prospects and customers will be alert to the value of the messages they send. They will constantly endeavour to see that their messages are positive, friendly, and aimed at building a foundation of strong and enduring relationships for their salespeople. As salespeople, we are in direct contact with the customers and prospects, so it is important that we not only understand every aspect of the advertising campaign but also that we support by our actions the message it is sending. We care about you. We are interested in you. We value both you and your business. What can we do to make life more enjoyable and less stressful for you? It is critically important that we say thank you. As George Crane says: 'Appreciative words are the most powerful force for good on earth.'

Providing they believe what we in the business say, the results will be fantastic — for them, for the business and for us. Why should they not believe our organisation? What will cause them to doubt what is being said? The answer in most cases is simple. They won't believe the message if the actions of the organisation don't match the message the organisation is sending. The whole critical issue is one of matching actions to words. When in doubt, people tend to believe actions not words.

Whatever you do as a salesperson, you must ensure that your messages are true and consistent. You need to know and understand how your employer uses advertising and communications. If it causes problems in the marketplace, then take the problem to someone who can fix the communications so that it enhances your chances with your customers and prospects. No business can afford to work against itself by condoning poor communications and creating a negative climate for its salespeople.

Every person in the business needs to discuss this subject in depth and realise that it is a very critical issue. It is a case of leading and managing by example. 'What we say is what we do' must become our credo if we want to communicate effectively.

When we say the customer and prospect is king, our actions must show them that we really mean it. In order to maximise your chances of success as a salesperson, you need to understand how communication takes place and ensure that what you say is what you do.

Now let me introduce you to one of the great personalities and leaders of the advertising business. Alex Hamill is Chairman of George Patterson Bates Australia, one of the largest advertising agencies in the world. Not only has Alex had a wonderful career in advertising, in my opinion he is one of the great successes of the human race.

♦

JC: Alex, in this chapter I have said it is important for salespeople to understand the advertising done by their employer. Do you agree, and if so in what way can salespeople get the most mileage from that advertising?

AH: Jack, one of the selling sins that must be avoided is for the sales force not to understand the advertising created for their product. A greater sin is for the company not to communicate to the sales force what it intends to say in its advertising. The marketing process is complex, and advertising and selling are important components. But like any jigsaw puzzle, every piece has to fit in place for the picture overall to make sense.

Advertising's role is to create a feeling about a product which is positive and eventually helps in the purchase decision. It can never substitute for face-to-face selling. Most successful companies I've worked with spend a great deal of their time making sure the sales force are aware of upcoming campaigns, understand the strategic planning behind them and, wherever possible, reflect the brand personality in the selling process. If the sales force contradicts the essence of the brand being portrayed in advertising, then you get consumer confusion which inevitably makes closing the sale all that more difficult.

JC: Alex, what are the key issues that in your opinion can help salespeople to be more effective in communicating with their prospects and customers?

AH: Advertising agencies spend a lot of time, money and effort on research. Very few advertising campaigns are created simply because a bright young whiz copywriter had a brilliant idea. Most are strategically driven, heavily researched, and tested with consumers before they see the light of day.

Salespeople can certainly be more effective in communicating with prospects and customers if they are prepared to mirror the advertising message. Importantly, they can add the personal touch not possible through mass communication. This is an important discriminator in the decision process as markets become more competitive and products more similar.

Great salespeople, like great communicators, understand the value of the service equation, before, during and, importantly, after the sale. In the same way, understanding the strategy of your own products' advertising campaigns can help salespeople to review competitive activity. It can provide a very clear understanding of just who you are competing against. You will be aware of their strengths and able to capitalise on their weaknesses.

Advertising will never be a substitute for personal contact, Jack. It can, however, dramatically change a customer's view of a product. A sales force that is cognisant of the role that advertising can play will recognise that it is a most powerful tool for opening the door. The task of closing the sale then becomes just that little bit easier.

JC: Alex, what qualities in a salesperson do you consider are valued most by those who are prospective buyers?

AH: The qualities should be no different in a salesperson to the ones you are looking for in a person with whom you want to build any relationship. There are obvious ones like honesty, integrity and a sense of humour.

Jack, I also believe there are two qualities that stand out and seem to be common in all of the great salespeople I've come across. The first is the ability to give a hard 'no' when an easy 'yes' might suffice. The second is the ability really to understand that selling, or indeed any career, requires balance and perspective. Balance comes from knowing that no one part of your lifestyle should be dominant and own you completely. Perspective is understanding that even the most difficult problems eventually go away.

The opening line of Rudyard Kipling's great poem *If* sums it up nicely: 'If you can keep your head when all about you are losing theirs and blaming on you. If you can trust yourself when all men doubt you make allowance for their doubting too.'

◆ — ◆ — ◆

There are many powerful messages in what Alex has to say. Life will be easier and more productive if we follow his advice.

THE COMMUNICATION PROCESS

Many factors are involved in the communication process, each influencing the final interpretation placed on the communication. To understand these influences and to become more effective in our day-to-day dealings with other people, it is necessary that you understand the process and how you can use it to improve your total approach to selling. The process of communicating takes place between a sender and a receiver of a message. The message may be written or spoken. If spoken, it can be by phone, face to face or via an audio cassette. For our purposes, we will assume that the communication is between a prospect and a salesperson and that the salesperson is speaking to the prospect face to face.

Before the salesperson can send the message in spoken words, they must first see it as a picture in their mind. When they see the picture of the message they want to send, they must then change the picture into words. This is called encoding. When the prospect hears the words, they must change the words into a picture they can see in their mind. This is called decoding.

The degree to which the prospect understands what the salesperson has said depends on how well their picture matches the picture the salesperson has sent.

The more complex the message, the greater the chance that it will be misunderstood and the less overlap there will be. The degree of overlap is demonstrated in the diagram following. If it were a perfect communication, there would be a complete overlap.

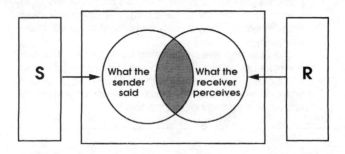

Difficulties in communicating

The most common causes of misunderstanding and barriers to effective communication are:

◆ Complex messages
◆ Technical language
◆ Jargon that is not understood by one of the parties
◆ Poor pronunciation
◆ Hard-to-understand accents
◆ Speech impediments
◆ Hearing defects
◆ Prejudice
◆ Poor listening
◆ Background noise, etc.

Any of these factors may cause problems of understanding on the part of both the prospect and the salesperson. However, most are within the control of both parties, and if care and patience are exercised the problems can be overcome. We should accept that the responsibility for communicating clearly in customer and prospect relationships rests with us. We need them more than they need us. They are our business.

Here are some ways we can help our customers and prospects to better understand what we say:

◆ Speak slowly and clearly.
◆ Speak loudly rather than softly.
◆ Avoid using jargon.
◆ Use easily understood words.
◆ Listen carefully.
◆ Ask questions if you need more information.
◆ Nod to let your prospect know you are listening.
◆ At intervals, repeat back to your prospect what you think they have said.
◆ Don't interrupt while your prospect is speaking.
◆ Select a location for your sales presentation that is free of distractions.
◆ When you are sure you understand, offer your solution.

SPEAK SLOWLY AND CLEARLY

It will assist your prospect's understanding of what you are saying, if you speak slowly and clearly. Speech specialists suggest that a rate of

140 words a minute is a good speed at which to deliver your message. It is a useful exercise to select a block of text containing 140 words and read it aloud at your normal rate of speech while you have your delivery timed so that you know how fast you speak. If you are faster, you should practise slowing down. If you have an accent, it is critical that you speak slowly to increase others' understanding of what you say, especially if you are delivering your message on the phone. If you find you are speaking too slowly, then speed up because it is not good for your prospect to be wishing you would hurry up.

Including the heading, and excluding the single letter 'a', there are 140 words in the above paragraph. Time yourself.

SPEAK LOUDLY RATHER THAN SOFTLY

While loud speech may cause some discomfort to the listener, it is preferable to speaking softly and not being heard and understood. Listeners can always move back a pace, or hold the phone away from their ear and still get the message clearly if it is too loud. When it is too soft, the only remedy is to ask the speaker to speak up or say, 'Sorry, I can't hear you', which may be embarrassing to both listener and speaker.

AVOID JARGON

I'm sure you have at some time been the receiver of a message delivered in the jargon of the sender and haven't understood what was said. All of us at some time have committed this crime against understanding, for it is so easy to fall into the shorthand of our own particular jargon. While specialised jargon may make it easy for us to communicate with someone familiar with that jargon, it has no place in a communication when we are not sure our listener will understand us. Always be on the side of simple explanations; that way, you will greatly enhance your chances of being understood.

USE EASILY UNDERSTOOD WORDS

The purpose of communication is to have your message understood, not to impress the receiver with your vocabulary. The more complex your message, the simpler your words should be. Remember: understanding is the goal. Winston Churchill is famous for his great wartime speeches, and if you read those speeches you will know why they were so effective. Simple, easy to understand words with great emotional impact, delivered with clarity and feeling. This description of his speeches should be the benchmark for all communications of the spoken word, especially sales presentations.

LISTEN CAREFULLY

If you want to contribute to effective communications, become an active listener. Pay attention; if you need clarification or more information, ask for it. The subject of listening is so important in our work as salespeople that Chapter15, 'Listening to Understand' has been devoted to it.

ASK QUESTIONS

There is an art to asking good questions to get more or specific information. Sometimes a good question can win you a sale. At all times, effective questioning techniques will improve the standard of your communication. Chapter 14, 'Questions are the Answer', deals with this special skill. Study it closely because it has a great deal of excellent information for those who want to improve their selling skills.

DON'T INTERRUPT THE SPEAKER

Patience pays off, and never more than when you let your prospects speak and tell you what you have to do to get their business. Too often our chances are diminished because we just can't wait to express a view or challenge a statement. As a general rule, assume you will receive more valuable help and information by patient listening than you will impart by speaking too often and too soon. Patience signifies interest and courtesy, both of which build trust and empathy. Be patient.

AVOID INTERRUPTIONS

If the location where you are to make your sales presentation is subject to interruptions by people, noise, or other distractions which are likely to have a negative impact on your sales communication, you should try to have it moved to a more suitable location. Otherwise you risk losing out because of those interruptions. Most prospects will try to overcome the problem if you alert them to it.

Written communications

The principles that apply to spoken communications apply also to the written word. Write clearly and use easy to understand words. Write in short, concise sentences and try not to have paragraphs that exceed four lines unless absolutely necessary. In face-to-face communication, both the sender and the receiver of the message have the advantage of body language and tone of voice to add degrees of meaning to what is being said. With the written word, you need to be very specific in terms of what course of action you are proposing and any time frames that are to be observed. Choose words and expressions that are not open to double meanings — unlike this example: 'My decision is maybe, and that's final'. Be courteous and friendly, and use the prospect's name as often as possible — remember most people like the sound of their own name.

Be particular about names, addresses and the style of your communication. If your communication is complex, then follow up your letter with a phone call and go over each issue until you are certain that your message has been understood. Finally, only write when it isn't possible to use the phone or to meet the prospect face to face.

The feedback loop

Effective communication should be two-way. There should be constant feedback from both the receiver and the sender. The sender who discourages or fails to provide for such feedback risks misunderstanding. The receiver who fails to use the feedback channel takes the same risk (see the diagram following).

Feedback on communications can also be given badly. Telling someone 'I didn't understand a word you said' is not going to be as useful as asking, 'What exactly did you mean by . . . ?' In other words,

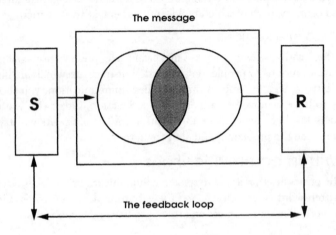

The message

S   R

The feedback loop

relating feedback to specifics is far preferable to sweeping generalisations, which often lead to bad feelings later. Be alert to every opportunity to seek clarification if you think it is needed. The best course of action is for you to take responsibility for making all your communications as effective as possible.

Selective listening

We tend to listen to and remember mostly the things that interest us, or the things we agree with. For example, in an election campaign, how much of a Labor Party speech would a Liberal supporter remember, and vice versa? Probably not much. In most cases, we hear only that which confirms what we already know and believe. We communicate selectively:

> *We hear and see what we want to hear and see.*
> *We perceive what we would like it to be, and*
> *we retain what we consider to be important.*

Communicating effectively is not only about how the communication process works; it is also about the means we have to communicate. Although the most obvious means is language, there are many other ways of conveying our thoughts and feelings and, indeed, identifying both the thoughts and feelings of our prospects.

In face-to-face communications, it is estimated that only one-third of the speaker's meaning gets through to the receiver from what is said. The remaining two-thirds is conveyed in non-verbal ways. To most of us, that means body language.

THE BASICS OF BODY LANGUAGE

People are more ready to believe what we do than what we say. This is probably because it is easy to say something which covers our true feelings, but much more difficult to control our body movements, many of which are unconscious movements. The ability to observe and to understand non-verbal behaviour will greatly assist you either when sending or receiving messages.

You should be constantly looking for body language clues which help you to understand the true meaning of what your prospects are saying, while also using actions and expressions to reinforce your own communication.

Some of these body language clues are:

◆ Head and facial expressions.
◆ Change of position.
◆ The distance between people.
◆ The voice.
◆ Gestures and posture.
◆ Eye contact.
◆ Physical appearance.

Head and facial expressions

Many emotions can be communicated by the face and the eyes. We are all familiar with the expressions which convey anger, surprise, affection or puzzlement. It is important to compare expressions with other non-verbal signals to check your interpretation.

Apart from the face, the way people hold their head can signal different attitudes and emotions. *Head erect* is seen as meaning high self-esteem, self-confidence, courage and strength. *Head tilted* indicates that interest has been aroused, or thought or consideration. *Head down, chin on chest* is seen as a negative attitude, non-acceptance or a lack of interest.

A *bowed posture* indicates humility, resignation or guilt. *Looking aside* signals embarrassment, a wish to hide or discomfort with what is being heard. An *elevated chin* signals high interest, empathy and general agreement. *Both hands pressed into the temples* is a sign of distress, despair, disappointment or a general negative response to the message being received. The forehead is also a good indicator of both physical and emotional health. For example, a *furrowed brow*, read along with other facial expressions, can indicate puzzlement, deep thought, tension, worry, fear or concern.

These types of signals are constantly being sent and received during a normal sales communication. You should become expert in recognising and acting on them, because they are telling you what you need to know in order to achieve understanding of your message and to increase your chances of success.

Change of position

This usually indicates a change in mental attitude. Quite often, when we are communicating face to face, if a person has decided to terminate the session or wants to leave, they will turn their body towards the nearest exit, finger their watch or squirm in their chair. If you see these signals, you should do something to regain the person's involvement and interest or, alternatively, finish the conversation on your terms, which allows you to maintain control.

Distance between people

The distance between the sender and the receiver varies according to relationships. For instance, strangers stand further apart than family. In business situations, the comfort zone is generally around one metre. Desks and counters usually solve the space problem; however, you should always be aware of people's need for their own space. Too close, and you will be seen as pushy. Too distant, and you will be seen as unfriendly.

Voice

The tone of voice and fluency of our speech have probably more influence on the meaning of what we convey than the words we select. The tone of voice can change the meaning of a statement entirely and quickly gives clues about the mood and emotions of the speaker. Listen carefully to how your prospect is speaking. Your prospect's voice will give you reliable feedback as to how they feel about your offer. If they like what they are hearing, their tone of voice and words will reflect their good feelings. The reverse is also true. If they are not impressed, their doubts and uncertainty will be reflected in their voice, words and general body language.

Gestures and posture

Maintaining an open posture with arms and legs uncrossed is an important sign which signals involvement. Tightly crossed arms and legs often communicate closeness and defensiveness. Drumming fingers indicate that the listener is not tuned to you mentally, so don't waste your time unless you can capture or recapture the person's interest. Body language is the way to see what others are thinking. Sometimes you will feel uncertain about how your message is being accepted, so pay attention to body language and be receptive to what their body is saying. If the messages are negative, then lift your performance. Ask an open-ended involvement question, such as 'How do you feel about making that particular change?' Now that they are involved, you may get the information that will help you to change pace, or tack, so as to get them involved again.

Eye contact

It is important as part of your greeting to maintain the correct amount of eye contact, particularly when you are meeting someone for the first time. The eyes have often been described as the windows of the soul. During a conversation, there are three simple rules of eye contact to follow:

1. Too much eye contact makes you appear dominating.
2. Too little eye contact is indicative of a lack of strength and purpose.
3. Avoid the 'non-person' stare. This means that in making eye contact you must focus your eyes, rather than give the person you are speaking to the impression that you are looking right through them.

Maintaining steady eye contact is critical, because if we keep changing eye contact the message we are sending is 'Shifty, not to be trusted'. You will judge the other person the same way if they don't maintain steady eye contact. The truth may be that the offending person is shy, but we usually apply negative reasons when confronted with this type of body language. Making eye contact as soon as you meet a person, whatever the circumstances of the meeting, generally works in your favour.

Body language is a whole subject in itself. *Body Language* by Allan Pease provides a full discussion of how to read and use non-verbal language as part of your communication skills. You can also read his interview for this book in Chapter 16, 'Making Powerful Presentations'.

Physical appearance

People tend to judge us by our dress and how we present ourselves. Always dress in a manner appropriate to the work you are doing and the way most of your prospects would dress if they were in your position. The more you look like them, the easier they will find it to communicate with you and the more value they will place on your message. How they dress gives you a great deal of information about who they think they are, and if you apply this information correctly it will help you in the selling process. Appearance is critical to our sales career. Read Chapter 22, 'Presenting Yourself', which discusses the need to consider all aspects of appearance and the role it plays in the day-to-day sales scene.

CONCLUSION

Understanding how communication takes place between people is important if you want to be effective in communicating with your prospects. Understanding is essential; however, putting it into practice is the critical issue. Wanting to communicate is the motivation that produces the desire to act. Without it, nothing happens.

The whole purpose of interacting with another person is to communicate. For the message to be effective, the receiver must understand it. Yogi Berra nearly got it right when he said: 'Remember, whatever you do in life, 90 per cent of it is half mental.' The constant need on the part of both the receiver and the sender is to seek out to what degree understanding is taking place.

Be patient when sending and receiving information. Some people communicate better than others. They absorb information and reach understanding more quickly. Others need more time and more involvement to reach the same level of understanding. You can improve your own and others' communication effectiveness by using the skills we have been discussing and paying special attention to the art of listening and questioning, which are the two critical elements of the process of communicating. So important are they that separate chapters on each are provided so that you can study those particular skills. They should be read and combined with the information in this chapter to give an overall understanding of how the communication process works and how you can use those skills in the key areas of that process.

CHAPTER 14

QUESTIONS ARE
THE ANSWER

*Every time you ask a question, you are inviting
someone to talk. People like talking, so don't
be surprised if you finish up being
popular and very successful.*
ANON.

SELLING HAS BEEN described as the art of solving problems. The truth is, it is the art of having prospects identify problems they are willing to solve. Discovering what they want and how willing they are to solve their problem is easy if you ask the right questions: soft questions, attitude questions, feeling questions. Soft questions get information about what prospects think, what they believe in, what they want, what they are willing to do, and how best they see themselves solving the problem.

SELLING USING SOFT QUESTIONS

Questions are the key to having your prospects buy from you rather than you sell to them. In many cases, your prospects will buy from you if you help them to establish and accept that they have a problem they are willing to solve. Many will accept that they have a problem, but you will succeed only when they are willing to solve it and only in proportion to your ability to provide, by way of your product or service, a solution which is acceptable to them.

Just about everyone I know would like to be shown how to get what they want. Your prospect may *need* a four-bedroom, two-bathroom house but *want* a three-bedroom, one-bathroom house. Your prospect may *need* a two-bedroom unit close to public transport but *want* a four-bedroom house with two bathrooms on five acres remote from transport. Your prospect may *need* a four-cylinder economy car but *want* a two-seater, fire-eating sports car. What people need and want is an entirely different question. If what they need and want is the same thing, there are no difficulties. Whether you spend your time trying to convert people from what they want to what, in your opinion, they need, is up to you. My money is on selling *wants*.

Use your skills in negotiation, not confrontation

In the selling presentation there is a need for a lot of discussion, and good (soft) questioning techniques, instead of the virtual confrontation that exists when a salesperson decides to sell a product or service, come what may.

Soft sell, not hard sell

By this I mean the iron fist in the velvet glove: the technique of making presentations without appearing to be hard sell. Learn these techniques and practise them at every sales presentation. Persistence is different from hard sell. Taking 'no' for an answer is a sign of being a mature person. After all, your offer must stand or fall on its merits and on your skill in presenting all the options in a simple but powerful presentation. If you have done your best, be gracious in accepting a 'no'. Don't blame the prospect for not buying, blame yourself for not selling well enough.

The main characteristic of soft questions, sometimes called open questions, is that they cannot usually be answered simply by a yes or a no. The soft question is designed to get information on how your prospect feels. For example, asking 'What do you feel is the main advantage of this colour and finish?' is a better question than 'Do you like this colour and finish?' because it solicits information, not just a yes or no answer. When this happens, you will have to ask 'Why do you feel that way?', which means you have to ask two questions to get the same information you would get from asking one good soft question.

If you continue to ask soft questions directed at finding out what your prospect thinks and feels about what you are suggesting, you are in effect finding out how to satisfy them. Soft questions are the way to build good relationships. When you are interested in others, they will be interested in you. As Lee Iacocca said, 'To succeed, all you have to do is make someone like you'. Soft questions will build relationships for you.

When you ask soft questions, you discover wants. You identify solutions, and you begin to understand how your prospect feels about what it is you are talking about. If, during your discussions, your prospect says they don't favour your product or service, you need to find out why by asking: 'Why do you feel that way?' No matter what your business, you want to know how your prospect feels, what they believe and what they want.

'Why do you feel that way?' is a very powerful question if asked at the right moment, and *how* you ask the question is as important as the question itself. You should pause, be still, gain eye contact and then speak. Be aware that feelings are instructions on what you should do or say next.

The questions you are going to ask most often are the six Ws: who, what, when, where, why and which, plus how. Of these, the most powerful are how and why. Most of the questions you ask will start with one of these words. How you use the words depends on how you ask the question. You ask the question to get answers. In order to know what questions to ask, you need to know what answers or information you want. You are looking for answers that will tell you how your prospect feels about what it is you are presenting, so you need to ask questions that will help you get those answers.

For example, you have asked a hard question and received a yes/no reply. Now you ask a soft question: 'How do you feel about advertising?' If you get a non-committal answer, such as 'good', then continue asking soft questions, such as: 'What makes you feel good about it?' Keep asking soft, non-threatening questions until your prospect is encouraged to communicate their feelings, attitudes, beliefs and desires.

HARD QUESTIONS

Hard, or closed, questions are about facts, not about how prospects feel or what their attitudes are. Hard questions require no real involvement from your prospect. Asking hard questions is a one-way communication process. Hard questions can be answered with a yes or no and rarely give any insight into how your prospect feels. For example, if you ask: 'Do you like this colour and finish?', the answer will be yes or no. You won't make any progress unless you follow with a soft question like 'Why do you feel that way?'. Although hard questions are necessary at times, soft questions are much more effective. Here are some more hard questions:

◆ Do you like being in business for yourself?
◆ Are you married?
◆ Where do you live?
◆ How much do you spend on your current advertising?
◆ What type of car do you drive?
◆ How much income do you earn?
◆ Do you own a computer?
◆ Are you interested in real estate investments?

This is information which can be put to good use, but it tells you very little about how your prospect feels, what they think, what they want, or what they like and dislike. This information is better gained by asking soft questions.

Another hard question: 'What type of car do you own?' Now that you know the make of car, ask the real questions, the soft questions:

'How do you feel about your present car?', or 'What would you like to be different about your car?' or 'What don't you like about your present car?'

Hard: What type of house do you live in?
Soft: How do you feel about your present house?
Hard: Where do you live now?
Soft: How do you feel about living in your present locality?
Hard: How much do you spend on your current advertising?
Soft: What is your current philosophy on advertising?

Hard questions are final and discourage an ongoing dialogue. You are finished unless you ask soft questions. Answers to soft questions tell you what you need to know to make a sale. You discover wants and identify solutions. You begin to understand how the prospect feels about what it is you are talking about.

If you are selling investment real estate, you want to know how the prospect feels about investment real estate. If the answer isn't favourable, ask another soft question: 'Why do you feel investment real estate isn't a favourable investment for you?' If you are selling advertising, you want to know how your prospect feels about buying advertising: 'How do you feel about advertising?' or 'What is your philosophy on advertising?'. If the answer isn't favourable, you need to know why, so ask: 'Why do you feel that way?'. Remember to pause and make eye contact before you ask the question.

If you are selling money, you want to know how your prospect feels about getting rich. If the response is favourable, you still have to find out which of all the available options they favour, such as property, banks, shares, building societies or credit unions. If your prospect doesn't favour your product or service, you need to find out why by exploring their various options of how they intend to get rich. Your prospect will always *have* options, so get them out in the open where they are not likely to become hidden objections.

You can do this by asking soft questions such as:

◆ How do you see yourself achieving your goal of getting rich?
◆ What, in your opinion, are the other alternatives?
◆ Which do you favour, and why?
◆ Why didn't you include . . . ?

Wait for an answer to each question before proceeding with the next one. If your option is not included in their answer to which options they favour, use the last question to identify your option and get a definite reaction from them.

By now you know where you stand. If your option doesn't rank highly, you have more work to do. Don't criticise the prospect's choices, because that only builds resistance. Your only real choice is to build the benefits of your option until they exceed the prospect's current choices. Perhaps they need help in understanding the benefits of your option. If so, spend the time until they understand.

Here is an example of a winning soft question. I believe it is the most creative question I have ever heard, and it won the person who used it a $1 million sale. Here is how it happened. The salesperson involved sells financial services. His name is Jim and he became involved in the possibility of securing these funds for investment when he was approached by the person with the $1 million to see

---

SOME DOS

✓ Explore options.

✓ Emphasise the problem.

✓ Match your questions to your sales track.

✓ Use strong statements or powerful questions to get attention.

---

what returns were available through the organisation which Jim represented. The money was currently in a bank, which was also trying to get the funds long term. The investor held a number of meetings with both parties and was considering his options. The bank's people had a final meeting with him and made their case for the funds. Jim was invited to make his final presentation.

The meeting became bogged down, with the investor trying to decide on the alternatives available from each party. It was making little progress until Jim remembered that the bank in question had its head office in a building in Sydney which was owned by the organisation which Jim represented. Jim had a flash of creative brilliance — he asked if his prospect was aware of this information. When the prospect replied that he wasn't, Jim said: 'Mr Investor, I think the real question you have to answer is simple: do you want to do business with the landlord or the tenant?' The investor replied: 'When you put it like that, I want to do business with the landlord.' Jim had his $1 million sale.

ALTERNATIVE QUESTIONS

No matter what you sell you want to know how your prospect feels, what they believe, what they want. Sometimes you simply want to know their choice among alternatives, so you ask an alternative question — for instance:

◆ Would you prefer to pay cash or charge it?
◆ Would you prefer to pay yearly or monthly?
◆ Would you prefer red or yellow?

◆ Would you prefer one floor or two floors?
◆ When would you like to travel, Monday or Friday?
◆ What size would you prefer, the large or the small?

These questions tell you your prospect's preference, but they don't tell you how they feel or why they prefer that option.

Constructive questioning can soon bring out all the key information you need to know in order to offer a solution to the identified problem.

DIRECTIVE QUESTIONS

With the help of directive questions, you can lead your prospect to talk about particular subjects. The subjects in the question should be those for which you have already received a positive reaction. By answering your question, your prospects are actually selling themselves. A directive question can also be used as a detour when you are discussing subjects that aren't bringing you closer to a decision or taking you in the direction you wish to go.

For example:

◆ You mentioned before that you thought you might . . .
◆ Earlier in our discussion, you raised . . .
◆ How would you define the problem?

If you ask your prospects directive questions, they will usually enlarge on the subject and you will get additional information. At the same time, they tend to understand more about the problem because they are taking part in the problem-solving process. A directive question consists of a leading statement followed by a request for agreement on a previously agreed point in order to confirm it. The following is an example of a directive question which also provides us with feedback:

'When delivery was discussed earlier in our conversation, you said that it was important it be done on Tuesdays. Would you tell me why this is so important to you?'

The question following the leading statement solicits information about how the prospect feels or thinks about what was said. As a result, it confirms to you, by giving feedback, that you have understood the problem correctly.

Feedback questions are often a mix of soft and hard questions. For example:

◆ Which of these products would sell best in your situation?
◆ In your opinion, which will attract more attention?
◆ If you went ahead with this idea, would you want to expand its use in the future?

LISTEN TO THE ANSWERS

Asking questions is futile unless you listen to the answers. The purpose of the question is to get information. Whether you agree, disagree, believe or don't believe is not the issue; you have your answer — you might not like it but it is the prospect's answer, it's their life, their wants, their beliefs, their feelings, their money and their problem.

Listen attentively, while they decide on their problem and their solution. This is putting the power of silence to work for you, and, as Charles de Gaulle said: 'Silence is the ultimate weapon of power.' Just keep posing soft questions to help them get the answer to their problem. When you get the answer, you only have to provide the funding and the sale is complete.

If your sales presentation style depends on getting a particular answer to your questions, then it is better to make statements and seek agreement rather than ask questions and provide the answers.

Spend 80 per cent of your time on the problem and 20 per cent on the solution. Once your prospect accepts the problem and shows a willingness to solve it, the sale is made. The solution only completes the process. If you have a satisfactory solution, the sale is yours.

To keep your questions in sequence and use them in the right order, they need to match the sales track you are using. If you are organised, you will have a sales track. If not, you will have to match wits with your prospect. Matching wits soon turns into a contest. In contests someone generally loses, and too often it is the salesperson. So be organised, have a good sales track, and use the power of soft questions to match your presentation to the wants, needs and beliefs of your prospect. This way, you will greatly enhance your chances of sales success while at the same time building an enduring and profitable relationship for both your prospect and yourself.

SOME DON'TS

✗ Don't interrupt. When the prospect has finished
answering your question, if you need more
or different information then enlarge
or rephrase your question.

✗ Don't answer your own questions. By doing
this you restrict your prospect
to yes or no answers, which defeats the purpose
of asking soft questions.

✗ Don't criticise your prospect's choices.
Work around them by asking selective
questions which will expose any weaknesses
in their choices which they may have overlooked.

In the attention part of the sales track, you can use either strong statements or powerful questions to get attention. Research shows 75 per cent of all sales presentation failures occur in the attention phase of the presentation. Therefore, it is important to design powerful statements and questions.

Most of your questions will relate to the interest, desire and action part of your sales presentation. Many salespeople think that if only they could make their prospect want what they are selling just by telling them what they are selling, then they would have it made. Most attempts to develop successful methods for arousing this want have been inadequate. For example, one author wrote 'Arouse your prospects desire with a few well-chosen words'. *Which* well-chosen words? It's not possible to tell in advance what those words should be. They have to be well-chosen, but in relation to what? They need to be well-chosen in relation to what it is you perceive your prospect will respond to. You have to look. You have to find out what motivates your prospect. You have to detect the hidden motive. When you get to this phase of the sales presentation, you are dealing with people's emotions, and this is where you have to discover your prospect's real interests if you are to make a sale.

To motivate your prospect to buy, you must detect their dominant buying urge and then find a way to answer or satisfy that urge. The best way is by using soft questions. Prospects don't just want to save money;

they want to save money for a reason. It may be to travel, to buy a larger home, to buy a bigger or different car, for financial security, or maybe just to win the approval of friends and neighbours. A presentation on why it is a good thing to save is not as effective as a presentation on how your program will get your prospect what they want.

The only way to discover your prospect's hidden dominant buying urge is to ask related questions and listen for the answers. Our prospects are like us. Everything you have done since you were born was because you wanted or needed something. You need to ask prospects soft questions about how they feel in order to determine their attitude and what they really want and then you can show them how you can help them to get what they want.

All the while you are asking questions, you have to respond to the answers so that communication is taking place. Your prospect will judge by your responses how effectively you are helping them to solve their problem and how concerned you appear to be about *their* welfare, not yours.

Here is a classic example of how to show you are interested in your prospect's problems. I decided to buy a Macintosh computer — I'd heard they were easy to use and I wanted to network with several of my associates who used Macs. I called a computer company that sold Macintoshes and asked them to send a salesperson around to see me.

The next morning at 10 am the doorbell rang. It was the company's salesman. He was around 25, looked just as the perfect salesman should, and was carrying a large carton. I invited him in.

'May I bring your computer in with me?' he asked.

I said 'Yes' and gave him 10 out of 10 for 'Always be closing'.

'What do you know about computers?' was his next question.

'You could write on a stamp with a mop what I know about computers and still have room left over', I told him.

So he hooked up the computer and, for the next 20 minutes, demonstrated what it could do. He was fantastic! I've never seen anyone operate a computer so well.

'How big is it?' I asked and received an extremely technical explanation about megabytes and the like. When the demonstration was over, I thanked him, asked for his card and said I would think about it.

QUESTIONS ARE THE ANSWER 173

Then I called another computer company and asked them to send one of their salespeople to visit me. The following morning another young man arrived at the door. He looked much like the first one, except he wasn't carrying a carton.

'Poor memory', I thought, 'he's forgotten to bring my computer.'

'Mr Collis', he opened with, 'can I ask you some questions so I can understand exactly what you want a computer to do for you?'

'Go ahead', I said. He asked me a number of soft questions:

'What do you do in your business?'

I answered him.

'How do you do that? Why is it important to you?'

I told him.

He continued, finally finishing with:

'Mr Collis, what do you want this computer to do for *you*?'

When I replied, he said:

'It will do that. But what would you say if it could do this as well?'

'Fantastic!' I responded.

He continued to outline various options the computer could give me and at the end of the 10 minutes or so I had a completely different and more valuable picture of what the computer could do for me.

'How big is it?' I said.

'Big enough', he replied.

So I bought it.

Why did I buy from the second young man and not the first? Well, if I was hiring an operator, the first young man would have got the job. But I wanted a computer not an operator. He wasn't interested in what I wanted; he was busy focusing on what he could do. All his demonstration really did was to convince me of my inadequacy as an operator. The second young man focused on me and my problems. Not only did he want to solve them, he wanted to add value to what I needed and he used soft questions to find out exactly what it was I needed. He was the *real* peak performer.

The strongest criticisms made about salespeople are:

◆ They don't listen.
◆ They are only interested in selling something.
◆ They don't care about us.

In marketing terms, most research projects are about finding out what consumers want, so as to design a product or service to satisfy that want. Great marketing successes are all about how well research was used to provide a solution to consumers' wants. Why should selling be different? Do the research, ask soft questions, find out what the consumer wants. Then provide the solution. Match your product or service to the perceived wants and you have a great sales success. If your research shows that you have a mismatch, be graceful, build goodwill, leave on excellent terms and do more research until you have a match. Not everyone can or will buy.

You will sell more easily, you will get referrals and you will build a business. People will say of you that you really care, that you listen, and that you are concerned about them, not only about making a sale.

You will succeed beyond your dreams if you do this. In a market that is increasingly competitive, many salespeople respond to increased competition by taking short cuts which will only increase consumer dissatisfaction. The greatest need in the community today is for satisfaction. In every facet of their lives, people are asking for satisfaction. The demand is unlimited. The supply is diminishing. If you become the creator of satisfaction, then abundance will be yours in every part of your life. The way to win in selling is to sell satisfaction based on the answers to creative soft questions.

Donald Mehlig's technique is one of the best I have come across. The approach gets the prospect's interest and promises benefits:

'Mr Prospect, my purpose in calling you is to arrange a time suitable to you so that I can show you how you can benefit from those things your corporation can do for you more effectively than you can do for yourself, taking account of current tax laws. I am sure you would like to know what other successful people in businesses similar to yours are doing to increase their spendable income and after-tax profits. Mr Prospect, are you interested in increasing your after-tax profits and having more money to spend? It will take just 20 minutes to show you how.'

The approach is a straight appeal to self-interest. Who wouldn't be interested in having more money to spend? The objective is to open the prospect's mind, to make them willing to listen.

Don's next question is: 'May I ask a few questions so that I can understand what has been brought to your attention in these areas?'

Don says it is better that the prospect's advisers, not the prospect, appear not to know what's going on. For this reason, he says, 'brought to your attention'.

Don's next question is: 'I am here to bring current market ideas to your attention, which you can check out with your accountant if they appeal. Is that OK?'

Don has a shopping list of 20 good ideas which he goes through one at a time, asking approximately 20 questions. This avoids wasting time and effort on one idea which the prospect may not like. If he gets interest, he ticks that question and says, 'I'll come back to that one.'

When he has completed his shopping list, he goes back to questions which gained the prospect's interest. He has never drawn a blank. Then he asks mostly soft questions to find out how the prospect feels about the idea, and then he offers solutions.

Most prospects have many needs and wants, yet salespeople often offer a one-off specific solution to satisfy those various desires. Such salespeople are easily defeated with a 'no, thank you' answer. By that stage, offering other options just makes them look as though they are clutching at straws and desperate for a sale. It is more productive to develop a technique like Don's which allows you to explore possibilities while still covering what you think are your prospect's specific needs and wants. Use the specifics to get an appointment and then use that appointment to explore other possibilities and make a sale.

Questions really are the answer. Soft questions get you the information you need to offer solutions to your prospects' and customers' wants and problems; the hard sell technique is more likely to alienate your prospects and make them resent and ultimately reject you. The time you spend exploring and valuing your prospects' options is time invested in building relationships which then allow you to build your future. You can build yourself a bigger, better and more interesting career if you become a master at asking soft questions.

CHAPTER 15

LISTENING TO UNDERSTAND

If people listened to themselves
more often, they would talk less.

IF YOU WANT to know about listening, ask a blind person. You will learn why listening is important and how you can improve your own listening skills. Listening is sight to those who cannot see.

While I was writing the material for an audio cassette program, I interviewed Mal Able on listening skills. Mal has three per cent sight and is outstanding in terms of communicating, even though he has lost the advantage of sight. I have always been impressed by how quickly he is able to understand exactly what is meant by the spoken word. In our interview, I asked him what he considered the most important issues in understanding what others say.

LISTEN CAREFULLY

Mal said that listening carefully is the critical issue in understanding. Trying hard to understand what is being said, is different from hearing what is said. It is different because we listen at a much faster rate than others can speak, and while we are listening we are talking to ourselves about how we feel about what we are hearing.

According to research statistics, we use on average about one-quarter of our potential in terms of listening. It is estimated that within eight hours we have forgotten half of what we have heard. Over time, we forget, or misunderstand, 95 per cent of what we have heard, so in effect we understand only about five per cent of what we hear. On average, what we manage to understand and remember represents less than two per cent of our working day.

Research tells us that the main reason for this poor retention is that our attention span is on average 45 seconds. That's why most advertising commercials run for 30 seconds. After that, the mind begins to wander and focuses on other stimuli. Even while you are reading these words you are deciding whether you agree with them, and you are also exploring what value this information can be to you and how you might use it to improve your own listening skills. This process is always active. Even when a prospect is listening to your presentation, they are going through the same process. That's why you should constantly seek feedback to see if what you are saying is being understood.

When we put together poor listening, an attention span of 45 seconds, and the fact that we can think much faster than others can talk, and then add to that our own self-talk, it's no wonder that we fail not only to hear most of what people say to us, but also to understand what they are saying.

Mal also said that we tend not to listen to people whose voices we don't like, yet the message they have may be more important than the message from voices we do like. The important issue in any communication is the message, not the sender, yet we know that who the sender is adds weight to or subtracts from the message, because we give value and credibility to the message on the basis of the sender. It takes a lot of discipline to focus on the message to the exclusion of the other factors because they may become barriers to effective listening.

FOCUS ON WHAT IS BEING SAID

Mal believes that his listening improves dramatically when he focuses hard on what people are saying to him. Because he can't see, he depends almost entirely on what he hears. He also says that it saves him time if he listens attentively. It saves time because once he starts to listen, he gets it right the first time and it enables not only himself but others to focus more clearly on the communication taking place. It tends to drag people into the conversation and makes them feel important and understood.

Whenever he listens very intently, he notices that the person to whom he is listening usually becomes much more expressive. The interest levels of both himself and the speaker increase, and good listening tends to breed good speaking and positive relationships. The real payoff for him in being a good listener is that he understands the message, and surely that is the only criterion by which listening should be judged; it serves no other real purpose.

Mal said that the better he understands what he has heard, the greater the possibility that he can use what he has learned to his advantage. If he can't use what he has heard, then he has been wasting the speaker's time and his own.

BE AN ACTIVE LISTENER

Being a good listener is essential to being an effective communicator. The payoff is in superior relationships. Most of us enjoy a conversation more when we have an opportunity to express our opinions, especially when those listening show genuine interest in what is being said. Enthusiastic listening is an art and one you should cultivate if you want to increase your sales success.

When you are prepared to listen, it doesn't only mean that you are willing to listen but also that you have prepared yourself to listen by freeing yourself from other problems. You are able to devote the time, and you accept that the purpose of listening is to understand what is being said. Make sure you are getting the main points of your prospect's or customer's message, that you understand the key issues. Focus on meaning and listen to the supporting points. Improve your understanding of what is being said, and you will improve your chances of sales success.

Maintain concentration past the 45-second interest barrier. Be an active listener. Ask questions when necessary. Attend by nodding at intervals to let your prospect know you have heard what they have said. Give the speaker feedback on what you think they have said by paraphrasing their words and asking if you have got it right. Try saying something like: 'Ms Prospect, this is what I think you have just said to me. Have I understood you correctly? Is that what you mean?' Every time you do this, you pay your prospect a compliment, and genuine compliments work for you not against you.

DON'T INTERRUPT

For most of us, the desire to add to the conversation by making a telling point is irresistible. We simply cannot wait until whoever is speaking has finished what they are saying to make our point, so we interrupt. Not only does this say to the speaker, 'What I have to say is more important than what you are saying', but it also deprives us of the opportunity to fully understand the point they were making. It would be more helpful to listen to what they have said and then ask some good soft questions to find out why they have said it and how it impacts on the sale we are trying to make. The more courteous you are in listening, the greater your chances of success.

A noted author who only ever spoke about himself became concerned that he was being avoided and he asked an acquaintance why this was happening. He was told that if he wanted to overcome the problem, he should give others a chance to talk about themselves. He should ask questions about them and listen, and not always talk about himself.

Shortly afterwards the author met a person who had been avoiding him, so he decided to ask questions about them and to listen to what they had to say. 'Tell me', he said, 'What do you think about my new book?'!

Those who are willing to listen and to give others the chance to talk about themselves, and to express what they think, what they believe and how they feel, will always be welcome. Others will be more willing to share with you if you cultivate the quality of being interested in them. Whenever they are telling you what they think, they are giving you good advice. They are telling you what they want, and that is what you want to know.

Listening is critical to being a good communicator, and being an effective communicator is the key to building good relationships. If you consistently bring this quality to your dealings with prospects and customers, you will find they will seek you out and will choose to do business with you rather than with others who don't display the skills of a good listener.

BENEFITS OF BEING
A GOOD LISTENER

- You learn about the speaker by being a good listener. You also learn what to do about what you hear.

- Your prospects and customers will be more willing to communicate with you if you are a good listener.

- You will be better able to solve problems. This will save you a lot of time and effort.

- You will increase your effectiveness and build better relationships with your prospects or customers if you get it right the first time.

- Good listening skills are critical to your success in developing effective relationships.

- People are more anxious to talk about themselves than they are to listen to others. Good listeners are generally accepted as being good company.

- The better and more often you listen with empathy and caring to what your prospects and customers say, the more chances you will have of satisfying your customers' needs and wants and building yourself a long-term, enduring and successful business career.

TAKE THE ADVICE OF THIS VERMONT PROVERB:
'DON'T TALK UNLESS YOU CAN IMPROVE THE SILENCE.'

CHAPTER 16

MAKING
POWERFUL
PRESENTATIONS

*Imagination is one of the last remaining
legal means you have to gain an unfair
advantage over your competition.*
PAT FALLON

A PRESENTATION IS the process of delivering your
offer to a prospect or customer, and it can be made in three forms:
visual, verbal or written. All are highly effective when the method
chosen matches the needs of the particular situation. The majority of
presentations are made verbally, because what is being offered can be
described and communicated easily by the spoken word without the
need for technology. Many are made verbally because salespeople are
more comfortable when maximising the interaction between
themselves and their prospect through the exchange of words. In
written presentations, communication takes place differently and
requires the written word to do the talking and the salesperson to
maintain silence. The selling process is internalised within the
prospect with a written presentation and is often more powerful than
when it is done by talking. A film presentation requires a lot of
preparation and the use of technology and so is rarely used in day-to-

day sales interactions. They are used mainly for very large contracts, where seeing the actual product or service is a major requirement of the sales presentation. Film presentations are not discussed in this chapter.

VERBAL PRESENTATIONS

The verbal sales presentation is the real test of your ability to use all the different skills you have acquired. In the sales presentation, you have to put them together in a logical sequence and present them in a way that will not only be easily understood but will also open your prospect's mind so that they are more receptive to your message. If you deliver your presentation in a positive, creative and enthusiastic manner, then you will greatly increase your chances of success. It is assumed that you will support your comments with the aid of either a visual aid or a laptop computer.

Preparation

Much of the success of presentations depends on the initial preparation. At all costs, avoid going into an interview only partly prepared. It is a real problem to discover during the presentation that you are missing something, or that you haven't done enough background research. You will find yourself at a real disadvantage in such a situation.

Be a peak performer. Be prepared, and then make a perfect presentation structured to match your prospect's thinking process, strong in logic with high emotional appeal. Make it about life; sell real-life issues and fund your ideas with your product or service. That's real selling, that's a winning sales presentation.

Knowing your story word perfect and understanding its structure enables you to answer questions, deal with objections and return to your sales track without losing your way. That's staying in charge.

Don't let your presentation be like what Ashley Brilliant said of his life: 'My life is a performance for which I was never given the chance to rehearse.' You *have* the chance to rehearse your presentation so make the most of it.

Be prepared. Have everything you need to make a successful presentation. Check that you have your:

- Samples
- Pricing
- Recent correspondence
- Visual aids (see Chapter 10)
- Third party recommendations
- Technical data
- Order book
- Anything else you will need.

Having to go back to your car, phone your office or make excuses is a sure way to undermine your credibility.

Have a checklist in a separate folder for each call. Complete your checklist to ensure that you have everything you need. Be prepared.

Looking right is also important. Take care in your dress and personal presentation. Look like a successful salesperson. Dress to suit the occasion and to help your prospect feel at ease. If you are overdressed or underdressed it will lessen your credibility, and successful presentations are all about credibility. Be as much like your prospect as possible, and always try to show that you have taken extra care in your personal presentation. People are quick to sense when you are taking them for granted. When you look right, you will feel right — and when you feel right, you will act right.

While you are waiting, stand rather than sit. If you are sitting when your prospect comes to greet you, then you start off with less power. Standing gives you more power. If you read while you wait, read your material not theirs. Read positive material if you can. This will help to get you into the best possible frame of mind. When you are asked to enter the prospect's office, walk straight in. Don't pause at the door, or you will lose power and credibility. Walk with assurance to where you are to sit.

Arranging the scene

Most desks are rectangular in shape. If you sit exactly opposite, you are choosing the position of absolute confrontation. It is better if you move towards one of the corners. Before you sit, move your chair to one of the positions indicated in the diagram below, all of which imply less confrontation. If you are sitting at a circular table, then choose a position on the right-hand of your prospect. The person on the right-hand side of the chairman has more perceived power than the one on the left. Make sure you are not looking into a window behind your prospect, because this places you at a great disadvantage. Sit tall in your chair, as the tallest person has the most perceived power.

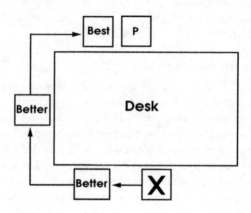

Choosing your words

Choose your words with care. Words are the tools of your trade. Choose words that are easily understood; the objective is not to impress, but to communicate and influence. Choose words that don't make your prospect feel uncomfortable. Speak on your prospect's level. If you speak down to them, they will resent you. If you speak up to them, they won't respect you. Speak to create equality. The more equal you become in your prospect's eyes, the better your credibility and your chances.

Using word pictures

To bring your sales story alive and make your presentation more powerful, learn how to master the art of using word pictures. Even the simplest of sentences can create a vivid image: for example, 'He lit up the room just by leaving' (Anon.).

Remember your sales story. It is built around pictures, and we tell it in story fashion because we know that we see in pictures and so does our prospect, and both of us were raised on stories.

Sales success depends on our ability to understand dominant thinking, because until we make what we want to sell the dominant thought in our prospect's mind, not only will they *not* buy, they *cannot* buy. You need to make what you sell real to those you are selling to. Do this by using words that generate the right pictures in the mind of your prospect. Sell life by making your product or service a real life issue. Show your prospect how your product or service will make their life more comfortable, more exciting or more rewarding. Too many people talk about the technology of what they sell, but forget to create meaningful pictures that work on the emotions and attitudes of the prospective buyer.

Revising your presentation

Your best tool for improving your selling skills is self-assessment after each sales presentation by filling out a simple analysis of how well you performed. Do it as soon as you come out of the interview. Answer the following questions:

◆ If I were to do it again, what would I change?
◆ What would I do more of?
◆ What would I do less of?
◆ What did I do well?
◆ Why did I think it was good?

On a scale of 1 to 7, rate your performance:

1 = very poor, 4 = average, 7 = excellent.

Follow-up checklist

The most crucial elements of the follow-up are:

◆ What you agreed with the customer.
◆ Who has to do it.
◆ When it is to be done.
◆ Why it is to be done.
◆ How it is to be done.
◆ The date it was done.
◆ What you want to achieve on your next call.

Making outstanding presentations, whether verbal or written, is the hallmark of superior selling. Putting all the elements together is crucial to increasing your sales effectiveness. The way to do it is to master all the elements and then practise until your presentations are perfect.

WRITTEN PRESENTATIONS

Written presentations are those that sell on their own, not presentations that contain relevant information to support a verbal sale. They should be classified as visual aids. For the purposes of definition, presentations that sell are those that do more than 70 per cent of the sales process. In most cases these presentations will be made on a second interview, because you need relevant information to make them work effectively and the best way to get that information is face to face so that you can do some selling while gathering the information.

It is assumed that the first interview will be a face-to-face approach to capture your prospect's attention and create interest in and desire for your offer. It's the time for you to give them the reason why you believe it is in their best interest to explore your offer in detail. You need to explain that it is necessary for you to obtain information which you will prepare in a written submission for them to consider. When you have made this sale and they have agreed to give you the information, you need to carry out your fact-finding activities.

During your fact finding, you will constantly work on developing more interest on the part of the prospect and focus on selling yourself while getting the information you need to make a complete written presentation of your offer. Your sale in this first interview is to convince your prospect that it is in their best interest to give you the information you need to properly prepare a solution to their problem or want. This should not be too difficult if the information is not of a personal or private nature. If it is, it may be necessary to convince your prospect that other people such as solicitors and accountants and some of their staff probably already have access to this information, because they deal with it when they are attending to the prospect's business. This can be done by saying, 'I appreciate that this information is given in confidence and you can rely on me to keep it confidential, just as your accountant or solicitor does'. During this first interview, it is important to sell benefits and to build your credibility. Here is an example.

My business is at home, because my art studio is at home and if I'm not presenting at a seminar, or writing, then I will be painting. As I was writing this chapter my doorbell rang. It was a representative from a painting contractor who had arrived to do an estimate on painting the outside of our house. (This visit came as a result of a cold call by a representative looking for prospects for house painting, so cold calls work if you are in the right place at the right time.) I was immediately impressed with the person who was to do the estimate — not only because of his appearance and demeanour, but because he knew how to sell. In a very discreet but positive way, he took every opportunity to build confidence in and the credibility of the people who would be doing the actual painting. He stressed how he would first do the estimate and then supervise the work and ensure that it was first class. He was an excellent salesman who obviously knew that this was the time to do the selling, rather than when he gave me the quote. If he waited until then, his sales work would look like he was trying to justify the price. Make sure that in your first fact-finding interview you do as he did: focus on why your solution will solve the problem or meet the want, and stress that you are the right person to see that whatever needs to be done to make your offer work is done to the satisfaction of your prospect.

Written presentations really work. They are compelling and powerful when used at the right time. In most cases, if you have written it correctly, you will only have to answer questions. Now let us consider the elements of a written presentation.

Length. The presentation can be can be as long or as brief as is necessary to do the job. Length is no problem, as long as it is interesting and entertaining to the prospect. They read 300-page bestsellers, they watch three-hour movies, they go to eight-hour conventions, and they do these things for the same reason you do — because they are interesting and entertaining. Make your presentation compelling and interesting for your prospect, while at the same time selling your solution. Once your prospect is interested, the sale can be made.

Self-interest. Self-interest is a major factor in every sale, so make sure your presentation is full of self-interest. Here is an example of self-interest at work. When I ran an in-house seminar on selling for a construction company, I was told that some of the engineers present were sceptical about selling techniques, yet they were the ones who were absolutely won over by the principles of selling by written presentations. They said they did a lot of tendering for projects and hadn't realised how dull most of their tenders were until they compared them with the type of presentation I was suggesting they should write. Their tenders included pages of facts and figures and met the requirements of the tender, but at no time did they do any discrete selling of why and how their tender had more value in it other than the price. They said they followed the usual procedures and used the normal words, and had never thought of changing the tender into a more interesting and sales-oriented presentation. They left the seminar with the objective of overhauling their entire written tendering procedures in order to encompass discrete selling of value for price. They now believed that, even though the process ensured that standards were met by all tenders, if they were written in a more user-friendly style it would influence their chances of success.

Quality. The presentation must be first class. Print error-free materials on good paper and use a presentation folder, not a binder. Staple the pages at a 45-degree angle in the top left corner so they are easy to turn.

Language. The presentation should be written in simple, easy to understand language. This is no time to try to impress with your vocabulary. If there is something complex or very technical which can't be simplified and must be included, ask your prospect to refer to you when that part is reached and, if necessary, include an appendix containing the supporting material for that part. When they refer to you, use the support material in the appendix to provide a short explanation. Don't introduce anything new. When you are finished explaining, ask your prospect to continue reading. Sit quietly and follow them as they read.

Format. The format of your written presentation should be as follows:

◆ Head page 1 with your prospect's name and address placed in the centre of the page.
◆ Underneath, in a separate paragraph, write: 'The following summary and recommendations have been prepared from information supplied to me at our meeting of [*date*]. Following are details of that information.'

   By stating that your presentation is based on information the prospect has supplied, the prospect now 'owns' this part of the presentation.

◆ List the essential information on which your recommendations are based. Be brief and specific, but make sure you list all the information that will be discussed in your presentation and include the statement 'as supplied by you'.

Making this declaration reinforces in the mind of the prospect that he has provided the information. If there are any errors of fact, they are his errors and he now has a chance to declare them. It also has the effect of validating your presentation.

◆ Now summarise what your prospect wants to achieve, and include any information or views you have on the matter that are relevant to what he wants to achieve.

This part establishes that these are the prospect's stated objectives in terms of the problem or want. You are not trying to convince him that he should have these objectives; he has given them as his own. He owns them, and so far there is nothing in the presentation that he can be opposed to.

◆ Now give your recommendations. Deal with each recommendation in a separate paragraph. State clearly and in detail what the situation will be after the prospect accepts your recommendations and describe the benefits he will receive by doing what you suggest. If it is necessary to have any support material as an appendix to a recommendation, refer to it in the presentation and ask the prospect to tell you when he comes to that part. When he raises the matter, go through the information with him and clarify anything that is involved or contentious. Make sure the prospect has understood what you want him to know before you move back to the main report. Follow this procedure for each recommendation.

The purpose of this part of the presentation is to isolate what you recommend from all other parts of the report, because this is the only part the prospect doesn't own and which he may disagree with. If you have written the recommendations so that they include plenty of benefits and describe what the prospect may lose or have to go without if he doesn't act on your suggestions, then the written word is doing its job and the prospect is selling himself. There is great power in letting prospects sell themselves. Don't try to close each recommendation separately; wait for total acceptance. So far you are in great shape and your prospect is doing all the selling. If you wait until the end of the report, it now becomes selling in reverse. The prospect has to sell you that he shouldn't proceed. He knows this and it gives you a distinct advantage.

◆ Now close your presentation by outlining what has to be done and how it will be done to put the recommendations into effect. Try to avoid having multiple options for how they can be put into effect. If that's not possible, then give your preferred option last.

   This part makes it easy for the prospect to make a decision, while also putting him in the position of having very little to discuss other than how and when to put your suggestions into effect.

Presenting your written presentation. Make sure that you have a copy of the presentation for each person at the interview. When you hand your written presentation to the prospect, simply say: 'Mr Prospect, I have taken special note of what you are concerned about and what you want. I believe you will find the solutions in this presentation. Would you please read the presentation, and ask questions as you go along if you need additional information or anything clarified.'

As the prospect reads the presentation, read your copy silently. When he turns a page, you do the same. Don't talk — silence is golden. The process of self-selling is taking place. If the prospect wants information, or has doubts about or an objection to something in the presentation, then answer his questions and wait for him to continue reading.

When the prospect has finished reading, don't talk. Wait for the verdict: have you made a sale, or do you have more to do? His first statement will give you the answer. Whatever you do, don't be the first to talk. It's a lot like poker: the looker generally loses. My experience at this time is that most people will say, 'That's good' or 'I like it' or 'You have done a good job'. To me that's acceptance, and I close on a soft option by saying, 'The next step is to do. . .' and then name what is needed to complete the sale. Most of my biggest sales were made with no more effort than that.

If objections are raised — for example, 'I like it, but I want to talk to my advisers, my boss, etc.' — check that the objection is genuine by asking: 'Am I right in believing that if they approve you will go ahead?' If the answer is 'yes', then try to get to the person they will refer it to. If they agree make sure you follow the same procedure with that person as you did with your prospect. If they say, 'No, I don't intend to go ahead if they approve', then you know it's a false objection. Try to find the real one by saying, 'Mr Prospect, I would like you for a client for myself and my business. What do I have to do to get your business?' They will tell you either what you have to do to get their business or why they won't do business with you.

If they say, 'Yes, I intend to proceed if my adviser says to proceed, but no you can't talk to the adviser', then ask the prospect to make sure the adviser sees your written presentation. You have a much better chance in this case, because it will sell the offer better than your prospect will explain it. I have never had one adviser cause me problems. I did have three of them ask if I would do similar work for their clients.

Your presentations speak for you and about you — about what you know, how good you are at your work and how much care you take. They also tell your prospects how much you are willing to put into your work on their behalf. They really add value to your image as a successful salesperson.

If you hand a presentation to your prospect and they put it aside and say, 'I'll read it later', it leaves you with the option of selling without it. Don't take this option. It is a put-off. Sink or swim now. Say:

> 'Mr Prospect, I can appreciate it's not convenient for you to set aside the time now. Can we make another time, please?'

Stand up, pick up your presentation and prepare to leave.

Or say:

> 'Mr Prospect, there is no point in reading it without me, because I need to explain those points which are too complex to put in writing.'

Now the onus is on the prospect: to go ahead by making time now, to set another time at which you will get attention, or to call the whole project off. I have never had that happen to me. Most people will say, 'How long will it take?' Most presentations should take only around 30 minutes.

Now that you have a presentation that will work, prepare a master copy with blanks where specific prospect details were contained in your original presentation and where you believe the presentation will vary from prospect to prospect. All you need to do each time you want a good written selling presentation is fill out one of your blank presentations and give it to your typist. Written presentations will work very effectively for you with very little effort on your part. Most of the work is in getting it right in the first place.

PAYING ATTENTION TO NON-VERBAL SIGNALS

Understanding and watching for the non-verbal signals given by your prospect is critical at any time, but especially so in the first few minutes of your approach and presentation. I interviewed body language expert Allan Pease on the issues he feels are most important to salespeople in the early part of making a presentation. Allan is one of the foremost experts in the world on this subject. He is an international speaker and author who has enjoyed worldwide success. I am sure you will find his views very helpful.

◆

JC: Allan, what in your experience are the critical issues for salespeople when they are making a presentation or approach?

AP: Jack, the first common factor is that 60 to 80 per cent of the impact of the presentation is non-verbal. One difference between men and women is that women are very aware of the non-verbal aspects and can read attitudes and emotions. Men are more concerned with giving facts and data and miss many of the non-verbal attitudes.

In the first four minutes of an interview or presentation, people form 90 per cent of their opinion about you. In fact, we know they form most of their opinion in the first minute and spend the next three minutes justifying what they think. The task is to create trust: if they trust you and you identify with them and have rapport with them, they are likely to buy. First they buy *you*; they are then likely to buy what you are selling because they have bought you first. One of the best ways of reading whether you are creating trust and enjoying rapport with people is to observe whether they are mirroring you. If people like you, they will mirror what you do. They will sit, stand and move in the same way. As a strategy you can intentionally mirror in a way that will create rapport. So, for the first four minutes, mirroring and creating trust, and understanding that 60 to 80 per cent of your impact face to face is non-verbal, is very important.

Things to avoid in the first four minutes: avoid any hand-to-face touching as you are speaking, because we know that when Westerners aren't telling the truth, hand-to-face contact increases. If you have an itchy nose, it is better to twitch it than scratch it!

Smiling is the first thing that you must do to create trust, but it is the one thing not usually taught in sales schools. Smile so that the prospect can see your teeth and the inside of your mouth. When you laugh hard, within four minutes your brain releases endorphins which give you a warm, tingly feeling. Smiling can create the same effect. If you make yourself smile, you can change the way you feel. If you get your prospect or customer to smile, after four minutes they will get the same warm feeling. So smiling is critical, while also maintaining the amount of eye contact that is acceptable. For Westerners it is 60 to 70 per cent eye contact in a non-threatening situation, compared to 20 to 50 per cent for Asians and less than 20 per cent for South Americans. If you use Western techniques on a Chinese prospect in the first minute, they are likely to think you are pushy, and you might think they are sneaky because they won't return your gaze. It is also important to avoid crossing your arms and legs or lacing your fingers during those critical first four minutes.

Paying attention to these behavioural traits will pay off for you in increased sales and better relationships.

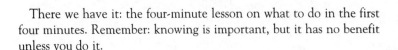

There we have it: the four-minute lesson on what to do in the first four minutes. Remember: knowing is important, but it has no benefit unless you do it.

CHAPTER 17

FOLLOW UP WITH AFTER-SALES SERVICE

This is where you win in the long term.
Selling is the easy part; keeping the customer is the
real test of any business.
ANON.

PEAK PERFORMERS KNOW that when their prospect or customer says 'yes' to an offer, the sale has just begun. From then on, everything you do to fulfil your promise either raises, or lowers your credibility, so it is critical that you follow up to ensure that the outcome is exactly what you want.

If your prospect or customer says 'No' to your offer, you will have to decide whether that is the end of the matter or whether it has just begun. There are always decisions to be made after your presentation has been completed. Here are the main issues that require follow-up:

◆ Your prospect has delayed a decision and wants you to call back.
◆ Your prospect has said 'no' to your offer, but you want to follow up for future business.
◆ Your prospect has said 'yes' and you want to ensure that the order is completed to their satisfaction.

YOUR PROSPECT SAYS, 'CALL ME BACK FOR A DECISION'

This is a common occurrence in selling. You make your presentation, ask for the order and your prospect says, 'I can't make a decision now. I have to discuss the matter with our financial controller. Call me in three days.' All too often, when you call back in three days, the prospect's answer is: 'We have decided not to proceed.'

Never call back for a decision. Let's analyse the situation. You make a presentation, and are asked to call back for a decision. Why? The answer must surely be because you didn't sell your prospect the first time. Ask yourself, 'After I leave, how much time is my prospect going to spend going over my offer and seriously considering it?' The answer is probably: very little. Over the next three days, your offer will get dimmer and dimmer in the mind of the prospect. So, when you call and say, 'You asked me to call you today about my offer. Have you made a decision?', they are likely to respond, 'We have decided not to accept your offer'.

Here is a better solution to the problem. Instead of calling back for a decision, get back to your prospect and sell them again, with more enthusiasm and additional benefits. Call after two days and say, 'I'm calling early because I want you to consider these additional benefits'. Arrange another 30-minute interview so you can show them these benefits. If you can't get the interview, sell over the phone. Anything is better than calling back for a decision. Go over the main parts of your offer again so they burn brightly in the mind of the prospect. Offer additional testimonials from customers in similar positions to your prospect, saying how they have benefited from your offer. Remember: most people have a built-in desire to act once they have evidence that says it is OK to do so. Your best chance is to resell your offer. Occasionally your prospect might genuinely have to consult with others, or have to await the outcome of something in process, however it is always better to try and resell the prospect instead of just calling back.

YOUR PROSPECT SAYS 'NO'

The decision you have to make in this scenario is whether to write this prospect off your list, or develop a strategy to follow up with the objective of building a relationship that will result in business in the future. A word of caution about keeping non-productive prospects in your prospect system: they make you feel better, but in the long run they will cost you plenty in terms of time and effort. Always consider how that time and effort might pay off if used on new prospects. Consult your ratios: what is your past success ratio in turning prospects who have said 'no' into someone who eventually said 'yes'? How does this ratio compare with the same time and energy spent on new prospects? When you have the answer, make your decision. I am amazed when a salesperson says to me, 'Persistency paid off. It took me 16 calls, but I finally sold him.' Sixteen calls? If those calls had been applied to new prospects, the effort would probably have resulted in three sales. The only saving grace in that situation might be the size of the sale and the size of future business. *You* have to decide, but base your decision on fact not fiction.

As a first step in developing a relationship, go back over your presentation to find what the prospect is interested in. Then provide information on, help with or recognition of those interests. At the same time, focus on supplying information and ideas that will help to build their business. Be helpful, not pushy. Keep the prospect up to date with any new products or services your organisation may produce or be about to produce. Try to find a third party who knows them and you and explore the possibility of that person referring your services to the prospect with whom you are developing the relationship. Have a senior executive in your organisation write a letter thanking the prospect for the time they have given you and saying they value this developing relationship.

Your objective is to earn the prospect's trust and respect, based on the value of the ideas and information you have given them. It may be a slow process, and only you can decide if your decision to build this relationship is a wise one.

YOUR PROSPECT SAYS 'YES'

Congratulations, well done. It is always a great feeling to have a prospect say 'yes', because it is a positive judgment of you as a person. Second, it affirms the value of your offer and gives you confidence to make that offer again with other prospects.

With acceptance of the offer comes responsibility for delivering all you said would be done. Don't leave it to the system to do it all.

Remember: Murphy's Law, which states that if anything can go wrong, it will, is always waiting to strike the unprepared. The time for you to implement your follow-up procedure is when you have made a sale.

Get in touch with key people in the delivery chain and advise them of any issue that is different, or unusual or very important in this case and, if possible, arrange for feedback so that you will know that what you have asked for has been done.

Make sure that you are advised immediately if anything arises that will make your promises uncertain. It's too late if your customer has to tell you about the problem.

When everything has been delivered just as you promised, send a thank-you note, or make a phone call to ask if everything is OK. If it's not, now is the time to know. If you have to fix anything, do it immediately and check again that your customer is satisfied.

Establish a call pattern with your new customer and make sure on your first call that you take some information or an idea that will be useful in building their business.

Follow-up is the last step in the selling cycle and is as important as any other part of the cycle. In building relationships, the key issues are trust and value.

CHAPTER 18

DEALING WITH COMPLAINTS

*Listen with empathy . . . focus all
your attention on the customer . . .
decide with speed . . .
listen to your customer.*

FOUR PER CENT of dissatisfied customers complain; the other 96 per cent don't talk — instead, they go to your competitor, and it costs six times as much to replace them as to service them as existing customers. Seeking out dissatisfied customers is potentially one of the most profitable activities a business can undertake. Some businesses have special programs for seeking out customer complaints and, as a result, are very successful in keeping their client base together. It is better to encourage complaints so that they can be dealt with as a process rather than a problem.

WHY CUSTOMERS COMPLAIN

When customers complain, it is because they believe they have been treated unfairly. Those customers should be treated as special because they are giving your organisation an opportunity to solve the problem and to retain them as a customer. Because you are the human face of the organisation for which you work, you will probably have to deal with most of the problems and complaints. You will not only get those that arise directly from your area of responsibility, but also those that come from other parts of the business for which you aren't responsible. Every complaint, no matter from where it comes, impacts on you. Salespeople have lost good accounts because the customers see closing the account as the ultimate punishment for a business that won't solve a problem that has nothing to do with sales. You should always be alert to problems, whether they are yours or someone else's and do everything you can to have the problem fixed as soon as possible.

Many customers don't complain; they simply go somewhere else to do business. Quite often, what they considered unfair was caused by a misunderstanding which would have been corrected in their favour if the business had known of the problem. The solution is to seek out customers who aren't happy; waiting for them to tell you they are unhappy will be too late, as most will simply leave.

RESPONDING TO CUSTOMER COMPLAINTS

When customers are angry, it is important to understand what is happening to them and what we need to do to make them feel better by solving their problem. They aren't the same thing. How people feel is essentially a human problem. They get angry, upset, defensive, aggressive or difficult, and it is our responsibility to make them feel better. Simply solving the problem of a faulty product or a failure on the part of the business to do what it promised may not always change how the customer feels. It is possible to fix the problem and still lose the customer, unless we pay a lot of attention to their feelings.

A good general principle to follow in all complaints, disputes or negotiations is to separate the people from the problem and be soft on the people and hard on the problem. Any time you spend on repairing damaged feelings will be time well spent. Preserving the relationship is always the key issue in dealing with complaints.

Prevention is better than cure. It is good policy for a business to let its customers and prospects know that it not only welcomes complaints, but actively encourages communication with its customers on any topic, including complaints. This can be done in many ways.

At the point of sale

Every customer should be told when the sale is made: 'Your satisfaction is our business, and your views are welcome. If for any reason you aren't satisfied, please let us know. We appreciate you and your business, and welcome your views so that we can serve you better.' Sales dockets and account forms should contain the same message, plus words to the effect of: 'Thank you for doing business with us. You and your business are appreciated.'

In advertising

All advertising should constantly reinforce all other actions taken by the business to get across the message: 'We welcome your views and appreciate your doing business with us.'

Whatever method is used to pass on the message to the customer, the critical issue will always be how the customers are treated when they *do* complain. If they are made to feel welcome and valued, and their problem is solved to their satisfaction on the first occasion, research shows that 95 per cent will do business with you again and that a satisfied customer on average tells five other people of their favourable experience. Research also shows that those who complain and have their complaint resolved to their satisfaction tend to be more loyal in the future than those who don't complain.

The choice seems to be either to encourage those who feel they have been treated unfairly to tell you of their dissatisfaction and try to solve their problem and retain them as customers, or to discourage complaints and lose the customer. Remember: research indicates that it costs six times as much to replace customers as to retain them. It would thus appear to be in the best interests of a business to retain its existing customers.

How they are treated at the time of making a complaint is the most critical factor from the customer's point of view. If the complaint turns into a contest of who wins the argument, then the outcome has been decided. The business will lose, no matter who wins the contest. If the business 'finally' decides in favour of the customer, the customer will probably still leave and do business with someone else. Even those who don't leave will generally resent the way they have been treated and may become an ambassador against your business. They will tell others of how they were treated. It generally costs businesses more to repair a damaged relationship than they save in winning a contest with a dissatisfied customer.

TECHNIQUES FOR DEALING WITH COMPLAINTS

Let's use the example of Mr Carter, one of your customers who is making a complaint against your business. Here are some techniques for dealing with his complaint:

- Treat Mr Carter as a valued customer. At the time of making the complaint, he is feeling anything but valued and so any time spent on repairing his hurt feelings will be productive.

- Give all your attention to Mr Carter, and in a face-to-face situation, make eye contact with him as soon as possible. You may have to use all your skills to preserve your relationship with him as your customer.

- Act and speak calmly. Care and consideration are your best chances of limiting the damage to the relationship. If care isn't taken, the complaint can erupt into a confrontation.

- Use his name often and with care. The sound that people most like to hear from others is the sound of their own name. Use expressions like, 'Mr Carter, I appreciate your concern and I can understand why you feel the way you do.'

- Listen patiently and attentively to his complaint. He may be angry, upset or defensive, and may even become aggressive. If this happens, hear him out. Patience and understanding are your greatest assets. Once Mr Carter has had his say, he will generally calm down. The quicker you can get him to calm down, the quicker you can deal with his complaint.

- Be sure and get all the relevant information. If necessary, ask questions and repeat Mr Carter's complaint back to him and get agreement that you understand his point of view on what has been said. If he says, 'You haven't got it right', never say, 'You don't understand what I have said'. Always say, 'I'm sorry I haven't made myself clear'. Always take responsibility for being heard and understood.

- Whenever possible, offer a solution that meets Mr Carter's expectations. Remember: the objective is to maintain the relationship and keep him as a customer, and that means satisfying him. The saying that 'The customer is always right' is never truer than in dealing with complaints.

• If a solution is becoming difficult, ask the magic question: 'Mr Carter, what do you think we should do that will solve the problem and be fair to both of us?', and then wait for his answer. In most cases, customers who are complaining will require you to do less than you were willing to do, so accepting their solution will not be difficult. You may decide to ask this question before you have to negotiate. The benefit of asking it earlier is that you can nearly always settle on the customer's terms, which is an advantage.

• Follow up to see that the arrangements you have made about fixing the complaint have been carried out as you promised. When you are certain that everything is in order, write Mr Carter a simple thank-you note saying that you appreciate having the problem brought to your attention and having the opportunity to make it right for him. Tell him that both he and his business is appreciated.

• It is good policy for a business to have a choice of simple, inexpensive gifts to enclose with thank-you notes. It's the thought, not the gift, that counts. Too much trouble? Yes, it *is* extra effort. You can't afford it? Of course, you can. Remember: one small gift may bring you more business than an expensive advertisement. Imagine the surprise and pleasure your gift will bring. Above all, you can be sure that most other businesses won't make this effort.

• When you have solved the problem and repaired the relationship, make sure you take whatever action is necessary to see that the complaint is used to correct current procedures so that this type of complaint won't arise again.

INVESTING YOUR TIME AND MONEY IN YOUR CUSTOMERS IS AN INVESTMENT THAT ALMOST ALWAYS PAYS OFF HANDSOMELY. CUSTOMERS WHO COMPLAIN ARE A LUXURY ALL BUSINESSES CAN AFFORD. CUSTOMERS WHO AREN'T SATISFIED AND DON'T COMPLAIN ARE A LIABILITY THAT FEW CAN AFFORD.

WHY DO CONTESTS ARISE?

Contests arise when a complaint is dealt with on a 'who is right basis', when 'being right' is more important than preserving the relationship. They arise when egos get in the way of preserving the relationship, because many staff who deal with complaints aren't trained to do so effectively or are emotionally unsuited to the task. Two common criticisms made by customers are: 'Why do businesses keep staff in complaints departments who are emotionally incapable of handling complaints?' and 'It's no good complaining to them. They're not interested in fixing the problem.' The onus is on you to make sure that no one can level those criticisms at you or the business you represent.

WHY PROSPECTS COMPLAIN

Prospects are usually driven to complain by a procedure they don't like, or by their belief that they deserve a concession which is outside normal company policy. Often the prospect believes that before they buy is the time to negotiate special terms and conditions or demand a concession. The leverage to get what they want is their business so the question you must resolve is twofold: (i) do you want their business enough to make changes in company policy or to do a one-off deal? (ii) will this be the end of the matter, or the start of an ongoing campaign for other concessions? Whatever the outcome of the original request, don't get into a contest of wills. The objective is to win the prospect, not the contest. Your main objective should always be to develop the relationship by creating mutual trust and adding value whenever you can.

CONCLUSION

Dealing with complaints is part of a salesperson's everyday life. The more effectively you deal with them, the better your long-term success, not only with the complaining customer but with all your customers. Complaints should become a process at which you excel. That things can go wrong is a fact of life, and most customers and prospects know this. What they won't accept is a continuation of the same problem, or problems caused by incompetence or neglect.

Every problem becomes an opportunity for you to perform. If you do it in a way that earns you credit, you win. If you respond in a way that doesn't, you lose. The outcome is always up to you.

CHAPTER 19

NEGOTIATING YOUR WAY TO SALES SUCCESS

*Whatever difference of opinion you may have with
a person, or persons, that difference is a product
of thinking — either theirs or yours.*

NEGOTIATION COULD BE described as a process in which two or more parties who have both common and conflicting interests bring forth and discuss explicit terms of possible agreement. Negotiation is part of our life. Every day, we all negotiate something. You negotiate with your husband or wife or partner about which film you will go to see. You negotiate with your teenage children the hour they will come home. You negotiate with tradespeople about getting your house painted, your lawn mowed and your car fixed. You negotiate a raise with your boss and a better price if you buy in bulk from your suppliers. We are all negotiators, and we negotiate all the time.

Our natural desire as human beings is to satisfy our own particular needs and wants, and in order to get that satisfaction we generally use negotiation as a means to obtain it and to decide the conditions under which we get what we want. Both you and the person with whom you are negotiating have something that you share — that is, some shared interest — as well as things you don't agree on. Generally speaking, it's the things you don't agree on that take up the time in negotiating. As a first step in negotiating, it is always helpful if you find out what you *do* agree on; you can then focus on the areas of disagreement and use your negotiating skills to reach agreement on them.

Today, conflict is a growth industry. People are increasingly acting as individuals and, as a result, fewer of them are willing to accept without discussion the decisions made by someone else. From the boardroom downwards, independence is ruling the day. Whether in business, government or the family, people reach most decisions through negotiations. Wherever there is conflict, there is a need to negotiate. If a product doesn't perform the way it should, there is a need to negotiate. In a divorce, there is a need to negotiate who gets the property and how much, who has the children and for how long.

The dilemma in most negotiating is the critical issue of how tough you should be and how hard you should push to win. People generally fall into one of two schools of negotiating.

1. *Soft negotiators* want to avoid personal conflict. They want to reach an amicable agreement, and they want to do it with the least amount of fuss and bother, so they give concessions and often they end up feeling they have been exploited and that the other party has taken advantage of their desire to be fair.

2. *Hard negotiators* believe that negotiating is simply a contest of wills, and the tougher you are the better off you will finish. Tough negotiators want to win at any cost, and so hard negotiations often damage relationships.

So the first issue to be resolved in negotiating is whether you are going to be soft or hard in your negotiations. You could, of course, adopt a strategy that falls between soft and hard and attempt a trade-off between getting what you want and maintaining good relationships with the people concerned. This is probably the least effective strategy, because there are usually no clear guidelines as to when to be soft and when to be hard.

PRINCIPLE NEGOTIATION

A third way to negotiate is called the method of principle negotiation. This is a combination of both hard and soft negotiation. It was developed at the Harvard negotiation project and is about deciding issues on their merit, rather than going through a haggling process focused on what each side says it will or won't do and what they want and don't want. Principle negotiation is about how to obtain what you are entitled to and still preserve relationships, because it makes it possible to be fair while ensuring that others cannot take advantage of your fairness. Principle negotiation can be used in any situation by any number of people, whether they are experienced or not. Principle negotiation has three critical elements:

1. Separate the people from the problem.
2. Focus on interest not position.
3. Develop options.

This chapter will focus on these aspects of principle negotiation.

Separate the people from the problem

It is important in every negotiation to consider the position you want to achieve. The most important issue in any sales negotiation is usually to preserve the relationship, and from now on in this chapter we will consider negotiation from the point of view of a sales negotiation. All efforts so far in building our sales career have been aimed at developing and maintaining relationships. Our objective is to make sales, to have the prospect become a client, to develop the relationship with mutual trust and to keep the client as the basis of our business. So, in terms of negotiating, it is critical to separate the people problems from the business problems. You may be negotiating during the very first interview even before you have a client. You could be negotiating price, terms and conditions, or any one of a dozen issues. This is why negotiating skills are so critical from your point of view. When making a sales presentation, you need to know when to move into negotiation mode so that you can get the best win/win result and arrive at an agreement that preserves the relationship.

The first step in separating the people issues from the problem issues is to put yourself in the other party's position so that you can fully understand their needs as well as your own. At this time it is as well to remember that you must not only deal with their people problems, but also take into consideration your own.

Perceptions are always the problem, for perception is the reality of the situation. Whatever you or the other party perceive to be true is, in fact, true to each of you. The more you deal with the people problem, the more you should focus on perception. If you support your perceptions with effective communications and handle your emotions and theirs effectively, look forward to solutions rather than backwards to the causes of the problem, then you are more likely to reach a win/win solution.

In dealing with people, you deal with emotions, so use standard techniques. If emotions run high, speak calmly, make eye contact and look at the person directly. Let them talk until they have said what they want to say. Keep nodding to show that you are listening. If you need information, ask for it calmly and inject whatever calmness you can into the situation. Remember that both your own and the other person's way of thinking is not just the cause of the problem but also something that may help you to solve the problem. Thinking is the problem, and thinking is the product of people, so focusing on people and not the problem is more likely to result in a solution. You are at a disadvantage if you keep on assuming that both of you need to know more about the issue that has caused the problem. Conflict is not about reality; it's about perception, and perception is a product of people's minds.

Whatever difference of opinion you have with the person you are negotiating with, that difference exists because it is a product of thinking, either theirs or yours. Understand that people have fears and hopes, and that fears are very real and need to be dealt with. Hope is something people hang onto and need to be satisfied. Then there are facts, and even if all the facts are established clearly in the mind of each party it will not do much to solve the problem. How you see the problem depends on your point of view. Remember what we said in Chapter 13, 'The Gentle Art of Communicating' — that people see what they want to see, hear what they want to hear and believe to be true what they want to be true — and this is part of the problem with every negotiation.

Listening is better than attacking. If you make a forceful attack on the person with whom you are negotiating, they will become defensive and resist your views. They will dig in their heels and become more entrenched in their point of view. The best strategy if the other party wants to let off steam is to simply let them talk, listen quietly, don't respond even if they attack, and occasionally give them encouragement and lead them to speak. When they have said all they have to say, it is time for you to say what you need to say.

Negotiation is a process of communicating back and forth with the purpose of reaching a win/win solution. If there is no communication, there is no negotiation. Communication is not easy, even between people who have similar values and shared experiences. What either side says may be misinterpreted by the other side and so compound the problem. It is better in a negotiation to talk about yourself, rather than them; it is better to discuss the problem and how it impacts on you, rather than what they did. It's better to say, 'I feel let down' instead of 'You broke your word', better to say, 'I appreciate your concerns, but here's how I feel'. Understanding the people problem makes it possible for a negotiator, using the method of principle negotiation, to be soft on the people and hard on the problem. Remember that people and their perceptions are the difficult part. The problem itself is probably the easiest thing to solve, though when it comes to the actual agreement on how to solve the problem be tough, hard, relentless with the problem, for it must be solved and it must be solved effectively.

Focus on interest not positions

If you want to get to a solution that is win/win for both parties, then focus on interest not position. Interest works effectively because behind the different positions of the opposing parties are their shared interests. As well as compatible interests, there are the conflicting ones which cause the problem. It is very easy in a negotiation to assume that because the other side has a different position to you, their interests are also different and must be opposed. This, of course, isn't true. If you are soft on people, ask questions and listen carefully, it won't be long before you discover that behind their positions they have interests that are quite similar to your own.

Here is an example. When we lived in the country we were renting a house, so we had a landlord–tenant relationship and a real estate agent to whom we paid the rent. The rent was fair, but we were still making our way and every dollar counted. After we had been a tenant for two years, the agent said that the landlord wanted a 20 per cent increase in the rent. My position was simple. Although I believed that the rent increase was fair, we simply couldn't meet it, so the position I conveyed to the agent was that if the rent went up we would have to find other premises. He advised the landlord, whose position was that she would prefer us to stay as a tenant but that if we couldn't meet the rent increase then she would have to get another tenant. Negotiations went on for several weeks, with the agent moving backwards and forwards between us, but in the end it became obvious that it was pay the new rent or leave. At this time I wasn't a skilled negotiator, but in desperation I said to the agent, 'Why does she want the rent increased? She's a very wealthy woman and she has many properties. Why a 20 per cent increase?' The agent said, 'Jack, she doesn't need the money, but the home in which you are living is the house in which she was born. It's her family home and she wants the rent increase so as to get the property painted and to maintain it in good order.' Now that we were talking interests, not positions, there was a possibility that the conflict could be mutually resolved. In looking for a solution, it became obvious to me that in order to have the house painted the landlord not only had to buy the paint but also had to pay a painter. It was also obvious that I could do the painting, and so I offered to paint the property if the landlord didn't raise the rent and would pay for the paint. Now I was stating my position. The agent said the landlord was happy with this arrangement and gave me an account number to operate on in the general store in town. I learned that behind every position there are shared interests, and if you focus on interest not position you are on the way to becoming a first-class negotiator.

There are always multiple interests. For example, securing a price rise from a customer is one interest, but the second and most important interest is to get the price rise and keep the customer. One of the basic problems of most negotiators is that they become so concerned with their own position that they overlook the interest of the other party. If you give the other party an opportunity to tell you their concerns and draw out their interest, you will go a long way towards solving the problem.

It is a good idea to stop arguing about the past and focus on the future. Ask the other party not to justify what they did yesterday or what caused the problem, but what both of you should do in the future that will solve the problem. As Dr Tony Campolo says: 'Your past is important, but it is not nearly so important to your present as is the way you see your future.' Always be hard on the problem, but soft on the people. You can be as hard as you like in talking about your interest. Every time they talk about their position, respond with your interest. Focus on the people not the problem, and whenever you have to be forceful in your negotiation make sure that they understand you are attacking the problem and not them.

Developing options

When you focus on developing options for the other party, you are working towards a solution based on interest not position. Creative solutions to a negotiation problem arise when you start to invent options. There are basically four rules for inventing options.

1. *Create first, judge later.* Nothing comes as naturally to most people as saying something can't be done. There is nothing that creates as many problems as someone just waiting to knock down every creative or helpful suggestion as not being possible. By creating first and judging later, you remove the judgmental process which hinders most creative thinking and delays reaching a mutually satisfactory solution. So create first, judge later.

2. *Increase the size of the pie.* The size of the pie can be the size of the possible solution before you invent options. If both parties believe that the pie is a fixed size, then both parties conclude that whenever they make a concession they are giving away part of their pie. If, on the other hand, you increase the size of the pie, then perhaps both parties can get what they want. When you increase the size of the pie by 100 per cent, the pie can be divided equally and both parties can get 100 per cent of the original pie.

   For example, two sisters were quarrelling over who should have an orange. In the end, they agreed to divide the orange in half. One sister cut the orange, and the other sister had first choice of the halves, which kept the first sister honest when she divided the orange. After the orange had been divided, the first sister took her half, ate the fruit and threw away the peel. The second sister threw away the fruit and used the peel from her half in baking a cake. If the sisters had focused on interest not position, then one sister could have had all the orange to eat and the other sister could have had all the peel and baked two cakes, but because they fought over position — which was, I want the orange — the obvious solution was to adopt the Solomon solution, which was to divide it in half. If they had focused on interest, they could have peeled the fruit and both had 100 per cent of what they wanted from the orange. This is a classic example of how most negotiations are conducted and why so many negotiators fail to get full value from their negotiations.

3. *Believing that the other side must solve the problem because it is their problem.* Nothing could be further from the truth. A good negotiator

focuses on helping the other person to solve their problem. By doing so, they generally solve their own problem, as long as they focus their attention on interests not positions.

4. *'What if'ing.* One of the most powerful methods of solving any problem is the 'what if'. Once you start 'what if'ing with the person with whom you are negotiating, both minds become focused on one problem, which is to create solutions which will satisfy the interests of both parties and, in the process, solve the problem. A creative way of 'what if'ing is to look through the eyes of someone else. For instance, you are a salesperson; how would an accountant look at the problem? What would a lawyer say? How would a marketing person deal with it? What about an investor? Once agreement looks a possibility, then make it easy for them to make a decision and remember that your opponent will probably accept the solution if it seems to be the right thing to do and is fair. It will look more right and fair if you have focused on their interests rather than their position.

THE PROCESS OF NEGOTIATION

The process of negotiation starts with the adoption of a broad strategy that will get you the desired result from the negotiations you are about to enter. This strategy should look at the best possible outcomes for both parties to the negotiation. Your objective in a sales negotiation where you want to preserve the relationship and keep the customer is obviously a win/win solution. A critical part of your preparation in terms of negotiation strategy is to decide your negotiating style.

Basically there are five styles:

1. *Competitive*: A win/lose approach which leads to confrontation.
2. *Compromise*: A win/win approach which is sub-optimal.
3. *Co-operation*: A win/win approach which creates joint problem solving.
4. *Accommodation*: A lose/win approach which leads to capitulation.
5. *Avoidance*: A lose/lose approach which leads to withdrawal.

The diagram opposite illustrates these styles.

Because you are focusing on preserving the relationship, your concentration will be on the co-operative style in order to achieve a win/win solution. You should also focus on the competitive style in

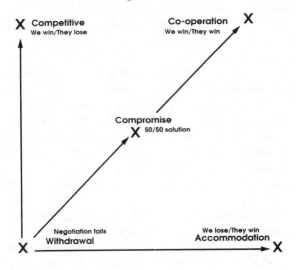

order to avoid becoming too involved in winning. The main thing that will stop you from achieving a win/win solution is when you or the other party are so competitive that it becomes a win at all costs situation, which you should avoid if you possibly can.

Conflict resolution

The above diagram shows the working of each of the five conflict resolution styles. When you move towards your own goal, your only interest is in yourself and not in your opponent. It becomes a win at all costs situation, which is fraught with danger and will probably lead to the loss of the customer. This competitive style usually inhibits resolution and creates more competition.

If you move towards your own goal as well as moving towards the other party's goal, then you set up a situation where you will finish in a co-operative mode and the solution will be win/win. Both parties will get the payoff.

If the negotiation bogs down because neither party is willing to make concessions or to consider the other party's point of view, then the negotiation will become deadlocked: you don't move towards your goal, and you refuse to move towards theirs; they don't move towards their goal and they refuse to move towards yours. The result is avoidance and the lack of a resolution, and therefore the negotiation fails.

If you move too freely towards the other party's goal and you don't cause them to move towards your goal, then you are in accommodation style. The result will be that you will lose and the other party will win.

It is rare for a negotiation to move constantly in one direction and to reach an outcome without deviating from the direction of the first move. For that to happen, you would have to conclude there was no need to negotiate in the first place, for negotiation is between two or more parties who have views which create conflict and they want to resolve the conflict. Usually the path to resolution is a process of give and take, winning and losing, trading concessions and making demands, which results in numerous changes in direction as a result of the trade-offs.

If you were to graph a negotiation process, the finished graph would show rises and falls and would look something like a temperature graph. When you create an option which is favourably received, you move up. When you trade a concession which is favourably received and accepted, or, you win a concession, you move up. When you have to give away a concession or agree on an option, you move down. So the negotiation is in constant flux: up and down, moving forwards and backwards.

The negotiation quadrant

This is the name often given to the negotiation matrix. What you need to do is to get the quadrant fixed firmly in your mind so that during the whole negotiations you keep asking yourself, 'Where am I on the quadrant?' Am I moving too far towards accommodation, or am I too close to being competitive? Do I look like I'm compromising, or is there an opportunity for a win/win solution?'

It is my belief that, once the quadrant is memorised, it is the best tool that you can take into a negotiation because at any time you can ask yourself which direction you are heading in, how you got there, whether you want to change course, and how you can do so. If you get the answers to these four questions you are always in control, and being in control is a critical issue when it comes to being a successful negotiator. The example given in the diagram opposite reflects the way a negotiation is most likely to proceed. In this example, I have shown a win/win resolution.

In sales, you will negotiate with a number of people who have no qualms about trying to force accommodation on you because they believe that the reality of the marketplace is that you need them more than they need you. You may find yourself in a position where you have to fight hard to get cooperation, but that is the skill of a negotiator and that's the reason why you focus on interests and not positions. If you keep focusing on position, you can easily finish up in an accommodation situation and set up a win for your opponent and a loss for yourself.

If you refer back to the sisters and their orange, then you will see that they finished at a compromise. This is known as a Solomon decision: you take half and I'll take half. Unfortunately, too many negotiations result in a compromise. For instance, you go to trade in your car. You believe the car is worth \$21 000, but you go into the negotiation asking for \$22 500 because you want room to move, usually downwards. After looking at the car, the salesman assesses its value at \$19 000 and he goes into the negotiation offering \$17 500 because he wants room to move upwards. Both of you have decided in advance that when you split the difference, it will come to \$20 000, which is the Solomon decision, so no real negotiation takes place because the issue was decided in advance. This type of solution is not

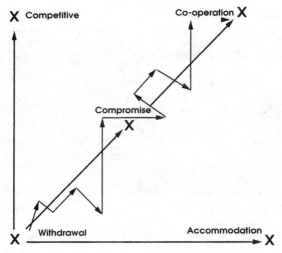

Course of Negotiation Matrix

as good as a win/win solution, but it is better than either of the other alternatives if you are looking at satisfaction as being a part of the deal. This brings us to the subject of negotiation range.

Negotiation range

Implicit in every negotiation is the knowledge of each party that they will have to move once the first offers are made. If neither moves, then you get avoidance and no negotiation takes place. If one moves and the other fails to do so, then a win/lose situation is created. In order for a win/win solution to come about, both parties need to move. So, generally speaking, the first offers decide the range of the negotiation. Let's go back to the car example.

You believe your car is worth $21 000 and the salesman believes it is worth approximately $19 000. You have asked for $22 500, but if pushed you will settle for $19 000 but nothing less. The salesman, believing the car is worth $19 000, offers $17 500, but knows that if pushed he will offer $21 000 but no more. So the real range of the negotiation is between $19 000 and $21 000, and anywhere in-between will be acceptable to both parties, although if you get a little more than $20 000 or the salesman pays a little less than $20 000 you will both be happier. So $20 000 will be a win/win or Solomon decision.

Range of Negotiation

Seller's asking price	$22 500
Buyer will not pay more than	$21 000
Estimated worth of the car	$20 000
Seller will not take less than	$19 000
Buyer's offer price	$17 500

The shaded portion represents the real range of negotiation

If the salesman's highest price is lower than your lowest selling price, you probably won't accept the offer and will go somewhere else with your business. This, of course, may not mean that the negotiation has failed, because sometimes it is better not to do business if you can't get the prices together. However, the important point is that if you both agreed on $20 000, the salesman could have bought it for less if he was a good negotiator, and you could have got more if you were a good negotiator. So the art of deciding final offers is a very real skill in negotiating. If both sides settle for a compromise, they have both lost the opportunity to do a better deal.

BEHAVIOURAL PATTERNS

Co-operative mode

Let's look at some of the behavioural patterns of opponents in the co-operative mode:

◆ They are more open to and willing to discuss alternatives.
◆ They are more willing to compromise.
◆ They tell the truth and are willing to provide information that you seek.
◆ They are more relaxed and intent on achieving a solution.
◆ They tend to focus more on interest than on position. They listen and ask questions and are open in their communications.
◆ They seek solutions and appear to want to understand your problems. They give and seek feedback and are willing to spend time on solving problems.

Competitive mode

In the competitive mode, the behavioural characteristics of the opponents are likely to be:

◆ They communicate poorly.
◆ They tend to make demands rather than offer solutions.
◆ They focus on winning at all costs.
◆ They tend not to listen but make statements.
◆ They give few concessions, but demand many.
◆ They tend to focus on position not interest.
◆ They only give information when they have to and sometimes it is false.

When you are conducting a win/win cooperative negotiation, keep these guidelines in mind and focus your attention on the positives, and try to get the other party to do the same. If you recognise a number of traits that lead you to believe your opponent is running in the competitive mode and is only interested in himself, then you need to try and make the communication more open by focusing on interest not position. When bringing interests to your opponent's attention, be very specific in describing them and what you believe would be the outcome for each party if a win/win situation was accomplished.

NEGOTIATING TACTICS

In terms of tactics, you will be in the stronger position in the negotiation if you can get the other party to state their opening offer first, because this focuses their attention on stating what they want to settle. It also helps you to understand your opponent's position and it allows you the luxury of giving your reaction. In most negotiation processes, one of the parties generally waits for the other to open the negotiation in order to get the other party to state their opening offer first. You can do this by saying, 'Why don't you tell me what it is you would like to achieve through this negotiation?' Always ask open-ended questions so that the other person has to explain their feelings.

If you find that you have to start the negotiation, then make your major demands at the opening because this leaves the other party in no doubt as to what you want to achieve. It also helps to minimise the time wasted on minor issues early in the negotiation. These tend to fall into place as the negotiation goes along, so it is better not to waste time on them at the start. It is also a good idea to make your major demands at the start because that's when compromises are more often freely acquired.

Make your first demand high, because research shows that if you do make a high or even an extreme initial demand, it is more likely that you will get a better outcome in the end. If you make your opening demand too small, it is very difficult to raise the stakes as you go along. If you are asking for something that wasn't supposed to be in the negotiation, then you can raise your demand by saying, 'OK, I'll be happy to concede that, but in return . . .' and then raise the stakes.

It is better to avoid miscalculations, so make sure the other party understands what you are trying to achieve. When you make your opening demands high, this communicates clearly to the other party what your expectations are. Their response to your high opening demands will give you a good idea of what you are up against.

If the other party is not anxious to talk or appears unwilling to negotiate, then a good gambit is to demand a precondition, which can be as simple as: 'Unless you can make a final decision at this meeting, then I'm not willing to proceed.' When you make a demand like this, you need to be in a position where, if the meeting doesn't proceed, it creates no problems for you. If that's the case then make the demand, because as soon as you can get the other party to concede an issue you have gained an important psychological advantage.

Here are some of the issues that may create a need to negotiate a settlement:

◆ Price. (This comes up more than anything else.)
◆ Exclusivity.
◆ Assurances.
◆ Repeat business.
◆ Method of payment.
◆ Scope of service.
◆ Guarantees and warranties.
◆ Signage and advertising support.

None of these issues are very complex, providing you focus on the people not the problem, on the future not the past, on interest not position, and as long as you have a fall-back alternative to an agreed negotiation. In negotiating terms, this is usually referred to as your BATNA, which stands for the Best Alternative To a Negotiated Agreement. Before you go into a negotiation, you need to be clear about your BATNA. If it is a better alternative than the negotiated agreement, you should quit the negotiation and implement your BATNA instead.

These are only some of the tactics that you could use in a negotiation. The main purpose of tactics is to get the other party to change their position or to prevent them from changing your position. Remember: the other party also has tactics, and in preparing your own you need to be ready to recognise and combat any tactic of the other party that may prevent you from achieving your objective of a win/win result in the negotiation.

Here are some more important tactics:

◆ If you want to diminish your opponent's argument and minimise their tactics, then you can start by drawing attention to what they have omitted and focus on any weaknesses you have discovered in their presentation. You could suggest that, because of certain information you have, they should revise their position.

◆ You could raise doubts about some of the assumptions their point of view is based on, which you can do by questioning the facts. Whether they are true or not, the fact that you have questioned them makes it necessary for your opponent to defend them, which puts them on the defensive.

◆ Support your own argument. You can do this by becoming a master of detail. Point out the reasonableness of your position and in the process make appeals to both emotion and reason. Outline the benefits of your opponent accepting your position and point out the adverse consequences if they don't do so. You can then add the burden of proof to the other things you are asking your opponent to defend.

Here are some important tactical defences:

◆ The less you talk the more you learn, and you learn most by listening to the other person and drawing them out by using soft questions.

◆ It's good practice never to negotiate anything on the telephone if your position is weak. If you are negotiating from a strong position, then you can do some of the preliminary, or perhaps even all, of the negotiations over the telephone.

◆ Never give lengthy explanations or give away too much information. If you are asked questions, answer them briefly and specifically but don't enlarge because you may provide extra information which could be helpful to the other party.

◆ If you are working with another person or persons in a negotiation, agree before you start who is to be the leader and who is to speak and when. Don't let your team members speak freely with the opposition.

Concession trading

To make concession trading productive from your point of view, try to make your opponent give the first concession. If circumstances dictate that you should make the first concession, then make it but at the same time make it a condition of giving the concession that in turn you receive a concession and state what concession you want. For example, you have been asked to agree to new trading terms, which increase your customers' 30 days credit terms to 60 days. You could say, 'I'm willing to agree, but in place of the 30 days I'm agreeing to, I want your discount on purchases reduced by one per cent'.

Before you make concessions, always think about the consequences both in the long term and the short term. The concession that you give away easily today in the short term may come back to cause you problems in the long term. When you are making concessions, add a proviso that they aren't forever, because future events may dictate that the concession has to be taken back. You could, of course, limit the concession so that it will apply for x time or under x conditions and then a review will be conducted. It is worth outlining the conditions under which such a review will be conducted.

When you are trading concessions, never trade multiple concessions. If you are willing to make more than one concession, trade them separately and get value for each concession. Sometimes you can get so wrapped up in the negotiation, particularly if it starts to go your way, that you start to feel generous and give away concessions without extracting any value in return. Remember that the law of payback that we discussed in Chapter 8, 'Why People Buy', is at work during a negotiation. It works against you as well as for you, so be careful when the other party grants you a concession that you don't give an immediate payback. Whatever concessions you give, make the other party work hard for them. Never give a concession easily, but when you do give it gracefully.

Concession trading is part and parcel of any negotiation and the active word is *trading*, the implication being that if you give a concession you expect one in return and always ask for one bigger than you gave. The law of payback also applies to you: and if your opponent gives a concession and you fail to give one, it may cause some difficulties, so the principle is to give back less than you get. In trading concessions, always talk up your concession and give it as much value as you can. Try to emphasise why this concession is important to the other party.

Deadlock

If either party fails to move, you will reach a deadlock. As a result, withdrawal will occur and no solution to the negotiation will be achieved. If you want to break a deadlock, then you need to review what you think has not been done for the other party that, if done, would have made it possible for them to agree. Then review how you can make that possible. Do you have to create an option? Do you have to define another concession? Do you have to change your style? It is essential at this time to define clearly what has to be done by both parties in order to get a negotiation under way, and this requires that the other party not lose face or they won't cooperate.

Here are some ways to break a deadlock:

◆ Attempt to get an agreement in principle, by discussing what alternatives are left to both parties and explaining why it would advantage both parties to agree to an in-principle agreement.
◆ Go back over the issues and the progress that has been made, and discuss what the outcome of a non-negotiation agreement may mean and what benefits each party may lose through not concluding the negotiation.
◆ Go back to 'what if' ing and introduce more creative solutions.

Your final offer

As with closing a sale, timing is the critical aspect in reaching settlement of a negotiation. Just as in a sale, you should be looking for buying signals while the negotiation is in progress. If in the middle of a negotiation the other party is giving signals which indicate you could bring the negotiation to a satisfactory close, you should do so. Don't go through the whole negotiating process if it isn't necessary.

Remember when making your final offer that many negotiators leave profit on the table because they didn't prepare well enough in terms of the negotiation range. Reread the section earlier in this chapter that deals with the range and memorise the procedure so that you can easily prepare your range figures for any negotiation. Then prepare your BATNA so that you always know your best alternative to a negotiated settlement.

When you make your final offer, do it with authority and give it some teeth. If necessary, tell the other party why it is your final offer and how you can both benefit from the offer. Leave them in no doubt that this is it; it is not up for further negotiation.

CONCLUDING THE NEGOTIATION

At the conclusion of any negotiation, analyse your performance and assess how successfully you performed. Follow the technique outlined in Chapter 16. Learn from each negotiation so that it strengthens your skills and focuses your attention on the critical issues of:

◆ Separating the people from the problem.
◆ Being soft on the people and hard on the problem.
◆ Focusing on interest not position.
◆ Creating options so as to enlarge the pie.

Your chances of real improvement will then be excellent.

All negotiating is about people: how they feel, what they believe in and what they are willing to defend. Once you are in control of those issues and fix the people problems, you effectively fix the negotiation. If you ask yourself which of the principles of negotiating you can use in your sales presentations and then practise them until they are an integral and effective part of your sales story, you will improve your sales results dramatically.

Here are some more important points on negotiating and selling from Australia's top negotiator, Harry M. Miller, who is one of Australia's leading businessmen. A great entrepreneur in the entertainment world by any standard, he represents many very successful entertainers and media people. When people want the skills of a high-level negotiator in the public arena they go to Harry.

◆

JC: Harry, in your opinion, what are the most important issues in negotiating?

HM: First, be sure you are prepared by knowing what outcome you want. Make your offer and stick to it. When you make your offer, keep quiet. Don't speak, shut up. Silence is your most powerful weapon, as while they are talking you are learning. Never exaggerate. You have an offer to make: make it exactly as it is and don't gild the lily, as it only weakens your case. Truth is a powerful weapon. Don't destroy it by making your offer better than you can deliver.

Jack, when I'm teaching my staff negotiating, it's always: make your point absolutely truthfully. Don't add anything.

If you can do 117, don't say 120. It's not necessary. Truth has a power of its own. When we are negotiating on behalf of our client, we know what they are worth to the other party and we show that party the benefits they will receive from using our client. We know what the client on whose behalf we are negotiating can do and deliver. If we are negotiating for a TV or radio commercial, we go to a lot of trouble to recommend the person who, in our opinion, is best suited to do the work and get results for the organisation that is hiring them. We do our homework. Always be prepared, know your next move and use silence. Too many salespeople are talkers and not listeners. Once you have made your point, listen and listen again and then listen again. Ask questions if necessary and listen to the answer. By *listen*, I mean not just hear what they say, but *understand* every bit of what they say. Then use that information to strengthen your claim.

If you want to build a reputation for great negotiating, be consistent. We have reached a stage that when we make an offer or a demand, we stick to it and people know that we mean it and they know we aren't discussing options. This is it.

JC: What are the most important skills that can help salespeople to become more effective in negotiating with their prospects and customers?

HM: Know your business. Be an expert on your products and services. Not just the main parts of them, but every last minute detail. This is the day of the salesperson who is willing to put in the time and effort to be world class in what they do. Knowing every last little piece of information about what you sell is critical today. It is surprising how often your first question can floor the salesperson. Here's an example.

We were approached about installing a voice mail facility. My first question to the salesperson was, 'give me the names of six people who have installed your system so that I can check it with them'. The salesperson didn't have testimonials with him. He was simply unprepared. The first question put him out of the game. What a disaster. The following weekend I rang six providers of voice mail. Not one of their voice mail facilities was working correctly. More disaster! What was I to think about my chances if they couldn't or wouldn't put their own house in order? Why hadn't the salespeople done the same test and said to their organisation, 'This isn't good enough. Some of my prospects may call us to see how good we are.' If the salespeople don't care, why should the others? Nothing but world class is good enough today.

Jack, salespeople need to focus on world-class selling practice in everything they do. Make that extra effort to meet people's needs and wants. If they sell a product and it is only available in black but the customer wants it in red, then try to get it in red. Go back to the factory and see if they will do a one-off order. Make the extra effort and show that you are willing to try on your customer's behalf.

Salespeople must be willing to sell the add-on. Add-ons are the extra sale. They are very important, because every salesperson should offer other products and services that complement what has just been sold. Give them a chance to buy. Ask, 'Have you seen this?' or 'Have you considered this?' or 'Would this be helpful?', because in my opinion people are always willing to consider other options and possibilities. Add-on selling is terribly important. I remember when I was on the board of Qantas and was addressing a conference of travel salespeople. I gave the example of a customer coming into a retail store asking for shoelaces. Why not ask about their shoes: do they need new ones, different ones, better ones. Keep going, they may need more: a suit, a tie or perhaps a shirt. When you have this person in this new gear, why not say: 'You look terrific, good enough for Hollywood', and then sell them a travel deal to match their new image. Now I know this is an exaggeration to make a point, but anything is possible if you ask and give them the opportunity to buy. Let them say 'no'. Perhaps it will be 'yes'.

Jack, there is so little difference between one product and another these days. The only real issue is the level of service. Whatever business we do with clients, as soon as we have delivered we check with them to see if we have delivered what we promised and that they are happy with what we have done. Yet this is not done very often because salespeople are afraid something will be wrong. For example, I believe that selling into the agriculture industry is the hardest business to survive in, because those you are selling to are generally conservative people. Some years ago, we were the biggest breeders of Simmental cattle in Australia and New Zealand. We had a fantastic Scottish studmaster who had been taught in Scotland never to ring clients and ask them how the bull they had bought was going because they might be unhappy with it. The best chance you have to put it right is at the beginning, *before* they have told a thousand people about how unhappy they are. Follow-up is terribly important.

The other thing I have found with many salespeople is that they are very reluctant to handle negative questions or unhappy customers. We teach our people here to deal with that issue by using the Nordstrom technique of saying, 'I'm really sorry, what would you like us to do?' That takes the wind out of the sails of the complaint, and now it can be fixed with a minimum of fuss. If you fix a problem for them better than anyone else ever has, your problem becomes a plus. They will remember you forever.

I believe salespeople are an arm of the manufacturing division, they are part of storage and delivery, part of the accounting department and every other part of the business, as well as having to look after the consumer. They have to have an interest in not just selling something but in looking after every part of what has to be done to deliver what was promised. This interest in the customer lasts for the life of the relationship. Selling at top-class standards is not easy, but it has a great payoff.

Salespeople must not give up. They have to be in touch with those who aren't currently buying so that when they are in a position to buy, they are at the top of their mind. Which is part of real service. I think that's very important.

Salespeople need to be constantly plumbing the depths, finding new customers. There are hundreds of thousands of new prospects out there. You've got to keep going. All the successes that I have had and that I have watched other people have come from keeping on going when everyone else has dropped dead or gone to bed.

My last suggestion is: remember the silence. It is the critical part of sales negotiating. Jack, thank you for asking me to be part of your book and I wish you and your readers every success.

◆ — ◆ — ◆

Well, there it is from Mr Negotiator himself. What you do with what he has said will decide how much you get from his suggestions. Go for it!

CHAPTER 20

CONCEPTS

*Creativity is a critical issue in today's fast-changing world
and imagination is the soul of creativity.*

ANON.

WELCOME TO CONCEPTS. It is my pleasure to introduce to you some creative and effective concepts that will improve your chances in the field of selling and management. Today we sell and manage in a different market to 10 years ago. Time frames have shortened, communications have speeded up, and the people who make up our particular market are better informed now than ever before. The media flood them with advice, and as a result our prospects and customers require more from us. They expect better service, and they expect it quicker. Not only do they expect to be educated as a result of our activities, but they also expect those of us who sell to be more creative and interesting than ever before.

Being different is important. It sets us apart from the mob and gives a special value to what we do. As Yogi Berra said: 'Don't follow the crowd; nobody goes there anymore, it's too crowded.' Part of being different is to understand that selling products and services first is not as effective as it used to be. Salespeople get so enthralled with their product or service they forget that no one wants what a product or service *is*, they want what it will *do* for them. In order to find out if people need or want what their product will do, the salesperson must adopt the technique of asking soft questions. By using open-ended questions you can explore what people want, and when you know what they want, you can sell them the idea of how your product will do what they want.

Those who sell product first, pay a high price in lost opportunities. Product is the solution to the problem, and solutions are best sold last. Don't sell products or services, sell solutions, philosophies, ideas and concepts. If you have no ideas on how your product or service can solve the problems of your prospects or customers, then you have nothing to sell. All we have to sell are our ideas, and we trade those ideas for the time our prospects and customers give to us. If our ideas are good, they will give us the time to explain them; and if we have creative ideas on how they can use what we sell and do to solve their problems, they will buy from us. We will prosper according to our ability to sell creative solutions to people's wants and needs.

As an example of selling ideas, philosophies and concepts, consider the following. Selling investments, whether it is real estate, shares or other financial services, is never about product; it is about getting richer. If you can't sell your prospects the idea that they should get richer, they will have no need of any product you are selling. If you can sell them the idea that they should be richer than they currently are, then they are in the market for a great variety of financial services and products. Sell ideas, concepts and philosophies on how to get richer.

If your product is real estate, then do the same: sell ideas, concepts and philosophies on how it will make them richer or more comfortable, or how it will satisfy their ego. If you sell computers, sell ideas, concepts and philosophies on how your product will make your customers more productive, more effective, more prosperous and their working life more enjoyable. Whatever you sell, the principle is the same. It applies to everything that is being sold. For you to unlock the door to selling success, identify your real sale and sell it, and fund it with your product or service. What you sell may be speed, safety, convenience, value, beauty or any other aspect of your product or service, but it is never product or service alone.

This chapter is about concepts that can help you to make your presentations more creative and interesting. If you master them and use them wisely, their use will set you apart from other salespeople in your field. They can be used with almost any prospect or customer by anyone who sells any type of service or product. The key to their success is in the timing, so that the concept you use creatively illustrates the point you wish to emphasise. A concept can be described as being an idea, a theory, an image, a view, a belief, an option or a conviction held by the person using it. To be effective it needs to be credible, easily understood and able to stand up to investigation.

Let's look at nine concepts you can use to make your selling more effective. These concepts can be part of your sales story or your approach, or can be a storehouse of interesting views that you can use in general conversation. They can be used to overcome objections or to close a sale. They can be used to reassure your customers that they have made a first-class purchase and a wise decision that will not only benefit them now but also in the future.

1: THE MAGIC OF 72

The figure 72 is a key figure in being able to do calculations in your head when dealing with earnings and rates of return over a given duration or of particular investments. For instance, if you make an investment with an interest rate of 12 per cent and you want to know how long you will have to leave the money invested before it doubles your initial investment, divide 72 by the interest rate of 12 per cent, which gives six. This means that if you invest $1000 at 12 per cent in six years it will have doubled to $2000. In a further six years, the $2000 will have doubled to $4000. Thus, in a period of 12 years commencing from the date of the first investment of your $1000, you will have accumulated $4000 without having invested any other money. Providing the interest rate remains at 12 per cent, this will be the case. It is possible, therefore, to calculate on into the future by doubling the investment every six years. By year 18, the investment will be worth $8000, in 24 years it will be worth $16 000, and in years it will be worth $32 000. So if you invest $1000 every year at 12 per cent and the rate stays constant over the time of the investment, at the end of 30 years you will receive $32 000 and you will continue to receive $32 000 each year for the next 30 years. In total you will have invested $30 000 and you will receive back $960 000. It's not difficult to get rich over the long haul.

If, on the other hand, you wanted to double your money every four years, then divide 72 by four, which will give you the interest rate you need to earn to double your money in four years. In this example it's

18 per cent compound interest. You can calculate returns and growth rates by dividing 72 by the interest rate, which gives you the duration over which the investment has to take place to double your investment. Or you can select a period of time in which you want your investment to double, such as 12 years, and then divide that into 72 to get the interest rate you need to earn to double your investment over the given number of years.

Let's do some calculations on the terms needed to double your investment at a given rate of interest. Six per cent divided into 72 is 12 years, 10 per cent equals 7.2 years, 15 per cent equals 4.8 years, and if you achieve an interest rate of 24 per cent then you will double your money in three years. Now let's do some calculations based on a given term. If you divide the six-year term into 72, it equals a 12 per cent interest rate, eight years equals 9 per cent, and 15 years equals 4.8 per cent. So if you have an interest rate of 4.8 per cent, it will take you 15 years to double your money.

This method of quick calculation is also useful to people who sell real estate, as it makes it easy to calculate very quickly the growth rate in compound interest terms that a property must get to double its value in any given time. Or you can establish the pattern of growth in real estate over the past x number of years and apply the growth rate that will give you the number of years it will take to double the value of the investment. You can do the same calculation on any commodity using the current rate of inflation. Divide 72 by the current rate of inflation and that is the period over which you will need to double your investment to maintain a rate equal to inflation. You can apply the principle to mortgages, buying or selling cars, or in any number of ways to a great variety of products and services to illustrate values in terms of earnings and growth rates. Being able to do these calculations in your head will certainly impress your prospects and customers, as well as set you apart from your competition and help to establish you as a creative thinker.

2: THE CREATION OF WEALTH

Leaving aside gifts, wins and inheritances, there are only two ways for a person to create wealth. The first way is for them to work, and the second is for them to put money to work for them.

How often have we heard the statement that time equals money? And yet the reality of life for all of us is that work equals money. If you think time equals money, stop work and see how much money you make. A man or woman at work or a dollar at work is the reality of making money and creating wealth. If you aren't working and have no dollars at work, I can guarantee you won't be making money but you will have still used up the same amount of time. Work, not time, equals money. In real terms, time equals decay.

For most of us, the wealth we accumulate through our working life starts with the income we earn — that is, a man or woman at work. If we can set aside and save some of that income, then we have dollars that we can put to work. Our chances of accumulating wealth increase dramatically once we put dollars, as well as our own labour, to work. If you win wealth, you win it as a result of the price that you invest to buy the ticket. Even when you inherit wealth, it is probably the result of effort for which you originally didn't get paid before you ultimately received your just reward in the form of an inheritance. In many cases, gifts are received as the result of extended effort, one way or another, on the part of the person receiving the gift. Because of the effort someone has made to help someone else, that someone is willing to make a gift because they consider whatever has been done as being worthy of the gift they are willing to make.

In reality, a man or woman at work or a dollar at work is the truth of life, and in many ways we can put that truth to work as a concept in our presentations. We may be selling money, real estate, or any other product or service. We may follow any one of a hundred occupations. We may invest our money in a thousand different ways, and yet the reality still remains: if there is no man or woman at work and no dollar at work, then there is no wealth and very little hope of wealth.

This concept can be used in many different ways. For example, when you are talking to a prospect or customer who believes that wealth will somehow magically accrue outside the concept of putting a man or woman or a dollar to work, you can use the concept to bring them back down to earth. Their options for creating wealth will forever be limited to their own work and putting their dollars to work and many people lose out because they can't see that. In the words of Ann Landers: 'Opportunities are usually disguised as hard work, so many people don't recognise them.' You can use the concept to reinforce a prospect making a purchase. You can use it to explain why a prospect or

234 The Great Sales Book

customer should pursue a certain course of action in order to achieve a long- or short-term gain. You can make it part of your overall philosophy of life and use it in general terms to show that you are a creative thinker. Overall, a man or woman at work or a dollar at work are the only real options we have in terms of creating wealth. It is a fact of life. You can easily apply the concept of 72 to the concept of a dollar at work to enhance your presentations even further.

3: LIVE, DIE OR QUIT

The live, die or quit theme is one of the most powerful themes used in selling. It is powerful because it is real and it applies to every one of us in almost every aspect of our lives. For example, if your current plan is to build a new home, then you will either live to see the home completed, you will die before the home is completed, or you will quit building the home for reasons unforeseen now and do something else.

If your aim and ambition is to earn $100 000 a year in your work, then you will either live to accomplish your plan, die before you accomplish it, or quit for reasons unforeseen now and set yourself different goals.

If your ambition is to retire before you are 50, then you will either live to accomplish your ambition, die before you do, or you will quit and change your plan for reasons unforeseen now. If you want to travel the world, then you will live to travel the world, die before you do so, or you will quit and change your plans for reasons unforeseen now. If you want to go into business on your own, you will live to have your own business, you will die before you get it, or you will quit for reasons unforeseen now and do something else.

You can use the live, die or quit theme in almost every presentation you make. Illustrate to your prospect or customer that the chances they have in life, no matter what they do or what they aspire to, are to live, die or quit. Whatever your plans, whatever you sell, you should try to make it equate to the live, die or quit theme. In other words, what will your idea do for your prospect or customer if they live? What will it do for them if they die? What will it do for them if they quit? As live, die or quit is a reality for every person, decisions should be based on these issues. What is the likelihood and what will happen if

I live? What would be the implications of this action on my family if I die? What are the options and possible outcomes if I quit?

For generations, live, die or quit has been used by the financial services market as a very powerful form of selling. It can be equally powerful, compelling and useful in a variety of ways for all types of selling. When you use this in your presentation, it immediately sets you apart from other salespeople, most of whom are so product-oriented they forget to add value to their presentations and enhance their image by using original and creative ideas based on life's realities. As part of mastering the art of using concepts in your selling presentations, you should build them first into your own life and then into your presentations. Find out how people relate to them. If being creative and having original ideas, so that you become a person recognised as being different from other salespeople, is important to you, then this is the way to start.

4: THE ONLY FOUR WAYS TO FUND A PURCHASE

No matter what we buy, when we buy it, who we buy it from or why we buy it, there are only four ways to fund a purchase. This concept can be used by every salesperson, no matter what they sell, because it is another fact of life. We have to use one of these four methods to pay for anything that we purchase. The four methods are:

1. Use income.
2. Use capital.
3. Borrow.
4. Sell assets.

The concept of funding a purchase is a very powerful one because every time we make a sale, someone must pay for what they buy. You should first do an exercise on your own products and services in terms of the purchases made by your customers. Fit each of those purchases into one of these four methods of funding a purchase to establish a pattern to see which methods are used most by your customers. The exercise will also show which methods are not being used. You should then do some creative thinking in terms of whether you can increase your sales by having your customers consider some of the methods they are currently not using. Let us look at the four methods.

Pay from capital

This method of payment uses accumulated funds. Most of us try to build capital to invest for retirement or to create reserves in a business. The use of capital is self-explanatory.

Pay from income

Day-by-day expenses are largely paid from income. House and home maintenance is largely paid from income. School fees and the like are usually paid from income. However, income is, by its very nature, restricted to a pay-as-you-go method. Paying as you go restricts your paying power unless you borrow or use capital. Most financial service products are sold on a pay-as-you-go basis from income, and often sales are lost because the salesperson hasn't explored the possibility of using one of the other three options of using capital, borrowing, or converting assets from their current usage into cash in order to fund the purchase of a different or better asset.

Pay by borrowing

Loans are usually arranged against the security of income or assets. If you have no assets, then you are left with borrowing against potential income. This is rarely a problem with small ticket purchases. However, when purchases are made of bigger ticket items and there is no capital and insufficient income against which we can borrow, then we should explore the possibility of arranging a guarantor and repaying from income on a pay-as-we-go basis.

Pay by selling assets

Many sales are lost because income is not sufficient to meet the prospect's needs, capital isn't available, borrowing for one reason or another isn't possible, and salespeople don't explore the possibility of converting assets from one type to another. For instance, if what you have to sell is an asset which can by its nature create income, then it is well worth exploring the possibility of selling some assets which may have a lower earning rate and be of little potential and using the proceeds of that sale to buy a new and different asset with a greater possibility of income or capital gain in the future. Very few people don't have some type of asset with a value which could be converted to income or capital. It is not unusual for people to have assets which they have forgotten about or which are making no real contribution to increasing wealth. It is my belief that there are millions of dollars waiting for some creative salespeople to unlock them and change them to wealth-building investments.

You are urged to explore these four methods of funding a purchase and find out whether you are using all the potential available to you. In many instances, when objections of 'I don't have the money' or 'I can't afford it' are raised, you should deal with the objection on the basis of the purchase being made from income or capital. If your prospect persists with this objection, explore the possibility of selling assets or borrowing. If they are not an option the sale is lost, but at least you have explored all the four options. If you do, then I am sure you will increase sales of your products or services.

These four methods of funding a purchase comprise a very powerful concept which should be used as often as possible. The very least that could happen is that you will impress your prospect or customer with your knowledge of concepts that impact on their lives. By showing your understanding of these options, you clarify thinking, promote action, and generate an image of being positive, creative and different from the rest.

5: YOU WILL EARN A FORTUNE

The concept of 'you'll earn a fortune' has been extensively used for generations. It has long been voted the most successful sales story in the history of financial services selling. Although this concept has been used almost exclusively by the financial services industry, it is just as effective in selling real estate, motor vehicles, and many other products and services. You can use this concept to close a sale whenever the prospect hesitates to complete a purchase because of the fear of not being able to pay in the future. Point out to the prospect that during their working lifetime they will earn a fortune. For instance, if you use as an example a person 25 years of age, take into account their normal earnings over their working lifetime of, say, 40 years. Add in the wage rises they can expect, plus an allowance for inflation, and you will find that even if they are moderate earners they will earn millions during their working life. If their income is higher, they will earn something like $5–$10 million. They will earn a fortune, and the only question at the end of their working lifetime is how much of it they will have accumulated for themselves.

You can prove this concept by doing the same exercise on a person 40 years of age earning a moderate salary of, say, $40 000 a year. If you just count their earnings, they will come to $1 million. If you allow for normal increases in earnings over the 25 years, you will find that they will earn well over $2 million between now and their retirement. The really important question is: how much of it will they have when the time comes to give up work? Will they have enough dollars at work to make the difference between subsisting and living?

The 'you'll earn a fortune' concept is based on the reality that all of us will earn fortunes, yet most people don't understand or appreciate this simple concept. To complete this concept, you need to add another which is called 'pay yourself first'.

One of life's great tragedies is that most of us will earn income, pay our way, and try to save something of what is left. The reality of life is that for many of us there is none left. So the fortune we earn simply gets spent. If, on the other hand, we were to adopt the practice of paying ourselves first and from every pay cheque investing at least five per cent of our earnings in something that earns a reasonable return, we would very swiftly accumulate a sizeable amount of capital.

As soon as we are able, we can use this capital to make a down payment on some real estate or another investment, and in no time at all the concepts of 'you'll earn a fortune' and 'pay ourselves first' will be working in our life to create the financial independence that most of us long for. If this concept does nothing more than focus your thinking on your own life, it will have proven of great value to you. No matter what you sell, how you sell it and when you sell it, when doubts arise in the mind of the buyer of their ability to pay in the future, then you can use this concept to show them that they will indeed have the money to fund the purchase. It is only a matter of priorities.

If you explain the concept of 'you'll earn a fortune' to your prospects and customers, you will be giving them some of the most important information they are ever likely to get from anyone and they should be forever indebted to you. Unfortunately, our education system doesn't teach these simple but valuable concepts. You can use creative selling and these concepts in different ways every day of your life to show your prospects and customers that you are indeed a person of value, and that you do have concepts and ideas that are very valuable to them and which will set you apart from the rest of the competition. Be sure to apply these concepts in your own life. Learn the lesson yourself before it is too late.

6: TIME IS LIFE

Time really is life, and life is all we have. If ever there was a valuable concept, it is this one. It creates urgency and focuses on priorities. There is no such thing as time as we understand it. Clocks and watches are only man-made devices which help us to know what to do and when to do it, how to co-ordinate our activities, how to be in the right place at the right time, how to catch the train, how to get to work and then home again. The reality is that time starts for each of us when we are born and (depending on our beliefs) finishes for us when we die. Between being born and dying, time flows on. We can't manage time because it is a non-manageable resource. It's there whether we like it or not. The only way to escape time is to die.

One way to realise that time is life is to ask yourself this question: 'What are my chances of getting younger?' Of course, the answer is 'None'. Time is simple: each day we get one day of our life, we take that day into the marketplace we call life, and we trade it for whatever we are willing to take in return. How well we trade depends on how much we value our life. Many of us give the days of our lives away and get very little of value in return. How are *you* trading, and what value have you placed on *your* life?

Time is not money, time is life. The value in understanding this is that it focuses your thinking on priorities that are important to you. Use this concept whenever it is necessary to focus your prospect's or customer's attention on the urgency of doing something now. When someone procrastinates and says, 'I'll think about it and give you an answer in a week/month/year', it's not difficult to bring them back to the reality that time really is life. Life is all they have, and every day that they procrastinate they are using up more of their allotted time and getting less value for it.

You can use this concept in a hundred different ways. You can use it in your presentation when urgency and prioritising is necessary. Time is life, life is all we have. Yesterday is gone forever, and tomorrow never comes. It's today, it's now or it's never.

7: THE INCOME CAPITAL TWIST

This concept is effective when present tax laws are taken into consideration. Very simply, if you spend capital it is not taxable, but income is. Therefore, whenever possible, we should pay out of capital and conserve our income in a tax shelter. This is especially applicable to those who have retired and those who sell to this market. For instance, if someone retires with $400 000 and they put that capital into an investment that earns income within a fund and then they draw out portions of the capital and use that capital to pay their living expenses, they are in a much better position net after tax than if they had put their $400 000 in an investment on which they earn interest, pay tax and spend the balance.

This concept is also valuable to those starting an investment, because the net after-tax position is the real worth of an investor. The old adage that we should conserve our capital and only spend income needs to be thought through again. For many people in the community today, the reverse is the best way to go. When we take into account tax on income plus provisional tax, we find that this concept is indeed a valuable one. Anyone investing for or during retirement will find it of great value.

8: SHARING THE RISK

This concept relates mainly to people involved in the financial services or insurance industry. If this is your work, you will often meet prospects who object to buying on the grounds that they either don't believe in insurance or they believe they can carry their own insurance. This belief may be expressed as 'my business is my insurance', or 'my investments are my insurance', or any other expression which indicates that, somehow or other, they have set up their own insurance.

Leaving aside the possibility that they may be able to accumulate the money they believe their family would need if they die or that they will need in retirement, the concept of sharing the risk can be used to show prospects that it is impossible for an individual to carry their own insurance. Impossible because the very basis of insurance is the sharing of the risk, which means the gathering together of a number of people whose premiums are accumulated to fund the minority at any given time. With an individual, this isn't possible. Individuals must join with others if they are to share the risk. Individuals can take the risk, but they cannot share the risk, as they have no one to share it with.

An individual can take the risk of when they will die and the possibility that it may occur at a difficult or inopportune time. There is rarely a good time to die. If they need to provide $400 000 for their family when they die and they leave that amount in assets, there is no guarantee that the assets will realise their value in cash. Perhaps the $400 000 worth of assets will return only $300 000 in cash. Assets are not always easily sold and are not always saleable on a dollar-for-dollar value basis. On the other hand, by sharing the risk with other policy holders in insurance companies they could very well insure that risk for five cents on the dollar, depending on their age, with the certainty of getting it when needed. So the concept is a very valuable one and is not used enough in terms of pointing out to prospects who are procrastinating about buying insurance that they can take the risk but they cannot share it. They cannot carry their own insurance; they can only carry the risk.

9: THE LIFE EXCHANGE PRINCIPLE

Most of us have a method of valuing our life. We may believe and say, 'You can't put a value on human life'. Others may say, 'Let's be realistic. Our value is the amount of our accumulated wealth at any given time.' Whatever the method we use, the ultimate value of our life is what we exchange it for. I call this the life exchange principle, and it is at work every day of our life. It works this way.

Each day we take one day of our life into the marketplace we call life and we exchange it for what we are willing to take in return for the day we have used up. On a day-to-day basis, that is the value we place on our life. No matter what we think it is worth, it is the day-to-day trading value that is the reality. Some of us are trading our days for very little; others are demanding a higher price. The choices are ours and we have no lease on life, no guarantees and no options; the clock is always ticking. The value to you of this concept is that it will focus your attention on the real issue which is the day-by-day trades you are making. Test what you are doing, each day for one month. At the end of the day, write down on a piece of paper, in no more than 20 words, 'My trade today was . . .' and then describe the value of your day. At the end of the month, place all the pages on your living-room floor and then walk around and through a month of your life, asking yourself, 'What value am I really exchanging my life for?' Remember, tomorrow is promised to no one. Create value while you can.

CONCLUSION

In this chapter, we have dealt with nine concepts, some of which may be familiar to you. The benefits you can get from these concepts will derive not from knowing about them but from using them. Remember: the knowledge you have and don't use will be no more productive than the knowledge you don't have and can't use. By selling concepts, ideas and philosophies, you focus your efforts on what products and services will do for your prospects and customers. You will demonstrate your abilities as a creative thinker and increase your worth to those with whom you do business and, above all, you will set yourself apart from the mob.

There has never been a time in our history when intellectual capacity has played such a key role in our society. Business is finally realising that the only asset of real value to an organisation is the abilities of its people. We need to realise that the only real asset we have as an individual is our intellectual capacity, plus the ability to turn what we know into effective results for those who do business with us and those who employ us to do business for them. Today we add value to what we do for others by demonstrating by our actions and thinking that we are such a person.

PART 2

BE YOUR OWN
SALES MANAGER

CHAPTER 21

YOU, YOURSELF INCORPORATED

Singleness of purpose is one of the chief essentials
for success in life, no matter
what may be one's aim.
JOHN D. ROCKEFELLER, JNR.

YOU ARE THE master of your own destiny. The cold, hard fact of human development is that it is all about self-development. You are the managing director, marketing manager, sales manager, accountant and chief motivator of You, Yourself Incorporated: you are the decision-maker in every aspect of your life. Other people and events may impact on your life in a negative and unhelpful manner, and you may have no control over what happens, but you have absolute control over how you react to whatever has impacted on your life. Zig Ziglar was right when he said: 'Others can stop you temporarily; you are the only one who can do it permanently.'

THE IMPORTANCE OF SELF-DEVELOPMENT

Most sales operations have a sales manager who is responsible for recruiting, leading, directing, developing and motivating the salespeople who make up the team. The objective of the whole exercise in managing a sales team is to ensure that the salespeople produce at a level that not only makes the sales team viable in financial terms but also makes a profit for the business. In simplistic terms, the responsibility of the sales manager is to meet the organisation's business objectives and to maintain and develop the individuals who make up the sales team. If you take the time to think through the above statements, several issues arise which are critically important to you and every other salesperson. Here are the issues:

◆ If the organisation for which you work is willing to meet the costs of employing a sales manager to enhance the chances of success of its sales team, why do so many salespeople resist the sales manager's efforts?

◆ If the sales manager has specific skills and tasks to perform which increase the effectiveness of the team members, why don't salespeople not identify those skills and tasks and acquire or perform them themselves?

◆ If your employer is willing to spend a great deal of money on developing your attitudes, skills and habits, so that you can make a contribution to the welfare of the organisation, why don't you make that contribution yourself to your own welfare? Why put your future in the hands of someone else?

The critical issue for all organisations and individuals in today's highly competitive and changing marketplace is the performance levels of the human resources that make up the organisation. As one saying goes: 'Among the chief worries of today's business executives is the large number of unemployed still on the payroll.' Intellectual capacity is an issue we must all face, so developing yourself and your organisation is a major safeguard against obsolescence. The real issue is not only having the capacity to learn what you need to know, but also having the ability to turn what you know into productive results for your employer, which in a growing number of cases will be yourself. In my view, freelance selling will be a growth industry over the next decades.

If self-development is so important, then you need to become your own sales manager and set yourself the goal of achieving the objectives a sales manager has to achieve. Their goal is to develop a salesperson who is highly productive and who can function with a minimum of management intervention. Remember: the sales manager is working to help you achieve the goals you want for yourself, so count that help as a bonus.

THE BENEFITS OF BEING YOUR OWN SALES MANAGER

You may wish to become a sales manager yourself, so learning how to develop yourself will build the skills you need. Once you demonstrate not only your willingness but also your determination to master the skills, attitudes and habits required to become a peak performer in selling, you have signalled your desire to be a success. Generally, that will lead to less intervention from your manager and more independence for yourself.

You are your greatest asset, irrespective of your current level of expertise. The more you hone, polish and shape your capacity in your chosen field, the more you are worth on the open market. When you can do more and are willing to do more, you will be worth more. Why is it that some people are paid $500 an hour, while others are paid $10 an hour? Is it because some employers are overly generous, or is it that some people are just lucky? Could it be that those who are paid more are perceived as being worth more? The truth is that you are generally earning at the level to which you have so far developed yourself. Become your own sales manager and increase your capacity and your worth. Build You, Yourself Incorporated into a million-dollar business. After all, you own it. But you must also manage and run it.

Your self-esteem and motivation will grow in proportion to the effort you put into your self-improvement program. Go for it! At the same time, your confidence will increase and this will be reflected in the way this influences more of your prospects and customers to buy from you. Much of the success that comes to peak performing salespeople results from their belief that they are a person of value and that what they sell is good for their prospects and customers. They expect to sell, they expect prospects to say 'yes'. This expectancy influences their prospects in a positive way, and outstanding results follow.

HOW TO BE YOUR OWN SALES MANAGER

Identify the main areas for which a sales manager is responsible and take over that responsibility for your own development. The four principal areas are:

1. Lead.
2. Direct.
3. Develop.
4. Motivate.

Lead yourself and others

This is a quality you have to earn by what you do. Leadership is not bestowed on anyone, it is earned by performance. Leaders are followed, and you can display leadership qualities by the way you perform in your work as a salesperson. As Emerson said: 'Make the most of yourself because that's all there is of you.' Show the other team members or your associates how they can benefit from following your example.

Set yourself high performance sales objectives and go after them with purpose and passion. Be proud of your ability to outperform your organisation's expectations and encourage other team members to do the same. It's *your* career you are building. You, Yourself Incorporated is looking good.

Be constructive in meetings by always looking for the positives. Focus on the future, not the past; on why an idea *will* work, not on why it won't. Focus on results, not the process. Once you develop this positive, can-do type of thinking, not only will you raise your own levels of commitment and confidence but it will also rub off on others, and then you will get the benefit of their enthusiasm and determination. You will find that working with a turned-on team has many advantages for all its members, including you.

Be a creative thinker and search constantly for new and innovative ways to perform your sales work without becoming a critic of present methods. When problems arise with current procedures, look for and encourage other team members to find a solution that will not only solve the problem but also raise productivity.

Become a can-do and will-do member of the team and you will find that these leadership qualities will not only make you independent of the system, but will also create a first-class reputation that will build your status in the eyes of your employer. Remember: the objective is not to take over the sales manager's responsibilities but to develop yourself. John Maxwell, a leadership specialist, said it so well: 'If there is hope in the future there is power in the present.' He was right. You have all the power you need to achieve the success you hope for. This is the era of the individual — go for it!

Direct yourself

Focus all your efforts on achieving your worthwhile objectives. Direct your behaviour towards developing attitudes and habits that increase your overall ability. Set up a client and prospect control system that will increase your call effectiveness. Don't wait for the manager to direct you; be one step ahead and direct yourself. Study your markets until you become an expert in identifying sales opportunities and industry trends. Do your own analysis of your sales performance so that you can discuss your actions in an objective way with your manager. Direct your own time management so that you can meet all the requirements of your work, in addition to selling. Meet deadlines for reports. Provide the information that the organisation and other persons require from you so that they can do their work more effectively.

If you earn a reputation for being one step ahead of the job requirements, and direct yourself in a positive way, then independence will follow. As your confidence and self-esteem grow, you will find that you are not only building a first-class reputation, but also a different, new and exciting you.

Develop yourself

If you want this new and exciting you, there is only one person who can arrange it: yes, it's *you*. Self-development is easy for some and difficult for others, but it is essential if we want to grow and prosper in an expanding universe. All life is an expansion. It's a learning process from birth to death, and even at the moment of death we are learning how to die. In sales, we are confronted every day with the necessity to learn and grow, and those who embrace the opportunities instead of resisting them make the swiftest progress. There will be development support from your employer, so look for it, embrace it, and if there isn't as much as you want or it is not about what you need, ask for what you want. Once you respond to development, you will draw more to you.

Here are some ways to develop yourself:

◆ At least once a month, read a book on a subject that deals directly with sales matters. If you have to buy them yourself, do so, because this is an investment in you. If initially funds are a problem, ask your employer to buy them. If that's not possible, explore your local library.

◆ At least every two months, read a book on a subject allied to business. It could be on marketing or negotiating, or on the changes taking place in society. Read anything that will improve your general knowledge of subjects that will be of interest to your prospects and customers.

◆ Read magazines that provide information that will help you to become better at selling. Read a paper each day that will keep you current on what is happening in the financial world. Watch the share market, and be up to date on what is happening to the share prices of your prospects and customers. Keep tabs on your opposition. There is no end to self-development, for the world won't stand still. Technology is driving the changes that are sweeping the world, and it is changing our life in the process.

◆ Go to seminars that will help you not only to become better at selling, but also a better, more capable and growing person. Feel-good seminars are great entertainment but offer little in terms of personal growth. Look for substance, not entertainment.

◆ Have tapes in your car so that you can learn while you travel. Search for those that will expand your thinking. Look for creative information that will enable you to pass on some of this learning to prospects and customers so that you get a reputation for being helpful and knowledgeable. When you do, doors will open more easily because of the added value you are creating through ideas and new information.

◆ Develop a network of people who are already successful in areas that you want to develop in your own life. Remember: there are three factors that will decide what level of success you achieve in your life. They are: what you see, what you hear and who you associate with. The choice is always up to you. If you want You, Yourself Incorporated to thrive, then make choices that will help you to build it the way you want it.

Motivate yourself

As the chief motivator employed by You, Yourself Incorporated, you have the task in this organisation of keeping the will and desire to succeed at a high level. Without your help and attention, nothing much will happen in this important area of your life. If you pay attention to the issues discussed in the sections on leading, directing and developing, and support them with specific goals, you will have done most of what needs to be done in terms of self-motivation. Read and put into practice the suggestions contained in Chapter 23, 'Self-motivation' and you will have few problems in this part of your life.

Self-development is a critical issue in all our lives and throughout life. It is not something we do now and again if we want to be successful; it is something we have to do all the time. It is not something separate from us; it is our life — it is the way we live. You, Yourself Incorporated can become a run-down, worn-out, tired and neglected entity, or it can be a dynamic, enthusiastic, growing, wealthy and successful one. The result is entirely up to you. No one has said it better than Ann Landers: 'The Lord gave us two ends — one to sit on and the other to think with. Success depends on which one you use the most.'

CONCLUSION

It is my pleasure to conclude this chapter with an interview with Carla Zampatti who is one of Australia's most recognised women. Carla has been honoured for her contributions to both fashion and business. Her achievements include the Medal of Australia, Designer of the Year in the 1994 FIA awards, plus many other distinctions. Her business is in wholesale and retail, with 30 Carla Zampatti boutiques throughout Australia.

◆

JC: Carla, what prompted you to go into business for yourself?

CZ: I went into business because there was a gap in the market for the type of garment that I was making: for understated quality, well-cut garments at a value-for-money price. That's the type of garment we make in our business and we are very proud of what we do.

JC: Carla, what do you think is the most important issue in terms of clothes when you are presenting yourself?

CZ: There is no doubt in my mind, Jack, that clothes need to be appropriate for the occasion. You have to consider the environment in which you are working and how you are presenting yourself, because you are essentially packaging yourself.

I believe you have to consider the people you are dealing with and whether what you are wearing is appropriate. Underdress rather than overdress. You don't want to be overly decorated, especially if you are a woman.

Colour is good, but it has to be used wisely. I would avoid prints and things like that. Too much elaborate jewellery in the business environment is not good. It is essential to think about the occasion, and then to dress for the occasion. Dressing appropriately is the key to personal presentation.

JC: How do you market your business and sell your merchandise?

CZ: Jack, we have 30 stores around Australia and in those stores we have consultants who advise their customers. They need to be people who like people, and they have to have an outgoing personality and relate to their customers.

They are the people who advise our customers on what is best for them — what is appropriate and what suits them — and they have to take them out of a rut because people do get into a clothing rut. Sometimes they have to be stretched a bit to get them away from always buying and wearing the same thing. Our consultants show them how good they could look in something new and different.

The consultants are expert at their business and we consult with them all the time because they are closest to our customers, so we must stay very much in touch with them. The people who look after our customers must make sure that our customers' money is well spent, because we generally put several outfits together for them so that they need not shop for another six months.

JC: What else is there that you would like to tell the readers of this book that might be helpful to them?

CZ: In dressing, I think that presentation is very important because it gives you the assurance that you are looking your best. The way to achieve that comfort zone of looking your best is a combination of good advice and experimenting with combinations that have you feeling very confident before you leave home. You have checked in the mirror and you like what you see. You know you are looking your best and you can get on with the task at hand. I think that's very important and I believe that's what we achieve for our customers.

The best advice I can give to your readers is to take the same care, pay great attention to detail, and work hard at achieving that feeling of total confidence in your personal presentation. When you feel good, you act out that feeling and great results follow.

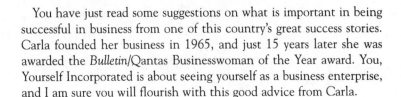

You have just read some suggestions on what is important in being successful in business from one of this country's great success stories. Carla founded her business in 1965, and just 15 years later she was awarded the *Bulletin*/Qantas Businesswoman of the Year award. You, Yourself Incorporated is about seeing yourself as a business enterprise, and I am sure you will flourish with this good advice from Carla.

CHAPTER 22

PRESENTING YOURSELF

You never get a second chance to make
a good first impression.
ANON.

IMAGE IS IMPORTANT. How you look, sound and behave sends messages to other people. In terms of communication, your appearance is of great importance. What you wear, why you wear it and how you wear it has a lot to do with your chances of success. Image is a critical factor in selling, because your appearance is speaking for you even when you are silent and it is important that you are sending the right messages.

HOW YOU LOOK

You have read in other parts of this book that you don't get a second chance to make a first impression. The impression you make in the first 40–60 seconds will be based on how you look and what you say, both verbally and non-verbally through your body language. The importance of how you look cannot be overemphasised. So let us explore some of the factors that impact on your image.

Let's start with your attitude to image. If you don't see your image as being critically important to your success as a professional salesperson, then you are hardly likely to take the care and trouble to package and present yourself in an image-conscious manner. In presenting your image in the best possible way, you are limited by who you are and how you look, so it's important to take advantage of your good points and to play down the others.

Personal grooming

How well you look has a lot to do with how much care you take in your personal grooming. Every day when you look in the mirror, you should examine your appearance and be careful not to take what you see for granted. You are so familiar with your own appearance that it is very easy to be casual in your assessment. A good haircut, worn in a neat and tidy style, is essential. If possible, wear your hair back off your forehead. Men should be clean-shaven. If you wear a beard or a moustache, be aware that you are technically at a disadvantage in the image stakes. Research indicates that people who wear beards have to work harder to create an initial image of success than those who are clean-shaven. So if you want to have a beard, you should take extra care with how you talk and act. You should trim your beard regularly and make sure that it looks good. A moustache falls between a beard and being clean-shaven, in terms of credibility. The most credibility is gained by being clean-shaven. Teeth should be clean and well looked after. Hands and nails should always be clean. Your clothes should be clean, tidy and well looked after, with creases in trousers and suits looking as if they have just come off the hanger. Shoes should be well soled, polished and of good quality.

All of these things can be easily overlooked in the busy life of a salesperson. We get so used to looking at ourselves in the mirror, that it is very easy to let our standards slip. In terms of image projection in today's image-conscious, competitive people market, that is a disaster. We should be bright-eyed, healthy-looking, trim and fit. If we look after ourselves, get sufficient sleep and eat the right food, our efforts will be reflected in our appearance.

Clothing for men

The saying that a person is what they wear has never been truer than in today's market, especially if you are selling in a prestige market.

Let's look first at clothes for male sales consultants. In terms of colour, the darker the suit worn the better, because it gives more power to the wearer. Dark colours imply authority, and the wearer appears more credible than someone in a light-coloured suit. Plain colours in suits are highly acceptable, as long as they are dark in colour. Dark blues and greys are fine, but avoid black or brown. A dark suit with a fine stripe has more credibility. So a dark grey or dark blue suit with a fine self-stripe or white stripe produces the greatest credibility in terms of prestige and power.

Whether you should wear a suit, or a jacket and slacks, or no coat at all will depend on the people you are going to be doing business with. The closer you dress to the way they dress, the more credibility and compatibility you will have with them. If you are in the country, then you are more likely to be able to wear a jacket and slacks. However, this again will depend on the people with whom you are going to do business. While a light-coloured suit is acceptable in the tropics, the same suit worn in the southern states will certainly lower your credibility. You should be more concerned about the reception you will get from the people you are going to deal with than with whether you like what you will be wearing. It is in your own interest to develop power and credibility with the people who are going to be your customers.

In terms of style, stay with the fashion. By this I don't mean following fashion slavishly. Your likely customers will be the measure by which you dress. In most cases, a single-breasted, two-buttoned jacket with a centre vent or double vents is the most flattering to the average male figure. If you wish to wear double-breasted suits, take special care because they only look their best on persons of above-average height and slim build. Coat cuffs should be buttoned, with at least three buttons, although four buttons give more credibility. The pockets should be flapped and jetted, and the flap should be worn out. Trouser length should be tidy so that the trouser just creases when it rests on your shoes. Cuffs and leg fittings both look best if they are slim. Trousers are most flattering when worn with minimum pleats. They should sit firmly on the waist and be held up with a good-quality belt. Side pockets are best. Many of the suit and clothing styles for young people today are very baggy, and so should be chosen and worn with care. The deciding factors about what suits or jackets and slacks you should wear are, first, the people you are going to be selling to and second, quality. It is rarely a waste to buy quality.

Wherever possible, shirts should be long-sleeved and when you wear your jacket you should show at least 10 mm of your shirt sleeve below the cuff. Nothing detracts more from personal appearance than bare hands coming out of jacket sleeves. Shirts are made in all sizes and can be bought in different sleeve lengths. It is worth making the effort to find the correct fitting. If your sleeves aren't long enough to extend beyond your jacket cuff, then you should go to a shirt shop and be measured for the right cuff lengths. The peaks of your shirt collar look best when of medium length, and the spread of the collar should not be exaggerated. Button-down collars are good. Pastels or stripes are OK. If you prefer a breakaway from solid white shirts, then white with a narrow stripe is acceptable. Be careful about prominent stripes in shirts or suits, and if you wear a striped shirt then make sure the stripe doesn't dominate when you are wearing a striped suit. Generally, it is better to have either the shirt or the suit, or both, plain. If you decide on pastels, make sure they don't fight with the colours of your suit or tie.

In terms of ties, a dark colour in red, blue or grey denotes prestige and power. If you choose stripes, they can be bold or subdued. Tie colours tend to be bold in both colour and design. This isn't a problem as long as you get the colours right. The tie gives men a chance to display their individuality without losing credibility, as long as the choice of colour is appropriate. Your tie length should finish at the belt buckle of your trousers. If you wear plain colours, they should be medium to dark with a small, discreet pattern.

Wearing a pocket handkerchief in the top pocket of your suit helps to produce a polished image. The handkerchief can match your tie, but in most cases it is better to buy some good quality, pure cotton, hand-rolled-edge white handkerchiefs and use those in your breast pocket. Make sure they don't look pre-folded.

Socks should match the colour of your suit, and again it is better to wear socks that are dark rather than light in colour. Plain socks are better than patterned ones, and you should wear them pulled up, not creased and crinkled around your ankles.

Shoes can be lace-up or slip-on. Lace-up shoes have more prestige and power. If you wear slip-on shoes, they should be as plain as possible. Avoid shoes with tassels and semi-bows on them because, while they are OK for the leisure market, they are inappropriate with suits. The current preference is for a plain, neat, well-made lace-up shoe that has a toe cap. Shoes should be dark in colour, such as black or dark brown. Leather is best; however, compound soles are now considered acceptable.

Overall, your appearance should indicate an attention to detail. When you acknowledge that there is a right and a wrong way to wear clothes and that there are right and wrong clothes to wear, you are in charge of your personal presentation. A golden rule in buying clothes is to buy the very best that you can afford if you wish to impress your prospects and customers with your professional attitude.

Whether we like it or not, salespeople have often been criticised for the style of clothes they wear. Indeed, some people have an image of salespeople that dates from the early days of film. The best way to describe this image is excessive. The clothes are too fashionable, the colours are too bright, the patterns are too large, and the combinations are too flamboyant. There is no attention to fit, and clothes are worn without flair. We want to project the exact opposite image: conservative in our approach, and a meticulous attention to cut, fit and quality. How we wear our clothes creates our image. Remember, perceptions and prejudices are difficult to overcome and it only takes a small slip on our part to plunge the image of salespeople back to that of those early days of film.

Clothing for women

The rules that apply to successful business dress for males also apply in most cases to women. If you want to gain a professional edge, then you have to look and act like a professional salesperson. Dress to match the buyer. Study your prospects and customers carefully and look at what they wear. If you are selling to the female market, you may not have the same broad choices in terms of colour, but in terms of quality, cut and style you can very easily match the way they dress. If you are selling mostly to males, then you only need to project a business image of good taste and conservatism to make them feel comfortable. Each time they talk with you, your image will be reinforcing their own good taste, because you are reflecting the values they hold. If you want to be taken seriously and treated as a businesslike salesperson, then you need to act and dress in the same manner.

Suits are excellent. Skirts can be any length from medium to long. The critical issue with skirt length is to avoid skirts that ride up and show a lot of leg when sitting down. It is distracting in a sales interview for a woman to constantly adjust her skirt when seated because she knows it is too short. This only diverts attention to the problem and away from the sales presentation. The time to fix this problem is when buying the skirt. A skirt and a long-sleeved blouse or shirt are good choices. There are many combinations of clothing that will make you look good and support your professional image, providing they are not too loud in colour and are well cut.

Women have more choice than men in terms of colour. However, light colours will diminish your authority whilst medium to dark colours will give you more authority, and credibility in the eyes of those with whom you are doing business. The objective is not to do away with femininity, but to play it down a little so that you are accepted as a businessperson rather than as a woman.

If you dress in light colours, soft fabrics, follow fashion slavishly, wear strong perfume and dramatic make-up, show bare skin, wear lots of jewellery and select shoes with very high heels, then, no matter how hard you work to build your business image, you will generally be less than successful at it. The objective is to be taken seriously as a professional salesperson so dress accordingly.

Successful women are very careful about their grooming. They wear their hair off their face, short to medium in length and always well cared for. They know that hair is the frame for the face and they pay particular attention to it. Nails are very important. They should be well cared for, and usually nail polish is best in natural colours rather than bright shades. Nails that are well buffed show care and attention. Successful women use subtle make-up, as they understand that less is best in business dressing. They tend to be conservative in their choice, they avoid fashions that are flashy, and they look as if they are dressed for work. They cultivate a businesslike approach to go with their businesslike image.

Bearing

You can have the best clothes in the business, but if you don't know how to wear them then you detract from your appearance. To make your clothes look good you should start by feeling good. Have a good self-image, and feel good about what you are wearing. Wear your clothes with a confident attitude and so that they hang well, which means stand erect. Cultivate a poised, confident bearing. When you are wearing coats, wear them buttoned up, not flapping in the breeze. If you have to carry things in your pockets, then minimise what you carry so that coat and trouser pockets don't bulge. Never put anything in the outside coat pockets or the hip pockets of trousers. Under no circumstances wear pens in your pockets where people can see them. Your actions should be discreet and should back up the quality clothes that you wear. Always move with confidence, and when you are standing it is best to stand with your hands behind you rather than with folded arms. Walk and act with a sense of purpose. Bearing is essentially a matter of confidence, which is shown by an upright stance and positive, easy, non-exaggerated movements.

Accessories

If you wear glasses, then choose frames that suit your features. Glasses are now a fashion item and it is well worth spending the money to get glasses that flatter your features. For men, dark-rimmed glasses have the most power and credibility. Rimless glasses don't have the same degree of credibility and don't promote a power image. If you don't like dark-rimmed glasses, then choose a pair with a dark bridge across the top and steel rims around the rest of the glasses. This will give you a degree of power and prestige in terms of your appearance. Women have much more choice in fashion glasses and are able to wear more colours and shapes than men. Colours should go with make-up.

Never wear sunglasses during a business conversation except when there are medical reasons for doing so. If you must wear them for medical reasons, then explain this to your prospect so that they will know they are not your normal choice for everyday wear.

For men, cufflinks add further credibility, so whenever possible wear double-cuffed shirts with cufflinks. Make sure the cufflinks are either plain gold or have a very plain design. Flashy cufflinks demean your appearance.

A plain, good-quality leather band gives the best appearance to a man's watch, with a round shape providing the most credibility and power. Roman numerals are more powerful than arabic numbers. The shape and size of your watch should be discreet and add to your overall appearance of credibility. Sports watches are very popular today, but if you want maximum credibility and power, then you should leave them for sporting occasions not for business.

Women have a broader choice of watches than men, and fancy bands are more acceptable. Jewelled watches are also acceptable; however, the trend among businesswomen is towards plain, round, masculine-style watches.

All of this care and concern for correct grooming and dressing has one objective, which is to match the buyer's expectations about how you should look. You can be certain that most of your customers and prospects will appreciate the care you take in your dress and grooming. When they meet with you for the first time, they will be making comparisons. It is in your own interest that this comparison should be in your favour and should not inhibit your chances of marketing and selling to them.

Finally, you must at all costs avoid what the customer would consider to be the brash salesperson image. The only way you can successfully avoid that image is to take the necessary care with your personal presentation. If you present yourself, in terms of your personal grooming, so that your customers feel at ease with you, you will win in the image stakes. The effort will put you on the road to success in terms of your self-image and self-presentation.

HOW YOU SOUND

Your voice

We use our voice to communicate, and how we sound has a great influence on the degree to which we can successfully communicate. If your voice sounds warm and friendly, you are more likely to be listened to. If the level of your voice isn't too soft or too loud, then you will be more easily understood. When you are speaking, watch carefully for reactions on the part of the listener. Not everyone has perfect hearing, and it is embarrassing for the listener to have to indicate that they have a hearing problem. It is better for you to take careful note as you speak and if you believe that your listener has impaired hearing then you should take whatever action is necessary to enable them to hear in comfort. The speed at which you speak is also important. It is generally accepted that if you speak at the rate of 140 words per minute, you will be easily understood. Take care to pronounce your words correctly so that you increase your listener's chances of understanding you.

From time to time, you should test your voice: how it sounds, and how well you communicate in terms of clarity, sound level and speed. To do this, you can record a sales presentation and make it as real as possible by having someone take the role of the buyer. Often it is a great shock to listen critically to how we speak and discover that our actual delivery is quite different from how we thought we sounded. We hear our voice so often that we tend to take it for granted.

People with an accent will need to take special care in their voice delivery to ensure that they are understood. Remember: the responsibility for being understood lies with the speaker.

Choice of words

Being heard and understood is one thing, having what you say accepted is another, so your choice of words is important. Choose your words carefully so that they add value to what you are saying. Use simple, easily understood words. The purpose of your words is to communicate, not to impress the listener with your vocabulary. Choose everyday, descriptive words. Choose words that add weight and meaning to your message. When you are describing technical specifications, use non-engineering terms if possible.

Whenever you communicate, use everyday language but use it in a manner that doesn't talk down to the listener. If the listener thinks that you are talking down to them, they may very well strike you down and out and thus destroy all your chances of a successful communication. If you are talking up to them, you can quite easily create the same problem. By talking down we create resentment, and by talking up we can easily lose the listener's respect. So the purpose of the way we deliver our words and our choice of words is largely to bring about understanding and, at the same time create a climate of being equal.

Every facet of your presentation will come under scrutiny. People don't consciously listen to every word with the objective of being critical, but they form opinions of you based on their own understanding of what represents good speech and then they mark you up or down accordingly.

Choose your words with care, because words are the tools of your business. Being better with words doesn't mean being glib. Make sure your presentation is free of jargon. Jargon may be very effective in terms of communicating with people in your business; however, the constant criticism of buyers, irrespective of product or service, is that often they don't understand what some salespeople are talking about. The more complex the subject matter, the more important it is that the message is delivered in a simple, easily understood manner.

Choice of conversational matter

During your presentation there will be times when it is necessary for you to engage in general conversation. This is most likely to occur before and after the sale, but sometimes it is necessary during the presentation itself. Subject matter is always a critical issue in the success of a presentation and the one golden rule that you should follow is to be well versed in subjects that are likely to be interesting to the buyer.

When you have studied the market and you know the profile of your most likely customer, then ask yourself what your prospective customers are likely to be interested in, other than what they are buying. When you believe you know the answer, gain a good understanding of those subjects. This may mean studying the share market, knowing the prices of commodities, or becoming an expert on something other than your product or service. You need to be well grounded in a broad range of subjects. Be up on the daily news and watch current affairs programs. Take an interest in politics. It is not necessary to become a walking encyclopaedia, but you should be able to converse in an intelligent manner with your prospective buyer. If you need to lead the conversation, you should be confident of your ability to choose a general purpose subject and to discuss it in an interesting and informative way. A last golden rule is: talk about your prospective buyer whenever possible and only about yourself when asked.

Being interesting

The decision as to whether you are an interesting conversationalist always rests with the listener. No matter how interesting you believe your subject matter is, if it isn't as equally interesting to the listener then it serves no useful purpose. Overall, your best chance lies with matching the buyer's expectation, in the sense that buyers expect their position to be recognised, to be treated with courtesy and to receive first-class attention.

Deal with your buyers as real people in whom you have an interest other than making a sale. The first time you sell to a buyer, you open the door to the possibility of an enduring relationship that will encompass many more sales. If you are genuinely interested in that person over a period of time, your relationship will grow to your mutual benefit. Enduring relationships are based on mutual trust. Without mutual trust, it isn't usually possible to build enduring relationships.

HOW YOU BEHAVE

Always be courteous and considerate to those with whom you do business. Look after their comfort, and make sure they are catered for in a friendly, cooperative manner. If you need to ask questions, then ask permission to do so. If you need to ask someone to do something, then do so in a courteous and considerate manner. If you have to interrupt someone or leave their presence, then excuse yourself, do what has to be done, and return to your presentation or conversation as quickly as possible. In paying compliments, be sure they will be seen as being deserved. A compliment is one thing, flattery is another. Flattery is generally perceived as being a compliment that has not been earned.

Structure your presentation so that you don't take up too much of your prospect's time. Find out how much time they have to spend with you, and stay within that limit.

Avoid doing anything that will startle, embarrass or concern your prospect. Don't make promises you can't keep. Don't criticise your competitors' products or services; simply acknowledge their existence and go on to the benefits the buyer will get from dealing with you and your organisation and from buying what you sell.

Display confidence and develop a sense of maturity about what you do. Don't react emotionally if your prospect says or does anything that offends you. Remember that most of your prospects will be comparing you with other salespeople. The comparison needs to be in your favour.

CONCLUSION

Few people are better qualified to discuss how to market oneself than Cyndi Kaplan, bestselling author, international presenter and speaker, and an authority on personal packaging and image building.

◆

JC: Cyndi, what in your opinion is the key issue that salespeople should consider when marketing themselves?

CK: Jack, I heard of an interesting observation by Mae West: 'It is better to be looked over than overlooked.' I believe that's true, that 'you never get a second chance to make a first impression'. The first thing to do is to take a good critical look at yourself in the mirror. Assess yourself.

Look at your clothes, hair, (make-up if you are a woman) and accessories. You don't have to spend a huge amount on your clothes, however I do believe in quality. Buy one or two well-cut suits in quality fabric. Clothing should be an investment. Buy the best you can afford. I would rather buy one stunning suit per season than many mediocre garments.

Your appearance can also be enhanced by good grooming and deportment (the way you carry yourself). To look appealing, consider the total image. The art of creating a positive image depends on personal style, attention to detail and well-chosen accessories. No matter what your height, weight or age, everyone is able to look great.

The initial impression that you make when you present yourself is very powerful. Part of how you market yourself is to create a strong identity with the product you are selling and the industry in which you work. For some readers, this will be your own business. You need to have a link between the product you are selling and your personality. If you are in real estate, consider the image you need to project to sell real estate. If you are selling clothes, think about the image you design. It is vital that there is a connection between the product you are selling and the way you look.

JC: Cyndi, what else could salespeople do to market themselves?

CK: I think that marketing yourself goes a step beyond presenting yourself. We have to deal with the total look. In marketing yourself, you are taking a more holistic look at the whole person. I think it is important for people to package themselves in terms of their skills, experience and accomplishments. A part of good personal marketing is to have a clear picture of the skills you have developed and your experience in different fields.

A very effective part of self-marketing, once you get into interaction with your prospect, is to show a lot of interest, be a good listener and ask a lot of good questions. The best salesperson is the one who does the most listening as opposed to the most talking. Although you need to know how to package and present yourself, one of the most powerful skills you can acquire is to be a good listener and show a lot of interest in your client.

JC: Cyndi, is there anything else you would like to add that would help those salespeople who are out there selling every day?

CK: Jack, what I have discovered is that you need to build a profile. Part of that can be accumulated through articles that are written about you and interviews you have with the media. As you go about your business you should endeavour to accumulate publicity about both yourself and the products and services you are selling. Use these as testimonials where appropriate.

You should make contact and network with people who can help you to achieve your goals. One of the best ways to do this is to adopt what I call the triple 'A' approach. It is: 'Anyone, anywhere, anytime' — speak to them. In other words, if you are on a plane, or in a queue at the post office or the bank, take the opportunity to reach out to other people. You never know who may become a friend or be influential in terms of making it possible for you to meet other people who can assist you. I have found that people influence is what one needs in the world of selling. Build a strong network of good and dependable people around you, and always be ready and willing to help them in return.

Finally, the quality of your relationships with your clients and prospects, plus the quality of your sales presentations and your attention to detail in every part of your proposal, should guarantee you success.

◆ — ◆ — ◆

That's good advice from Cyndi Kaplan, who has put that advice into practice herself and achieved success as a result.

CHAPTER 23

SELF-
MOTIVATION

Winning isn't everything, but wanting to win is.
VINCE LOMBARDI

TOO MANY PEOPLE think that someday, somewhere, something, somehow will motivate them. Not true. Motivation comes from within. You must make it work for you, or it doesn't work at all. The only motivation is self-motivation, and you *are* always motivated. It isn't true that people are demotivated. What is true is that from the day you are born until the day you die, you are always motivated. What is true is that you aren't always motivated to operate in your own best interests. You aren't always motivated to do what your employer wants you to do. Your children aren't always motivated to do what you want them to do. When you hear an employer say, 'I wish I could get this person motivated', what they should be saying is, 'I wish I could get this person to do what I want him or her to do'. When a wife says, 'I wish I could get my husband motivated', what she really should be saying is, 'I wish I could get my husband to do as I want him to do'. When parents say about their children, 'I wish I could get my children motivated', what they really should be saying is, 'I wish I could get my children to do what I want them to do'. People are always motivated, but they don't always direct their motivation in their own best interests or those of their family or employer. Even when you do absolutely nothing, you are fully motivated to do absolutely nothing. So the real problem is not to motivate people, but to have them direct their motivation so that it works *for* them, not against them.

When individuals feel demotivated, they are simply acknowledging that they aren't directing their activities towards achieving what is important to them, or they are working hard but getting no real results and feel the results aren't worth the effort. Each of us needs to know 'how to get what we want'. Mostly it's a case of not knowing the rules, or knowing the rules but not following them. Your objective should be to direct your motivation towards those things most likely to get you what you want out of life and your work, and this can only be done if your motivation is directed by goals which will help you to achieve those things you really want.

DEVELOPING A POSITIVE SELF-IMAGE

Self-image is the factor which limits your performance in life. As you see yourself, so you act. It is impossible to consistently perform at a higher level than your current self-image. If you want to improve your performance, become a more positive person and be more in charge of your life, then you need to improve your self-image so that you can see yourself doing and achieving the things you want.

Much of your self-image has been developed by interpreting the reactions of others to what you do and who you are. The views held by others may not be correct, but you still believe them and they are the reason why many of us suffer from fears and insecurities.

I have never seen a top-class salesperson who didn't have a healthy self-image. They believe they are people of value who are selling something of value, and they rarely take rejection personally. Rather, they see it as being about what they are selling rather than about them. Less secure salespeople are shackled all their life by the image they have of themselves. So it is very important to ensure that the problems you have in your selling aren't the result of a low self-image.

If you wish to improve your current self-image, you can do so by using your self-talk to send the right messages to your subconscious mind. The subconscious mind cannot tell reality from illusion, or fact from fiction, so one of the first things you need to do is to act as if you are already in possession of the high self-esteem you would like. You need to visualise yourself as a capable, confident person going about your business in a superior manner. You need to see yourself as being a valuable human being and someone worth loving, worth respecting and worth knowing.

Each day as you act out your newfound confidence and continue to visualise yourself as being the person you would like to become, you are in effect building that person. Each day, if you stick at it, you will get a little closer to your goal, and finally the change will have been accomplished and you will have become the person you have been practising to be.

REWARD YOURSELF FOR DOING WELL

If you were given the task of motivating a team of salespeople, one of the first things you would do would be to set up a reward system for those who performed well and achieved or exceeded their targets. It would probably be a money bonus, time off, a weekend away at a special place, or a meal at a good restaurant. All of these rewards are a good form of motivation.

If you would do this for someone else, why not do it for yourself? Pay yourself, even if your organisation also pays you. Give yourself some real incentives to perform. Set up daily and weekly goals and decide what reward you will pay yourself if you succeed. Remember: it's you who is doing the work, and superior performance deserves to be rewarded.

PRAISE YOURSELF

You would certainly praise superior performance to enhance team motivation, so why not praise yourself when you perform at a superior level? It is easy to focus on what you should have done, rather than praise yourself for what you actually did. It's OK to praise yourself when you have earned the praise. Don't be embarrassed — you're the only person hearing your praise, so don't hold back. Always follow the golden rule of giving praise as soon after the event as possible. The more you praise your superior accomplishments, the more likely you are to repeat the performance. What we think about ourselves is the critical factor in driving us on to greater accomplishments. In the words of Denis Waitley: 'It's not what you are that holds you back, it's what you think you're not.' Focus on building on the qualities you have — and remember, you are always better than you think you are.

STRIKE THE WORD 'FAILURE' FROM YOUR VOCABULARY

The words 'failed' and 'failure' are judgmental. There is rarely total failure or total success. If you don't achieve a goal, see it as a need to try again rather than as a failure. There are very few first-time total successes or failures. Build on what was good and try again.

Recently, a man who had been buying Lotto tickets for many years won in excess of $2 million. When asked about the numbers he had used, he said: 'I have been playing Lotto for 17 years and have never changed the numbers. I believed that sooner or later they would come up.' For Lotto that's good logic because, given enough time, any combination of numbers will eventually come up. But life is not Lotto; the rules and conditions are always changing. What won last year may be this year's big loser, and the quality that separates winners from losers is judgment. If you give away the concepts of failure and losing, with all their value judgments, and focus on the positives, you will enhance your chances of success enormously. You will increase your motivation, raise your positive expectancy level and, in a short time, you will have become what you have focused on: positive, motivated and successful.

How often do we hear the words, 'I tried, but it didn't work' or 'OK, I'll try'. We have to give up trying, because for too many people it absolves them from facing up to one of life's great truths, which is: we either do or we don't. No matter what the objective, whether it's to be a millionaire, or travel the world first class, or call your mother on her birthday, the result is always: you did or you didn't.

If you focus on doing instead of trying, two things will happen. First, you will succeed more often, because doing is more positive than trying. Second, because you will have removed the failure syndrome, your motivation will improve until you find yourself expecting to succeed, and a winning expectancy is the result of a positive, 'I can win' self-image. Very few people are totally successful. No matter what level you are performing at, it is always a case of you did or you didn't. Use the 'I did' occasions to build confidence and the 'I didn't' ones to learn how to improve so that next time the possibilities of success are increased. Nothing succeeds like success, so if it is necessary to tackle less difficult goals in order to achieve some positive successes, do so. It is better to have a realistic target and achieve it, rather than one that is beyond you and which will build a 'I didn't' pattern that hinders your self-confidence and becomes a self-fulfilling prophecy of defeat. Once you have established some successes, move the target up and it won't be long before you are wondering why targets were a problem.

Knowing how to motivate yourself is the key issue in improving and maintaining your performance. Getting things done is what brings the rewards and, in order to get things done, you must be committed to the task in question. Without strong commitment it is easy to lapse into old habits, and your drive disappears.

COMMITMENT IS THE KEY

Let me ask you a question: Are you getting what you expected from selling? When you entered your present position of selling, you must have had expectations, some goals you wanted to achieve. I believe that if you had what you wanted where you were before, then you would still be there. Now, I don't know what your expectations were or what motivated you to enter selling or to choose your present employer, but at a guess I would say you were seeking something more than you had, whether it be more money, more time, more excitement, more freedom, more ego recognition, more travel or more independence. Somewhere among those things is probably the key to why you chose to enter the sales profession.

Not enough of those who join a salesforce really achieve their expectations. So be clear in your mind what it is you want to achieve and understand that it is your responsibility to get it. No one owes you anything — not your company, not your boss, not your wife, not your fellow workers. No one is responsible for your career but you, and you need to be committed to getting what you want. Many people never get what they want because they never really committed themselves to getting it. How do you rate in this business of commitment? How long is it since you worked around the clock in order to achieve a goal? How long is it since you did something at great personal inconvenience in order to achieve a goal to which you were committed? There are no prizes, there is only the hope that you understand that commitment is the key to goal achieving, and that goal achieving is the driving force that powers personal motivation and motivation is the fuel of life.

Commitment is the result and evidence of strong motivation. Once one is motivated sufficiently to become totally committed to an ideal, a vision, a dream or an objective, the chance of success is multiplied. Commitment is the key issue. It's the bond you have with yourself. It's your personal contract to get the job done. It's the difference between talking and acting. Commitment is the fire you light within that won't go out whatever difficulties are placed in your path. It's the fire that can only be extinguished by the achievement of the goal to which you are committed.

Without commitment, we are at best lost souls. We wander the world seeking a place. We invent goals to which we are not committed. We dream dreams to which we have no commitment. We make plans to which we owe no allegiance, and invariably they languish through a lack of commitment and personal motivation. Those who are the world's winners are different. They really do march to a different drum. They are the ones who know the rules. They have a system and they apply a method. They are committed. They dream as a basis of accomplishment, and they make things happen. Self-motivation is the fuel of life and is driven by goals. Motivation is the force that drives us in every field of accomplishment. When you are without strong powerful goals, you are like a domino without dots, a guide without directions; you become lost in the daily ebb and flow of trying to get it together when there is no it to get.

Peak performers are outstanding salespeople not only because they have mastered the skills and developed the attitudes and habits of a successful person, but primarily because they have a positive, winning self-image. They expect to make sales and they expect to build a happy and rewarding life. They have problems just like anyone else, but they are confident of solving them to their advantage rather than letting them hamper their progress towards achieving their immediate goals. They are goal-oriented because they know that without them they have no direction or purpose.

How, then, can you do what they do? You can do it by first understanding the process, by understanding why you behave as you do. With understanding comes the possibility of motivation. With strong motivation comes desire, and with the desire comes commitment. From commitment comes action. From action comes results, rewards and further motivation, and then the cycle of goal achieving is complete — it becomes a way of life, the winner's way. But, sadly, not for all.

Many people spend their time on the lowest rungs of life's ladder waiting, hoping, longing for the chance that rarely comes, because life's not like that. Good things in life don't happen by accident. They happen by plan. Winning is not an accident — winning is planning your lifetime goals and going after them with every skill at your disposal.

The pleasure of achievement, the satisfaction of winning, the rewards of accomplishment are all made possible by commitment. Commitment is the driving force that makes it impossible to rest until you have accomplished your goal. And yet it seems to be the missing ingredient in so many of us. This may have something to do with today's quality of life, because it is becoming increasingly difficult to marry together the concepts of quality of life with goal seeking, goal achieving and commitment to objectives; too often, goal achieving loses out to quality of life. However, one of the rewards of success is that you are able to have both. The penalty for not succeeding is that our options in life are severely limited.

You are in the best business of all: selling. Give it all you've got, go the extra mile, share your success with others and more will return to you. Remember: you come this way but once — make it count.

CHAPTER 24

THE
MINDPOWER
ADVANTAGE

We are total mental creatures
and selling is a total mental function.
Sales are made in the mind.
Salespeople who understand and apply
mindpower have a distinct advantage over those
who either cannot or will not learn how.

MOST OF US have never made any real effort to explore the powers of our subconscious mind. Few of us have really tried to understand how our mind works. We take our existence and ability to function for granted and never attempt to unravel the *how* of individual performance. The all-powerful subconscious mind is the key to getting what you want for yourself and those you love and care for. The subconscious mind takes no account of whether what you want is good for you. It has no moral function, passes no judgments. Its main task is to get us what we want from life, to get us what we picture, imagine and think about. So be careful what you think, because sometimes we get what we don't want because we focus on what we want to avoid not on what we want to achieve.

THE POWER OF THE SUBCONSCIOUS MIND

This is how our mind works. The mind is different from the brain. Our mind is made up of the conscious or objective mind, and the subconscious or subjective mind. Throughout this chapter, the terms 'conscious' and 'subconscious' will be used to describe these two parts of the mind. The conscious mind decides your rational thinking and guards the entrance to your subconscious mind. The conscious mind is your capacity to think and reason. You make your choices and decisions through your conscious mind; it is the rational you. Your conscious mind determines whether information presented to it by way of your thoughts is true or false. Your reactions are based on what you currently believe and feel about this type of information.

Your subconscious mind cannot reason the way your conscious mind does. Your subconscious mind is the seat of your creativity and emotions. Your subconscious mind keeps your lungs breathing, your heart beating and your circulation and digestion working. All these functions are monitored, controlled and executed without reference to your conscious mind. Even when you are sound asleep, the subconscious mind is faithfully attending to its duties of refreshing and revitalising you for tomorrow, while at the same time resolving your problems, finding solutions to your wants and needs, and building a life for you which matches how you currently think.

The subconscious mind is the powerhouse of human existence. It is the storage place of our past experiences. All our previous thoughts and feelings are retained in our subconscious mind and produce our self-image. All the possibilities of expressing our life reside in our subconscious mind. Our dreams, fantasies and illusions come from this source. Through the power of your subconscious mind you experience ecstasy, joy, peace and contentment. You can also plumb the depths of despair, and be driven by fear and worry. The choice is always yours.

Life can be a feast or a famine — the decision is yours. You can attract infinite riches by your thoughts and actions. The great wisdom that you possess in your subconscious mind is just waiting for you to put it to work and be expressed in your life. It is through these powers that you can build a new, different, more successful and nobler you. Through these powers, you can express your life as you want it to be. Will this be difficult for you? No, it won't, because you are already using some of these powers. The question isn't: Is it all possible? It is: To what extent do you want to employ them in your life, and how can you ensure that they are always expressed in a positive way? It is only ever a matter of degree.

You are as rich as you are now because of the way you have used your thoughts in the past. Poverty thinking brings poverty living. Bountiful thinking results in bountiful living. You are currently as happy as your thinking. Happy thinking builds a happy life. Open yourself to the infinite possibilities with which you have been endowed and your life will change accordingly. The decisions that will make life beautiful and bountiful for you will always be up to you, and you can achieve any or all of them by learning how to unlock the power of your subconscious mind.

To direct your subconscious mind, you need to feed it with the illusion of what you want. The subconscious mind, not knowing the difference between illusion and reality, will accept the illusion as a reality and then will bring it about in your life. If you want to be a more successful salesperson than you currently are, feed into your subconscious mind by way of visualisation, self-talk, dreaming, desire and affirmations the image of yourself as a successful salesperson, and it will accept the illusion and direct you to behave, talk, think, act and work like the successful salesperson you have created by way of your thoughts.

Life will be as beautiful and successful as we can imagine, because, in some marvellous way we don't as yet completely understand, vividly imagined events supported by purposeful action and sustained by faith and belief come to pass. Remember: whatever you claim by way of thoughts which you believe to be true will be reflected in your life. The law of the mind is that you will get a response from your subconscious mind which reflects the thoughts your conscious mind has passed on to it. Is this difficult to do? Not really, because you are already doing it. This is how people build their life. It's only a matter of degree and focus.

LIFE IS A SELF-FULFILLING PROPHECY

There is a rightness about life that causes most of us to take it and our lives for granted and, as a result, few of us ever ask how human achievement occurs. What makes it possible for some people to win so often and so decisively, while others fail just as often and so disastrously? Why are some people so lucky? Does the Universal Mind select some to be favoured at the expense of others, or are others penalised in a monstrous game of chance which we call life? Is our existence ordered, our chances decided at birth, or are we endowed with free will and masters of our own destiny?

We must confront our beliefs. We must attempt to unravel the myriad fears, worries and beliefs we hold in our subconscious mind about ourselves and the world around us. Our storehouse of beliefs contains everything from mysteries to myths. The mysteries we can contend with by simply accepting that we don't know the answers. That's what makes them mysteries. Myths, on the other hand, are more difficult because, despite the fact they aren't always true, we have endowed them with truth and used them as a basis of decision making throughout our life. Myths and fables clutter our ability to believe. What we already believe gets in the way of the need to make a fresh start, to challenge what we now think by testing those beliefs. One of the best ways of doing this is to test them against the self-fulfilling prophecy. Ask yourself whether your current beliefs are really true, or whether you hang onto them like a small child clutches its security blanket. Are they really true, or have you just grown to believe them and hold on to them because they make you feel safe?

What do you believe? Are you committed to a course of beliefs that will cause you to avoid searching for the answer to how people achieve? Are you willing to explore the possibilities of knowledge that may profoundly alter your life and raise your consciousness to a new and higher level that will bring you sales success on a scale that is difficult for you to envisage at this time?

Is this knowledge some new and recently discovered secret? No, it's not. It has been available to mankind for as long as people have been able to think constructively. Then why is it that so many of us find it difficult to believe and use this power in our lives? It would seem to be because we have been brought up to believe in only those things we can understand and verify. Miracles cannot be understood by the rational mind; they defy logic. Can you understand and apply this knowledge in your life? Yes, you can. You use it and do it every day of your life now, because it is the way we get things done. The degree to which you use this power in your life decides the level of your success. Even people who don't believe in self-fulfilling prophecies create their life by using this power, because it is a universal law. With or without conscious knowledge of what they are doing, they will use the power to accomplish their thoughts and desires, whether they are negative or positive. You must decide whether you will take your chances on the self-fulfilling prophecy improving your life, or whether you will use it in a purposeful way each day in all parts of your life to create abundance for yourself and others.

The critical issue is not can you *use* it, but can you *believe* it, because belief is its foundation. If you cannot believe, it will be denied you. Your disbelief will cause you to constantly send negative messages that will cancel out your primary message instead of reinforcing it. No one is a complete unbeliever. Every day of your life, according to the law of belief, you either win or lose. This is a universal truth. It's the connection between man and his maker. It is the way of all accomplishment. It is the great wisdom passed down through the ages, and yet it is very simple: life is a self-fulfilling prophecy, and as you think, so it will be. You create the life you have by the power of your thinking. You will be as successful as you can imagine and believe. You will be as happy as you think you should be, and you will be as rich as you are willing to settle for.

This is the ultimate truth of all life. You have free will, you are in charge, you can influence your life by the way you think. Life is not a lottery. The quality of your future will not be decided by luck but by you. This is the wisdom of the ages, and it is there for all to see who are willing to look.

People from every walk of life have discovered the power of the self-fulfilling prophecy working in their lives. Because my work is largely in the area of self-development and I deal with all sections of the community, I have the opportunity to communicate with thousands of people each year and with few exceptions they are searching for new ways to create peace, harmony and meaning in their lives. Whenever I present 'Yes, You Can' to a conference or seminar, the positive response is overwhelming. Many people say they can finally see a way through the chaos, confusion and lack of knowledge that plagues them.

What you strive for and how high you aim is a personal choice. A goal has no value except that which you give to it. It is as noble and honourable to strive for something that is of value to you as it is to aim for great riches and material possessions, for they are no more worthy than peace of mind and happiness. Indeed, there is evidence that the more spiritual your aims, the more certain it is that you will achieve your goals of peace and happiness. One doesn't deny the other. You can have both. It is a fallacy to believe that wealth, prosperity and success are in some way tainted, and that in order to have peace, love and happiness in your life you must forgo material possessions. It is just as wrong to believe that we cannot be happy without material possessions.

The universe is a place of abundance. That so few people claim what is rightfully theirs is not the fault of our maker. The fault lies in our own inability to understand the real meaning of plenty. One of mankind's greatest failures is to believe that in order to justify poverty, we must denigrate wealth. We are meant to be rich not poor, happy not sad; we are meant to succeed not fail, be healthy not sick, and life is meant to be full of meaning and enlightenment. Life really is a self-fulfilling prophecy, not only in terms of all that is good and beautiful but also in the potential for evil. The mind makes no moral judgments; if you prophesise, it delivers — so be careful what you think. It can as easily destroy as build. Its power is limitless, and its purpose is to get you what you ask for.

Now that we know the self-fulfilling prophecy is the way that we build our life, we will explore how we can make it happen for us. There are two parts to understanding the prophecy. The first is the prophecy itself, and the second is how to make it happen.

1. *Life is a self-fulfilling prophecy. As you think, so it will be. By the power of your thinking you create the life you have.* The universe in which we live is made up of energy, and thought is energy. The law of attraction applies to thought, and so your thoughts attract to them similar properties and like energy. If you think success, your thoughts attract and manifest success in your life. If you think poverty, your thoughts attract poverty. It's impossible to think poverty and attract riches.

2. *In some way that we don't fully understand, Nature, The Universal Mind, The Infinite Wisdom or God ensures that vividly imagined events, supported by purposeful action and sustained by faith and belief, come to pass and are manifested as reality in our life.*

Vividly imagined events

We have considered the power of imagination in our lives and how it can create magic, wealth and happiness, or chaos, confusion and disaster. Be sure you don't fall into negative thinking and focus on what you fear rather than what you want. For example, you may want an increase in salary but you fear you may be retrenched, or you would like to buy a second-hand computer but you fear it will be a bomb and cost you more money. All these concerns are natural and may help you to avoid making doubtful and costly decisions, but if, when you vividly imagine what you want, your fear outweighs your desire, you may very well hold pictures of what you fear in your imagination rather than pictures of what you really want. If you do, you will surely get what you fear and least want.

Visualisation is the process of creating pictures in our imagination. We need to learn how to use our ability to visualise more effectively, as it is critical to successfully implementing the power of the mind. What you can't see on the life screen of your mind you can't achieve, so constantly visualise your goals. The key is: vividly imagine. Nothing in this life is ever accomplished before it is first imagined. This reality is being discovered every day. It is a cornerstone of the winning preparation of top athletes. They know that in order to win, they must 'see' winning as being possible. They are taught the techniques of relaxation and visualisation as part of their preparation for competition. You are a sales athlete in the game of life, and if you want to win for yourself and those you love and care for a happy, successful and prosperous life, then not only must you compete but you also need to prepare yourself by using the powers of your subconscious mind. These powers will ensure your success.

This technique is crucial to your success. You already do it every minute of every day. Everything you ever do, you first imagine and then you do it. What you need to do is to better direct your visualising so that it is specifically about your possible dream and the goals that will help you to achieve your dream.

Until you see yourself as a successful salesperson making the sales you want to make, it is impossible to make them. Until your prospects and customers see themselves buying from you, not only will they *not* buy, they *cannot* buy. That's why it is so important to present your offer in such a way that having it becomes your prospect's dominant thought. Then they will buy. If you want sales success, you must see it in your imagination. You do this by visualisation.

You can make visualising a creative part of your life by setting aside 20 minutes each morning and night to relax and visualise your goals.

Do this in a relaxed state, preferably last thing at night before you go to sleep. Let the cares of the day slip away, unwind, relax your whole body and your mind, and then as you enter into a dreamlike, peaceful state imagine your goals. See yourself in possession of them. Affirm in a simple way what it is you want. Do this again first thing in the morning when you wake and as often as you can throughout the day. Support your actions by belief. If you don't believe it can happen, it won't. Support your belief by working at what you want to achieve. Your success in life will be directly proportional to the extent to which you follow these universal laws.

Managing your mind is the most crucial issue in making your dreams come true. Those who cannot manage and direct their minds towards what they want out of life will have limited success. We live in a time of emotional abundance: you win and I win. You don't have to lose for me to win. I don't have to lose for you to win. You can, by your ideas, create what you want. You can multiply anything. Your thoughts and actions can create abundance, a world of plenty, because every time you create you enlarge and you don't have to take away from anyone else to do it. It's the double win: you win, and no one loses.

People are born to succeed not fail, to be rich not poor, to be healthy not sick, and they are born with the means of making it happen for them. The means is the power of thought made real through the function of the subconscious mind. Thought is the maker of your life — use it well and it will serve you well. There is no escaping the power of the subconscious mind, there is only the opportunity for each of us to use that power for good in our life. The option of not using it doesn't exist. All that exists is the choice of the instructions we send to it. If we choose to create beauty, peace and happiness in our life, so will it be. If we choose to create sadness, worry and guilt, so also will it be. If we choose sales success, we will achieve it; if we focus on the problems of selling, those problems will grow and fill our life.

Whatever your mind can conceive and believe, you can achieve. Through the power of your imagination and using the technique of visualisation, you can create in your life all the happiness, success and contentment you desire. Do you need anything special by way of mental powers to accomplish this? No, you don't. You are already doing everything that needs to be done, every day, because that is the way we create and run our life. All that is required is focus.

HERE IS A VISUALISATION EXERCISE

1. Close your eyes and relax your body from head to toe.
Slowly and peacefully unwind. Now relax your feet, your legs,
your torso, your arms and hands. Relax your fingers and finally
your neck, face and head. Imagine you are so relaxed that you
bend and sway like a willow in the wind.

2. Now imagine your favourite beautiful, peaceful place.
See yourself there. Enjoy the peace and solitude.
Surround yourself with quiet. Feel the sun on your face.
Feel good feelings sweep over you.

3. When you are completely relaxed, start your visualising.
See yourself asking for what it is you want —
in this example, sales success. Feel the power responding
to you in a positive way. Hear your prospects saying 'yes',
congratulating you on your good work and saying
how willing they are to give you the order. See your partner
in life congratulating you on your success. See the money
you earn from these sales in your hand or in your bank.
See yourself enjoying the extra income.
The more you can experience the feeling of getting
what you want, the more powerful your affirmation
to your subconscious mind will be.

4. As you visualise getting what you want, say this simple
affirmation to yourself: 'The universe has abundant wealth
for everyone. I am now enjoying great financial prosperity
because of my sales success.'

5. If you find your mind wanders, start again.
Keep on focusing and practising. Remember:
the universe is made up of energy, and thought
has energy. It is through this energy that thought
creates reality. If your focus is strong enough,
then results will come quickly.

The first thing to decide is what you want to achieve. Be specific. You might want to get a certain amount more in your weekly pay packet, or at Christmas you would like to go on a first-class trip around the world, or reduce your golf handicap by five strokes, or lose six kilograms in weight. Whether it is getting to the top in your business or claiming wealth and prosperity, it is waiting for you if you will send the message and make the claim.

The whole exercise of visualisation requires you to role-play in your imagination that which you want to attain in your life. The more vividly you can role-play, the better. Active visualisation is where you have decided the goal you want to achieve and you affirm by way of an affirmation what it is you want. An affirmation is the act of affirming by way of writing, or speaking aloud or silently to yourself, what it is you want to accomplish and have manifested in your life. An affirmation can be about anything you wish; there are no limits to the variety of affirmations you can make. Your affirmation may be about material possessions such as a home, car, boat, money, jewellery, or about a promotion, personal development, self-employment or acquiring qualifications. It could be about feeling good, travelling or simply having time to yourself. It could be about getting in touch with divine wisdom and putting it to work in your life. Affirmations supported by visualisation is a role-play of what you want manifested in your life, so always affirm the positive and focus on what you want, not what you want to avoid. Always see yourself already in possession of that which you are affirming. Don't worry if you find it difficult to use these techniques. Continue to practise the methods and you will surely succeed.

In writing your affirmations, remember that the objective is to finish with a statement that is positive and specific and that affirms you are already in possession of what you want. For example: 'I have abundant wealth, happiness and health in every aspect of my life.' When writing an affirmation, rewrite it as often as necessary to finish with exactly what you want. Then practise speaking it until you are completely satisfied that it reflects what you want and you feel comfortable saying it. You can speak your affirmations aloud or silently to yourself. Usually when they are spoken aloud, it is in front of a mirror and the affirmation is about building your self-image and self-confidence so as to achieve success. For example you might affirm: 'Everything I attempt is building my success.'

Here are some other examples of affirmations:

◆ Every day my life is filled with love and happiness.
◆ Sales success flows into my life.
◆ Learning new sales techniques is easy for me.
◆ I am filled with energy.

When you have made your affirmation and visualised it as clearly as you can, your work is done — now let go.

Going with the flow of life is an extension of letting go. It means that faith at work in your life will lead you to make a conscious decision to stop pushing, fighting and manoeuvring for what it is you want in life and what you want your life to become. Relax and follow your new feeling of inner power. Let this new contentment and peace become a permanent part of your life. The law of attraction works with certainty in all our lives: what you think will be attracted to you in your objective life. Let go, and go with the flow.

Purposeful action

Purposeful action reinforces your visualisation program. It means doing what you can to achieve your goal. Ask yourself: 'Is there anything else I should know and be able to do in my current position that is likely to increase my chances of achieving my goal? Should I take a course in something, attend a seminar or read a book? Is there anyone who could help my cause, and what should I do to get their help?' The more we help ourselves, the quicker we will achieve our goal.

Purposeful action to achieve specific goals is a powerful aid to affirmations and visualisation. Every time you take purposeful action to support your requests, you are using energy in the most positive way to convince your subconscious mind that you are serious, that you really mean to achieve this goal. Repeated actions and affirmations is the way to convince your subconscious mind. One of the best actions you can take is to make what you want a goal.

Faith and belief

The second thing you can do to assist your affirmations and visualisation of your goals is to support them with faith and belief. This seems to be difficult for some people. At my seminars, I am constantly asked: 'How can I develop faith?' My response is that faith comes a little at a time. Repetition is the way to develop faith. By repeatedly instructing your subconscious mind by way of affirmations, you build and develop faith. Any thought which is repeatedly passed on to the subconscious mind is finally acted upon by it and is reflected as reality in your life. Faith comes a little at a time, until one day you have it, and the more you use it the stronger it becomes.

Faith is a state of mind and can be created by auto-suggestion. If you pass on to your subconscious mind by way of repeated affirmations that you believe you will receive what you are asking for, it will bring it about because its main task is to get you what you want from life. It sees no obstacles and has no limits; it does what the conscious mind instructs it to do.

Faith has moved mountains, changed the course of history, cured afflictions and created riches. It has strengthened and sustained the human race through mankind's greatest triumphs and failures. Intuitively, we sense the power of faith in our lives. We use expressions such as, 'Have faith in yourself and in what you are doing.' I am sure you've been told by someone who was encouraging you to persist with a course of action, 'Hang on, have faith and all will be well.' Faith is the foundation of religions and the only known cure for failure.

Now is the time to decide. You can start here and now on one of the greatest journeys of your life. There are no limitations. Knowing what you want to do and not doing it is the greatest crime you can commit against yourself. Having an advantage and not taking it to weave magic in your life is a tragedy. Your powers were not bestowed on you accidentally. They are a divine blessing given to you at birth to enable you to fulfil your life in the way our maker intended. However, you were also given free will and the many enticements that can distract you from totally fulfilling yourself as a person.

It has been said a million times, and there is no better way to say it: 'The longest journey starts with the first step.' It is time to start your journey, and the best way is to implement the power of the self-fulfilling prophecy in your life and gain the mindpower advantage for yourself and those you love and care for.

CHAPTER 25

TIME
MANAGEMENT

*Time is like a precious jewel. It must be guarded
well and worn with discretion, or you will
suddenly find it has been stolen.*
GLENN BLAND

LIFE IS FULL of time problems and time is full of life problems, because they are one and the same thing. Whether we are in control of our lives and our work is essentially a matter of whether we are using our time effectively. It's a matter of being in charge, of understanding that our life will be as we make it, of accepting that life really is a full-time self-development course and that it's not about what we can be, but what we are willing to be. What we do with ourselves is our decision. How far we develop depends on how hard we work on improving ourselves and only we can do it, and only we can be held responsible for the final result. There is nothing wrong with being a self-made person, as long as we are not the result of unskilled labour.

Our world is full of opportunities. Some of them will be made available to us by others, but the real work, the seeking out and the improving must be done by us, for us. The universe places no limits on what we can achieve. For some it will be harder, but for none will it be impossible. The limitations on our self-development are essentially self-imposed. We create most of our own problems. If you want a better you, then you must *make* a better you. Your future belongs to you alone, and its quality and success will be decided by you. Time is a limited resource, so you need to decide how to use it effectively to improve the quality of your life and spend more time selling.

Tomorrow is promised to no one. There is no substitute for time: it's now or never. If you were building a house and had no bricks, you could use timber, cement or stone. There are substitutes for virtually everything except time, because time is life itself. We all get the same amount of time each day. Only the quality varies, and the quality is decided by what we do with the time we have. If we fill our thoughts with sales success, our time will be filled with sales success.

BECOMING GOAL-ORIENTED

The only choice we have with time is how to use the time we have. The real issue is not to save time, it is to achieve our goals within the time allotted to us. In order to win in life it is necessary to focus on contribution and effectiveness, not process and efficiency. You may be the most efficient performer of this decade, but if you are not focusing on identifying the main tasks you should be achieving, your efforts may count for little. Losers in life tend to focus on process. They fall in love with the methodology, rather than the result. Winners focus on results. They will endure the pain of any method as long as they achieve a positive result and make sales. Turning time-wasters into time-winners is a sure way of increasing your effectiveness and achieving positive results.

In terms of time effectiveness, there are two broad options we can consider. The first is to identify our top 10 time-wasters and try to eliminate them. The second option is to become wholly goal-oriented. In this chapter, we will focus on this second option. Our objective will be to remain focused on our high-priority goals. Irrespective of what other time may be wasted or ill used, if we continue to focus on what is crucial in our lives, we will make a dramatic impact on our productivity and effectiveness, and our sales results will increase accordingly. Not wasting time is a good discipline, but focusing on what matters is what counts, and for salespeople this is asking prospects and customers to buy what they are selling.

Let me give an example. A salesperson who had been in business for three months analysed his activities over that period and discovered that he was getting something like 5 per cent of his business from third, or later, calls or interviews, but was spending almost 40 per cent of his time on those calls. He made a simple decision: he wouldn't make more than two calls. That decision meant that the 40 per cent of his time spent on producing 5 per cent of his business now went into first and second calls which produced 95 per cent of his business. Immediately, his productivity increased dramatically. This is a simple example of how to spend time more effectively. No matter what you do, make sure that what you are spending your time on is important. Priorities are crucial in using your time effectively.

Plan your time, then plan your work, because time is limited and work rarely is. Then establish objectives that can be achieved within the time you have available. Peak performers take great stock of this principle, and the best way for you to put it to work in your life is to follow the suggestions given in this chapter.

Plan three types of priority activity:

1. What *must* be done.
2. What *needs* to be done.
3. What *might* be done if there is time.

Spend your time on priority 1 activities and then on priority 2 matters. If you follow this technique, your time will always be focused on what is most important. Remember: the issue is not to save time, it is to achieve your goals and make sales.

If you spend 50 per cent of your time on low-priority work, where will you finish? Where would you expect to finish? Would you really expect to finish on top? Keep a daily 'to do' list of your first and second priorities. On one side of the page, under the heading 'Must do today', list the six most important activities you should do that day. Don't list things you do as a matter of course. On the other side, list the appointments you have for the day and carry the list with you. At the end of the day, transfer those items which you haven't completed to the next day's list. If an item is carried over for more than a week, forget it — you're only playing games.

Discipline yourself to do what needs to be done until it becomes a habit. It has been said that our desire to learn about and become involved in anything increases in proportion to the amount of knowledge we have of that particular subject. So, to become good at and be interested in and get benefit from your sales activity, you need to learn more about selling techniques, your prospects and your customer's business. Your level of desire and activity will then increase and you will no longer find it a problem to do what needs to be done to achieve outstanding sales success. You will be a peak performer.

Keep your desk, office and car clean and organised. Only have on your desk what you are currently working on, and don't be fooled into thinking that time equals money. Time equals opportunity to work, and *work* equals money. There are only three ways to create money: by working yourself, by putting money to work for you, and by receiving handouts. If you think time equals money, stop work for a year and then see how much money you have made. The more high-quality work you do in the time you have available, the more likely you are to win and the more you will get paid for the work you do. In absolute terms, time equals decay. Success is the motivator, and using time effectively is organising how to get work done.

For those who want to succeed in sales, the critical issue at all times and in all situations is to focus on the required result, not the process. Be clear about what you want to achieve as a result of performing an activity and constantly ask yourself: 'Is this the best use of my time now?' If the answer is 'yes', then do what has to be done as well as you can. If the answer is 'no', don't do it. If it needs to be done, get someone else to do it.

TEN WAYS TO USE YOUR TIME EFFECTIVELY

Find out how you are currently using your time

Keep a time log of your activities for at least a month and at the end of that period analyse how you used your time. You will almost certainly find that some of the following have happened:

◆ You will discover that most of your time has been spent differently than you expected. A good discipline is to write down how you believe you are currently spending your time, keep your time log and then match your beliefs against the reality of how you are spending your time. In most cases you will be in for a shock. We generally do what we like doing and we rationalise our activities until in our mind we are doing what we are supposed to be doing, which is focusing on our highest priority goals.

A large sales organisation did a research project on the top 10 per cent of their salespeople. The question they asked them was: 'How much of your time do you actually spend face to face with clients or prospects asking them to buy what you sell?' On average the salespeople said they spent around 55 per cent of their time on this activity. The organisation then set them a project: for the next month, each salesperson had to keep a diary of how they spent their time. It had to be kept daily, and was broken down into half-hour segments. Their entries were to be checked each day by their secretaries to ensure that they recorded fact not fiction. At the end of the month the totals were analysed. The result showed that on average these salespeople spent 18 per cent of their time asking clients and prospects to buy what they sold. That's a difference of 37 per cent. Don't let this happen to you — keep a time log.

◆ Much more time than you expected has been lost on unproductive or unnecessary activities. You will be surprised at how often you spend your time doing what you like doing, even though it adds nothing to your productivity, effectiveness or sales results.

◆ The 80/20 rule has struck again. You will find that 20 per cent of your activities have produced 80 per cent of your effective results, and that you have spent 80 per cent of your time producing 20 per cent of your results. This is always a shock, but it happens to all of us unless we are constantly reviewing and analysing our activities and directing our efforts towards those activities that produce outstanding results.

The above are three very good reasons for finding out how your time is currently being spent. When your analysis is complete, write down the actions you intend to take to make yourself more time effective. Here are some issues you might consider:

◆ What did I do well in terms of using my time that resulted in my being able to give more time to selling, and can I do more of it?

◆ Where did I waste time which lost me precious selling time, and what should I do to avoid doing it again?

◆ What did I do that had to be done but could have been done by someone else?

◆ Am I doing some activities over and over again, and would I be more effective if I organised them into a procedure (for example, sales presentations)?
◆ Am I using other people's skills to lighten my workload?

Now write action plans to remedy any of the problems you found in your summary.

 ## Plan recurring events

Whenever you find yourself repeating an activity, ask yourself whether you can minimise the time spent on it by organising it into a procedure. Should sales presentations and quotations be reduced to a procedure that someone else can carry out?

There are endless opportunities to formalise and structure activities so that you lessen your involvement, save time, and increase your own and other people's effectiveness. Time spent on establishing routines which are easily understood and can be carried out by others is time well spent.

 ## Decide what doesn't need to be done

Make a decision not to get involved in any activity unless it multiplies your chances of sales success. If your organisation is creating time barriers for you, then you need to solve the problem so that you can spend more time asking your prospects to buy what you sell.

Identify what others do for you that, if it were done differently, would save you time and then ask them to do it differently. If you take care of their ego, they will usually meet your needs. You will probably be able to show them how, if they give you information in a different way, you will be able to use it without doing extra work. Give them credit for doing it differently and thank them for increasing both their own and your effectiveness.

 ## Decide what can be delegated

It is worth considering Peter Drucker's advice: 'Delegation as the term is customarily used, is a misunderstanding, is indeed a misdirection. But getting rid of anything that can be done by somebody else so that one does not have to delegate, but can really get to one's own work — that is a major improvement in effectiveness.' In other words, instead of constantly delegating less important work, transfer the activity permanently to someone else.

Have a number of 'In' baskets

The 'In' basket is the downfall of a vast number of people. They busy themselves with looking after the 'In' basket and at the end of the day judge their work by how much they get through. Their measure is quantity, not quality. Whether you have your mail sorted for you or you sort it yourself, the way to get control of the 'In' correspondence is to have at least three 'In' baskets. If you put all your mail in one basket you will spend a great deal of time each day looking for what you want. You might also lose what is important among what is of no importance.

Have one basket for reading matter, newsletters, brochures, periodicals and any other information you plan to read if you have time. If you have the time, read them; if not, pass them on to someone else or empty them into the wastepaper basket.

Have a second basket for all the internal mail that is circulated for your information. If it is expected that you will read it, tick the circulation list to say you have read it, and then send it to the next person on the list. Try to send it on the day you receive it. Don't forget to tick it, or someone will send it back.

In the third basket, put the things you *must* deal with because they fall into your area of responsibility. This is the basket which should get your time and which will give you the opportunity to perform. Be ruthless about what goes into this basket. Delegate what you can and deal with the rest as effectively as possible. The first issue in dealing with paperwork is to sort it into priority order so that you know what is most urgent. It is often good practice to deal with all the easy items first so that you can spend more time on the more difficult ones without interruption. It is also sound psychology to reduce the size of the 'In' basket as quickly as possible. Deal first with matters that can be handled on the phone. Then write any necessary letters in one session. Systems and methodology pay off handsomely when doing paperwork.

Have a hold file to clear paper

In your day-to-day sales work, you will find that you often need to hold onto some paperwork because you need to discuss the matters arising from it with someone else. That person may be away on holiday, ill, or at a conference or seminar. You have to hold the paperwork until you can deal with it, but you don't want it to stay in your 'must do' file, so you need a hold file. Last year's diary makes an excellent hold file; you can file what you hold on the relevant day or date. Let's say you have just called Fred from Marketing. He is on leave for 10 days starting today, which is the 15th. He'll be back on the 25th. File the relevant paperwork under the 25th of the month. Check your hold file first thing each morning and you will get it back on that date. You could, of course, use this year's diary, but you will find it soon gets clogged with pieces of paper you are holding and becomes unwieldy to use.

Handle paper only once

Winning the paper war and giving yourself more time to sell depends on your attitude and techniques. The battle rages incessantly. It seems the rest of the world has one goal in mind: to send all its paperwork to you. Start winning by making a decision on every piece of paper the first time you handle it. If you have to wait for someone, then at least decide to put the information you will need into your hold file. If no decision is needed, throw the paper into the wastepaper basket or file it. Remember: research shows that 85 per cent of all filed paper is never looked at again, so decide on the wastepaper basket if you can.

If you decide on none of the above, then work on it until it is completed. This will not always be possible or desirable, however. The least action you should take on it is to give it a priority number or a must complete by date and then place it in your hold file to come back to you with enough time to complete it by the desired date.

If you decide that you will handle paper only once and use these techniques, you will take most of the stress out of the paper war. One way to reduce the number of times you handle paper is to put a dot in the top right-hand corner of the document every time you handle it. If it starts to get the measles, deal with it or throw it out. When you adopt this technique you will soon find that you handle items much more often than you thought. Almost every salesperson I talk with complains of the paper war, so winning it is critical to your success. Your real work is selling, not shuffling paper.

Only have on your desk the item on which you are currently working

Have as few items on your desk as possible, because selling is your business, not administration. This technique will keep your mind on what you currently are doing. It is easy to fall into the habit of storing present, past and future work on your desk and losing valuable time looking for what you need to complete a task. Research studies have found that people who work with piled-up desks on average spend up to an hour a day looking for what they want. So stow it, or throw it. Stow it in a file, a box, a bin — some place where you can find it when you need it — but get it off your desk. If you have to carry correspondence with you, have a special filing system so that you can find what you want easily. Carry as little with you as possible.

Do clean desks always represent productivity and effectiveness? No, they don't, no more than time organisers make effective time users. Clean desks and time organisers are a process, and if they don't contribute to increased productivity and effectiveness they serve no useful purpose other than making us feel good about the way we work. Many time organisers actually reduce instead of increase effectiveness. Spending time on organising facts and information which are not always productive may make us feel good, but the real question is whether it increases our productivity and effectiveness. The effectiveness of many personal organisers seems to decrease with their thickness.

Plan your selling in blocks of time

You can decide how to manage your own workload, and the first step in doing that is to organise your work in larger blocks of time. If you spend the day trying to get important work done in 30 minutes here, 10 minutes there and 15 minutes later on, and this pattern persists through the day, you will have achieved little except put out fires. Use the exercise over the page to work out how to overcome this problem.

Eliminate unnecessary meetings

Meetings are ranked as the world's seventh greatest time-waster and you need to be constantly checking the amount of time you spend on them. Are meetings the bane of your life? Are they causing you to lose control of your selling time? Is each day spent preparing for or following up on meetings? Do you spend hours listening to other people listen to themselves talk? Do you often ask yourself, 'Why am I here?' or say to yourself you could be out selling instead of wasting time? Do you contribute to this slaughter of time, or are you a victim?

Not all meetings are time-wasters. People who work together in an organisation have to help each other so that they can get their specific tasks done. Co-operation and communication are vital if individuals are

1. Draw up a schedule that shows your working week in half-hour intervals under the working days of the week.

2. Fill in the times of the day over which you have no control — for example, travelling time, meetings, training sessions, meal times, and all other recurring activities which are done on a regular basis and at a specified time and which have to be done.

3. Identify how much selling time you actually have in each working day and when you have it.

4. Spend this time with prospects and customers, looking after their needs and wants, solving their problems, and asking them to buy.

AFTER SUCCESSFULLY COMPLETING THIS TASK YOU HAVE SOLVED THE MAJOR TIME PROBLEM OF MOST SALESPEOPLE: HOW TO FIND ENOUGH TIME IN THE WORKING DAY TO ACHIEVE YOUR SALES OBJECTIVES.

to become an effective team. It is also a fact of life that no single person in a team or organisation has all the experience, knowledge and ideas necessary to accomplish the goals of the organisation, whatever its size. As Ashley Brilliant said, 'Sometimes I think I understand everything. Then I regain consciousness.' It is understood that no matter how important it is for you to make selling your first priority, you will have to make a contribution to the whole team by being present at a meeting that is more important to someone else than it is to you. Make your contribution as soon as possible and leave as soon as you can. Here are some tips that will help you make the best use of your meeting time.

◆ Ask that the discussion be restricted to the current matter.
◆ Encourage the chairman to enforce basic meeting procedures.
◆ Encourage those who are running the meeting to have a short action plan session before they close the meeting. The purpose of this session is to ensure that all who attended the meeting know what actions were proposed, who is responsible for what has to be

done, when it is to be done by, and who has to be advised when it has been completed.

TACTICS FOR USING TIME EFFECTIVELY

Here are some useful time tactics that can help make your life and your work easier and more productive.

- ◆ If you travel by bus or train, read a book that will develop your skills. Many of us could do a complete course on a special subject each year if we adopted this practice.
- ◆ While driving, listen and learn. Play tapes that develop your knowledge, that inspire you to think big and motivate you to put what you learn into effect in your life.
- ◆ Make your last activity of the day a check of the day's 'to do' list. Did you get everything done? If not, start tomorrow's list with those activities that weren't completed today.
- ◆ Make your first activity of the day the preparation of your 'to do' list. Complete the list you started yesterday.
- ◆ Relax for 10–20 minutes each morning and afternoon. Learn relaxation techniques and put them into practice. You will find that these sessions will refresh your body and your mind, and that you will accomplish more and feel better as a result.
- ◆ Avoid becoming a perfectionist unless you are a brain surgeon. Remember: only mediocre people are always at their best. There are very few activities that require perfection. I am not saying 'Near enough is good enough' because it isn't, but becoming a perfectionist can cripple your effectiveness. Focus on results, not the process, and you will soon learn that being a perfectionist is in many cases a sure recipe for low performance.
- ◆ Don't let the process of time effectiveness take over your life to the extent that the process becomes a goal in itself. Records are helpful and information is important, but only to the extent that they help you to achieve your important objectives. Keep your eye on the result and minimise your involvement in the process, or it will become a self-defeating activity and your possible sales results may become one of the casualties. The goal is to make sales. Other parts of your work may be necessary, but sales are crucial. No sales, no future.

CHAPTER 26

ACHIEVING
YOUR GOALS

*All successful people have a goal. No one can get
anywhere unless they know where they want to go
and what they want to be or do.*
NORMAN VINCENT PEALE

ACHIEVING TARGETS AND meeting deadlines is a major issue in the life of every salesperson. No matter how well you do, the constant push is for more. It is the nature of the business: either you push yourself, or someone else will. To do better is the constant challenge, and it is one that strengthens those who embrace it and weakens those who fight it. So accept this challenge for what it is, a test of your willingness to embrace self-improvement, and do it with zeal and determination. There is no better way to start than by setting some goals that will keep you ahead of the mob.

SETTING YOUR GOALS

Setting goals is not only the way to accomplish your sales success, it is also a basic human need. If you want to fill your life with purpose and accomplishment, you need to set worthwhile goals that are important to you and those you love and care for. Just getting through the day is not enough. Sacrificing your potential for short-term comfort is too high a price for those who want a future full of pleasure and plenty. High expectations lead to high achievements, and your goals will be set in a way that reflects your optimism and belief that you will get what you want.

The ability to set goals correctly is a skill that can be acquired. The drive to achieve goals is a want which you can foster, and foster it you must if you want to succeed in turning your sales dream into a real-life accomplishment. Without motivation to achieve your goals, nothing will happen; you will simply perform at your comfort level. To move from the comfort zone is difficult, if not impossible, without strong motivation. To set and achieve worthwhile goals, you need to get your motivation, your mind and the clock in harmony. In this part of your goal-achieving plan, you will look at how to translate what you want into specific goals.

The good news is that goal setting really works, and it works because you are endowed with a brain that operates like a mechanical goal-seeking device. This is what separates humans from all other known life forms in the universe. It gives you the power to make judgments, to consider options and to choose alternatives. It makes your dream possible, because you have the power to choose. However, choose wisely, for as Mary Crowley says: 'We are free up to the point of choice, then the choice controls the chooser.' Above all, it sets you free, fills you with hope, and sustains you with a belief that empowers you to act out your beliefs until they become a reality in your life.

This marvellous goal-seeking mechanism operates automatically to achieve your goals for you. It is like a homing device on a guided missile. Once the missile is fired, the device is up and running, seeking the chosen target and automatically correcting itself if it gets off target. It is locked on to the target. So it is with your goal setting: once you have set a goal and started the activity necessary to achieve it, your mind's goal-seeking device operates automatically to achieve your goal. All you have to do is keep it on target, which means you need to constantly check your progress towards your goal and, when necessary, change or correct it to keep on target. If you constantly focus on the goal, the mechanism will ensure you hit the target.

We use this remarkable ability to set up either failure or success. There is no middle ground. You will either achieve your goal, or you won't. The result of your failure to achieve your goal may be much better than the result if you had not attempted the goal. For example, you may have set yourself the goal of increasing your income by 50 per cent in this financial year. Although you may have failed to achieve your goal, you are much better off than if you had never made the attempt. Always remember that when you fail to plan, you automatically set up failure. Keep your mind constantly on your possible dream and focus all your energies on it. Your mind will do the rest.

You build your life and your success by your thoughts, and the first step is to build yourself a winning self-concept. Who you believe you are and what you do with who you are is your potential, because:

◆ What you believe will become a reality if you have faith — faith in your mind's goal-seeking mechanism and belief in the relationship between you and your maker. Your mind is a magnet, so dwell on the sales success you want and you will achieve it. You really are a child of the universe, and the loving, creative power that flows from your maker to you is a guarantee of the self-fulfilling prophecy.

◆ What you believe grows from an idea, a vision, a dream or a want into reality in your life. It is impossible for a person to hold a thought constantly in their mind that does not manifest itself in some way in their life. The pictures in your mind are the screwdrivers, wrenches, nuts and bolts that build ideas into reality in your life. That's how all things are achieved in this world in which we live. Dwell on your sales success and you will achieve it. Focus on your sales problems in a negative way and they will grow and overwhelm you.

◆ You will always find what you believe. The images you see will become real. The more often you concentrate on them, the sooner you will have them. When building your winning self-concept, focus on the positive factors of health, wealth, happiness and success as a general principle and on sales success as a specific goal.

The next step is to set yourself a program. Set goals that are important to you, goals that will enrich your life and cause you to grow as a person as a result of having accomplished them. List the daily actions that will, if implemented, achieve your goals. This will be discussed in detail later in this chapter. List the attitudes that will help you to take these actions so that they will become a reality in your life. Train yourself to absorb these actions and attitudes into your nervous system until they become automatic.

You will achieve what you focus on, because it is an unalterable law of life that what you think and believe is what you get. Think and believe that you are shy, and you will act as a shy person. Think and believe that you are friendly and courteous, and you *will* be. Think and believe that you will be successful in life, and success will be yours. Think and believe that you can become a great salesperson, and you will. Remember, it is you who holds the key to your sales success, no one else.

Focus on the result, not the journey

When setting your goals, focus on the result not the process. This is a critical factor for those who want to win. At all costs, avoid shrinking your goal, which is the result you want, so that the process, which is what you do to achieve the goal, becomes pleasant and easy. This doesn't mean that achieving goals should be unpleasant and difficult, but that life seems to demand more than pleasure and ease. It is said that losers in life will do anything to achieve a pleasing method (process), while winners will endure any pain to get a pleasing result. For you it must be the *result*, at whatever price. Paying the price for what you want in life is a key issue for all who want to succeed above the ordinary and achieve their possible dream. If you pay little, you will get little from life; if you want little from life, the price is small. The more you want, the more it costs. Success is limited by the price you are willing to pay. The price is not paid in money. It is paid in knowledge, activity, creative thinking, innovation, identification, preparation, commitment and compromise.

It will be necessary for you to compromise. The need to compromise is a fact of life. All of life is a compromise. Trading off one aspiration against another is only a reflection of your willingness to pay the price. Everything demands a price. The trick is to pay the right price for the right thing, and to know when to compromise and which compromise to make.

◆ Do you know your price?
◆ Do you understand that you are currently paying only sufficient to get the current rate of success that you enjoy, and that if you want more success then you have to raise the price?
◆ Do you know what it is you want?
◆ Do you know when you want it?
◆ Do you know what you must do to get there?

- ◆ How will you know when you do get there?
- ◆ Above all, have you decided what you must give in return for what you expect to get, because there are no free lunches?

Clearly define your goal, prepare yourself for the journey and then commit yourself to the job ahead, recognising that it will not be easy, that everything has a price, and that if you are willing to pay that price and commit yourself to the attainment of your goal, then you are almost certain to get there. It is not possible to see into the future, but it is possible to predict the results of certain actions with a high degree of success. For instance, I promise you that if you make no changes but continue to live your life as usual and sell as usual, then you will get the usual result. If you don't change the cause, you won't change the result. If you do this year exactly as you did last year, then don't be surprised if you get the same sales results. Like begets like. Equally, if you run your life exactly as before and make no changes in attitude to take account of your dream, then don't be surprised if it remains a dream. Pay the price. If you want more, then give more, know more, do more — pay the price: the payoff is fantastic. Make a total commitment and focus on the result. You know that with success will come joy and fulfilment in plenty, and to ensure this success you must focus on the result, not the journey.

Your brain can function no better than the success program that runs it, so when you set your goals, think big. Expectations are a major limiting factor in our lives. We tend to live up — or down — to our own expectations. We are subject to both nature and nurture, yet we are still in charge. We have this marvellous goal-getting mechanism within our brain, and because we are in charge we can decide the size of the task we set. We can limit our brain to run a program that doesn't extend us, that keeps us within our comfort zone, or we can stretch our imagination and set a program that is inspiring and testing. *You* must choose for you, and now is the time to make the choice, so think big. You will accomplish anything to the limits of your self-concept program, so think big. Your brain is a wonderful machine, but it can only run the program you set it.

Time really is life, so time has to be translated into real-life goals. To do that, you should list your goals — business and private, long-term and short-term. This is where major difficulties arise for many people, because they fall victim to the 'I think I know what to do, but I can't make up my mind what I want' syndrome. This is a very real problem, with only one answer: action. The problem stems from thinking, 'I'm OK. I would *like* more, but on balance I really don't want to *do* more.' The desire for what you would like doesn't exceed the pain of what you might have to do to get what you want, so staying where you are is generally the result.

You don't get out of life what you want; you get what you expect, and not one bit more. Those who say they can't make up their mind are satisfied with their current lot. Only when they become dissatisfied will they act. Dissatisfaction is a great motivator. Only when you become sufficiently dissatisfied with your income, home, car or sales success will you be motivated to do something about improving it. Does that mean that if you are satisfied with your current situation, you must act to change? No, it doesn't. The choice is always yours. If you want to change, action is the answer, so let's start by trying to generate some dissatisfaction and create some desire. You can do this by asking yourself the following questions and writing down your answers.

1. What are my lifetime goals?

Answer: _____

_____

2. What would I like my situation to be five years from now?

Answer: _____

_____

3. What would I like my situation to be three years from now?

Answer: _____

_____

4. What is my most important current ambition?

Answer: _____

_____

Setting lifetime goals

Start with your lifetime goals, with whatever goal is most important to you. Don't judge at this time, just let your desire really work. Put down all you would like to have and do. Stay at it; even when it's difficult, write them down. Focus on what is important to you. Ask yourself:

◆ What do I want to do with my life?
◆ What do I want to achieve?
◆ How much of my potential as a person do I want to reach?
◆ When my time is gone and there is no time left to do more, will I have any regrets or will I be satisfied that I did my best? The life you lead today is building your future. The future consists of all your todays, so make sure your plans are focused on what you really want for yourself and those you love and care for.

When working on your goals, it is important to get a sense of urgency into them. This can best be done by moving on to the next step, which is your five-year goals.

Setting five-year goals

Write down your five-year goals. This requires more specific thinking, but it is made easier because you have already clarified your lifetime goals. When you have written down your five-year goals, amend and clarify them and make sure they reflect your lifetime goals and ambitions. Ask yourself more questions on matters that are important to you:

◆ Where do I want to be living five years from now?
◆ Would I like a different house, perhaps in a different suburb or state?
◆ What income do I want to be earning from my sales activities?
◆ Is a better car or a new boat important to me?
◆ Should I plan to improve my sales skills?

The list is long and diverse. It's your life you are considering, so give it plenty of time and effort. This is important, because if you don't get it right now you may later regret not giving your plans the attention they deserved. Remember: all this planning is about your life, not just work. So give plenty of attention to home, family, leisure and relationships. You only have one life, so you should work hard at making it enjoyable and satisfying. If *you* don't do it for you, who will?

When you have identified all the issues that are important to you, list them in order of priority so that you will know which are the most important.

Setting three-year goals

Now make your planning more urgent still by applying the same procedure to your three-year goals. Each time you shorten the time frame of your planning, you increase the need to plan now and decide now. Think back to three years ago. What were you doing then? What had you planned or hoped to achieve within the next three years? Have you achieved that goal? If the answer is 'no', then ask yourself why not. What did you do, or neglect to do, that prevented you from achieving your goal? Is it important for you to avoid doing this in your current three-year goal plan? If you *did* achieve your goal, identify what it was you did that was mainly responsible for achieving it. Can you do it again to help achieve your new goals? When you have made all the decisions necessary to get your current goals on paper, write them down in order of priority.

Identifying your most important current ambition

Having completed your lifetime, five-year and three-year goal plans, you have only one step left to complete your goal setting and that is to establish what is most important to you *now*. You can do this by writing down your most important current ambition. You now have a list of what you consider are the most important issues in terms of what you want to achieve. Your goals range from your most important current ambition through three- and five-year terms to your lifetime goals. Your next task is to reduce the list to a possible achievement level. Focus on the short term, because that is where you must start.

Prioritising your goals

Listing your goals in order of priority is a very important part of your plan. Select your most important goals and give them priority 'A' status. Give your next most important goals a priority 'B' rating. List the remainder as priority 'C' — to be done if ever you have the time.

Next list your most important 'A' goal as 'A.1', the next most important as 'A.2', the third most important as 'A.3', etc., until all your 'A' goals have a firm priority. Do the same with the 'B's. When all the 'B's are accounted for, do the same with the 'C's.

Writing valid goals

For a goal to be valid, it must contain the following four elements:

1. It must be specific.
2. It must be time bounded.
3. It must be measurable.
4. It must be achievable.

   If any one of these are missing, you are largely wasting your time, for the following reasons:

◆ If your goal is not specific, you will have no focus, no target to aim for. Your wonderful goal-seeking mechanism will be unable to start because it has no specific instructions. For example, you may write a goal that reads like this: 'I want to improve my selling skills'. To be specific, the goal should be written like this: 'I want to improve my selling ratios by successfully selling to one in five prospects instead of one in eight.' Now your goal-seeking mechanism knows what to aim for. Remember: your subconscious mind doesn't understand abstract terms. Terms like 'rich', 'happy' and 'beautiful' are not specific, as they may mean quite different things to different people.

◆ When do you want to achieve these new ratios — within the next six weeks, six months or six years? The goal needs to be time bounded. So your goal should read: 'Within the next three months my sales ratios will improve from selling to 1 in 8 prospects to selling to 1 in 5 prospects.' Now your goal-seeking mechanism is up and running. It knows what you want and it knows when you want it by.

◆ It can be measured because it is specific and time bounded, so checks on progress can be made at any time along the way.

◆ It is achievable within the time frame of the goal, because such a goal is within your grasp if you want it enough. Not all goals are achievable — for example, winning the lottery without a ticket is not possible. Don't be like Fred who went to his church each day for a month to pray for a win in the lottery. At the end of the month, he complained in his prayer: 'Why aren't you helping me? I have asked, but have won nothing.' A voice from the heavens replied, 'Fred, give me a chance — buy a ticket.'

Goals should be written in output terms rather than input terms. The following example illustrates the difference between input terms and output terms.

Input terms	Output terms
I want to learn more about our new product X	I want to sell 10 of our new product X within 28 days

The message is clear. You may learn and know more about product X than any person alive, but if you don't sell any it was all a waste of time. Learning is the process, sales are the result.

Input terms	Output terms
I want to increase my earnings this year.	I want to increase my earnings by 20 per cent this year.
I want to improve my selling skills.	I want to improve my sales closing ratio by 25 per cent within three months.
I want to take a course in short story writing this year.	I want to have a short story published this year.

The whole purpose of writing goals in output terms is to achieve a positive result. In the examples given above, all these goals could have been attained without achieving a positive result, because inputs largely focus on the process. Generally when a goal is written in output terms, the focus is on achieving a positive, worthwhile result. Outputs force you to focus and to act.

Now you need to test the validity of the goals you have written to see that they conform to the criteria of a valid goal. This means that you need to make sure the goals you have written down are specific. For example, 'I will achieve a 50 per cent increase in income'. Next, you need to ensure that your goals are time bounded. For example,

'I will achieve a 50 per cent increase in income within nine months commencing from the first of next month'.

Now make sure that your goals are measurable in a valid way. In the case of the example just given, you could measure its attainment by the fact that you have received 50 per cent more income in the specified time. You could measure it by your bank accounts, by your tax return, by your group certificate, etc. It can be measured in any way that meets the test.

A valid objective or goal must be achievable, which doesn't mean that you must be certain of getting it before you attempt it. Achievable means that it is a possibility. However, you should write goals that stretch you to your limits.

If a goal doesn't have these four qualities, then it becomes more of a wish or a dream — above all, it becomes non-specific. When it is non-specific and no time limit is placed on it, then it becomes impossible to measure. When this happens, it is soon relegated to the too hard basket and forgotten. It becomes just another exercise in dreaming.

By now you have the 'I want' part of your important goals on paper and you are on your way. However, this is where most goal-achieving attempts fall down, where most plans start and finish, because the 'I want' is just a dream and dreaming comes naturally to most of us. What is now needed is action. You are at your best when you are striving to achieve and at your most vulnerable when you are inactive.

Within you is all that you need to achieve all that you want. Happiness, prosperity, peace and outstanding sales success can be yours if you will but reach out and claim them. You have the power, all you need is the desire.

Your main objective is to achieve your goals, but so far all you have done is set them. Almost anyone can do that part; it's the getting that shortens the list of those who succeed. Remember: work in itself is not accomplishment; if it were, those who work hardest would always win, and you know that isn't true. If hard work in itself was the answer, then goals would be easy to achieve.

The paradox of work is simple. If you think you can be outstandingly successful without working hard, you will be bitterly disappointed. If you think that hard work by itself will make you successful, you will be equally disappointed. Success requires more than hard work: it requires imagination and creativity applied to real-life goals in a purposeful way. It requires faith and belief in yourself and in your goals. Don't be put off or inhibited by the words 'imagination' and 'creativity', as you have all that is needed within you now to achieve your most testing goal. You use the very same imagination and creativity to convince yourself that you can't or don't want to get involved in all this goal achieving. By simply focusing on the positive not the negative, on the *can do* instead of the *can't do* and the *want to* instead of the *can't decide*, you will go most of the way towards identifying what needs to be done.

Perspiration is necessary. Hard work is always on the side of those who want to win. But inspiration is essential. It is said that a drop of inspiration is worth a bucket of perspiration, so simply identifying and prioritising your goals will not accomplish your end. Something more is required, and that something is the creative twist to what you are going to do. Creative goals are the answer. Business or private goals which are worth working for, to which you are willing to devote your time, energy and skills. Goals that test and improve your abilities, strengthen your character, and that build a better life for you and those you love and care for. Goals that will be big enough to ensure that you grow as a person as a result of achieving them.

TEN WAYS TO ACHIEVE YOUR GOALS

☆ Balance your picture

Ask yourself whether your goals fit your total picture. Are they in harmony with your current lifestyle? Are they consistent with your aspirations? Are you heading in the same direction as your partner in life? Do they provide a balanced view of life from others' perspective? If not, it will make them more difficult, though not impossible, to achieve. Discuss your personal goals with your partner or a friend. Discuss business goals with, say, your sales manager. When others are involved in your life, you can easily increase your own motivation to achieve your goals by involving those people. Remember that goals are tools for getting what you want. They should not be seen as your master. *You* are in charge of you.

☆ Align your goals

This means working in an orderly and consistent way. As you work on achieving your first goal, try to contribute to the achievement of your second goal, and so on. As you work on achieving your most important current ambition goal, you can contribute to achieving your three-year, five-year and lifetime goals. As you work on your three-year goals, you can contribute to achieving your five-year and lifetime goals, and so on. Save time and effort by doing things once wherever possible, and never stop focusing on what it is you want to achieve. Make sure that every activity you undertake is contributing to the achievement of all your goals. If you don't do this, each becomes a separate operation requiring more time, attention and detail than if they were in harmony as an overall operation.

☆ Co-operate with others

If others are involved and you need their co-operation and help, ask for it. Most people from whom you want help will be glad to give it, sometimes even at the expense of their own goals. But you need to ask for their help and you can pay no greater compliment than to say, 'I have a goal that is important to me, and I believe you could help me. Would you do this for me, please? I am asking because I admire and respect the way you work and manage your life. I realise you are busy and I wouldn't ask if it wasn't important to me. I don't want you to do anything other than give me your opinions and advice when I need them. I will be happy to return the favour by helping you when you let me know what I can do to help you get what you want out of life. Is that fair enough?'

☆ Visualise what you want, not what you want to avoid

This law of life is critical to your success. At all times focus on what you want until it becomes your dominant thought. We cannot move away from what we *don't* want, we can only move towards what we *do* want. If you visualise what you want to avoid, it becomes your dominant thought and that is what you will surely get. That's why so many of life's negative people get what they least want. They focus on what they fear, rather than on what they desire. Always focus on what you want.

☆ Have a clear image of what you want

Traditional goal-achieving methods and systems don't take account of the power of your mind and the role that visualisation plays in goal achieving. As a result, those methods constantly fail to achieve the goals that are set. If you want to make real progress in achieving your goals, then you must acquire the skill of visualisation and back up that skill with belief in and understanding of the part it plays in achieving your goals. Your ability to succeed in life is linked directly with your ability to understand and employ the skill of visualisation.

Quantify it, time bound it, make sure it is measurable and attainable, for without a clear image of what you want you cannot visualise achieving it. If you can't see it, you can't do it. Nothing in this world is ever achieved before it is first seen on the life screen of a mind. It's impossible for you to accomplish anything without first visualising what it is you want to achieve.

This is a law of life, necessary to all achievement. In every instance, the idea, the image, the visualising, comes first and then plans can be made and activities carried out. Finally, that which was first imagined becomes a reality. No one has put it more simply or effectively than Napoleon when he said, 'Imagination rules the world'. In order to see the part visualisation and having a clear image of what you want plays in the overall concept of achieving your life goals, remember a time when you thought of someone or something, and within a short space of time the event occurred or the person you were thinking of called or wrote, and you said: 'I must be psychic, I was just thinking about you.' Or think of the times a problem has been solved or taken care of shortly after you wrestled with it in your mind. First comes the picture in your mind. With it all things are possible; without the picture, nothing is possible.

☆ Accept responsibility

It's up to you. If you don't do it, it won't get done. It's your goal. It's your responsibility. Once you accept absolute responsibility for your actions and your goals, you will look at life differently. Actions take on a new meaning, options look more real, possibilities unfold that previously you hadn't seen. Everything takes on a new meaning, and you begin to see that you really are in charge of your life and your career. This is one of life's great motivating influences: the power of choice to determine what you want. Before you can exercise this right, it is necessary to be in charge of yourself. For some, this is one of life's greatest struggles, but for those who succeed it is a wonderful victory. That so many choose to ignore or deny their right to self-determination doesn't mean it doesn't exist. It simply means they exercise their right not to act. For reasons known only to them, through their disbelief, they deny themselves all the benefits and opt for accepting what comes their way. It really is a sad choice.

☆ Set a time for accomplishment

I will have it done by . . . [date]. Nothing generates action more effectively than setting a date by which a goal will be accomplished. For example, 'One day, I'll be earning 50 per cent more than I currently earn' requires no immediate action, as against: 'Six months from today I'll be earning 50 per cent more than I currently earn.'

Those who constantly set firm dates by which they will have achieved their goal will be much more successful in most aspects of their life. Whatever the goal, the principle remains the same. Just set a time and do it.

☆ Measure your achievement

It's important to define clearly how you will know when you have successfully accomplished your goal. This means you need to measure what is done. It is also important that the method you use can be understood by others so that they, too, can see when you have accomplished your goals. In many cases, your goals, especially business goals, will involve others. So you need to have a prior agreement with them on the method of measurement to be used in determining when and if you have reached your goals. Without a method of measuring, it is impossible to decide how much progress is being made. Progress needs to be measured constantly. Salespeople can easily measure what they do. The result is what you sell, and so you know day by day how well you are doing and what you have achieved.

☆ Check your progress

Set dates of review. Be constantly checking how you are going, where you are going, and whether you are on time, on plan. If not, why not, and how do you plan to get back on target again? You would rarely if ever go off on a holiday without a destination and a planned time of arrival, yet many people journey through life without such a plan. If you simply take things as they come, it is almost guaranteed that you will achieve less than you could. Always determine your next goal as soon as you achieve your current one.

Knowing your next destination is important to your success. For example, when a ship leaves a port, the captain must plan his course, decide his next port of call and tell someone else of his destination and estimated arrival time. If his ship misses its destination, it's not the fault of the destination. Similarly, when you fail to achieve your goals, it is not the fault of the goals; it's *your* fault. You are the captain of your ship, and when your ship misses its destination it is because your navigation isn't good enough. The purpose of constantly checking against your planned progress is to ensure that if you depart from your plan, you know about it as soon as possible. Finding out too late may mean no possibility of recovery. At best, it will mean unnecessary work.

☆ Write down the 'how to' of your plan

Put your goals in writing. That's the key. Then prepare a detailed activity plan to achieve your goals. You will need a separate activity plan for each goal you set. That's the whole secret. Write your activity plan in detail. Most methods of goal achieving finish at defining what it is you want. The real issue isn't what you want; the real issue is how to get what you want, and that's what we will now deal with.

Until you make a list of the activities you are going to carry out in order to achieve your goal, you are largely only dealing with the 'want to', which is important for without strong desire nothing will be accomplished. However, the difference between success and wishing will depend on whether you take the next step of doing the 'how to'. It is only when you commence the activity, when you start working on how to achieve the goal, that it becomes a reality, and the key issue for you is what activities you must carry out in order to achieve your goal.

You might wonder why you should write down the activities, and the answer is because it is much easier than trying to do it in your head. Let's go through a simple exercise. Let's say you have six goals you want to achieve, and that each of them will require from 10 to 20 activities to ensure that you achieve that particular goal. That means on average you will have to carry out 15 activities for each goal, which over six goals means a total of 90 activities. Each of these activities will need to be carried out in sequence. Some will need to be done by people other than yourself. Many will be mini goals in themselves, and each of the activities, if you are to succeed, will need to be accomplished by a set time. You need to know who is going to do them and in what time order. Here is the important question: do you really believe you can meet all the requirements and handle 90 of these activities in your head? In the 20 years I have been asking this question at my seminar sessions no one has ever indicated they thought they could. So what are the alternatives?

- *Alternative 1:* Be positive. Take the time to write down all the activities which need to be carried out to achieve your goals then, day by day, week by week, month by month, carry out those activities and get the job done. The advantage of doing all this is that the planning has been done first: the thinking through, the relating of events, the sequencing in time and in order. The decisions about who will do best what you want done have been made. This is easier to do when you are looking at a total plan rather than working on a wish list put together under the constant pressure of having to do something about the goal today.

- *Alternative 2:* Don't write your activities down. Do them as they occur to you, taking the chance you will get it right.

Let me ask another question: which of these two alternatives do you think would be the most effective? In 20 years I have not had anyone say that doing it as it came to them, day by day, would be more effective, but I constantly hear this statement: 'If I write them down, some into the months ahead, circumstances will change and I don't want my goals set in concrete. I need to be flexible.' Of course, you need to be flexible. Some goals will need to be altered because things will change and you will change. You may even abandon some of your goals, but you will always be in charge if what you want to change is already written down. When the necessity arises for you to make alterations, you will know why you are changing your plans. You will know what you are moving from and you will know what you are moving towards — *you* will be in charge. Altering goals is no problem; suspending operations temporarily or permanently is no problem. Changing your mind is no problem, because whether you keep track of your goals and activities day by day in your head, or write them down, you will change your mind, events around you will change, and you will have to make allowances and do some activities differently. This will not preclude you from doing that. Experience shows that it is easier and more effective to change a plan that is recorded in detail than it is to make changes on the move.

Ask yourself this question: 'How long is it since I took an hour, two hours, a whole day or a whole week, to sit down and go through this planning operation as if my life really counted?' The answer will probably be that you have never done it. Does that mean you can't succeed without doing it? No, it doesn't. There are more roads to Rome than one. There is more than one way to do things. This is not the only way. But if you want to win more often, win more, do it easier and quicker, be more in charge, and have fewer problems, then plan what it is you want to do and write it down.

If you want to be a peak performer at managing your life and achieving your goals, if you want to do it smarter and not harder, if you want to work less and have more time for yourself and your family, if you want to get more and get it quicker, if you want to do more, if you want to be more, then write your plans down.

Let's assume you have now written down your goals, prioritised them, and decided on the measurement method. It is now time to tackle the payoff section: the 'how to' of achieving your goals. To complete this exercise, focus on one goal. Select the goal that is most important to you. Write down the activities that you consider would be necessary to achieve this goal. Use plenty of paper and take your time. Be creative, and list all the possible activities that will help you to achieve your goal.

Keep asking yourself, 'What if I do this?' and then write down your ideas. Remember: it is important to separate the act of creating from the act of judging. Create first, judge later.

When you have exhausted all the possibilities, then judge the merits of each idea and get rid of those that, in your opinion, will not assist you in achieving your goal. Now you are left with a list of activities which, if implemented in the right order, should help you to reach your goal. Now it is time to follow the procedure set out on the following page so that you can get your goal written down in a format that works. Write your activities on a goal record sheet like the one shown on page 320. While this example is of a product development and sales promotion, it could just as easily have been on writing a book, changing careers, or exhibiting a painting in an exhibition. You are only limited by your imagination.

Once you have created a goal record sheet you really will be making progress. You will have your goal written down. It will be one that really counts for you and will have a priority number of importance

THE 10-STEP GUIDE TO WRITING DOWN YOUR GOALS

1. Define the goal. For example: 'I want to increase my net income by 20 per cent within nine months.' Or 'I want to sell 10 of our new product X within 25 days.'

2. Write it down in the section of the goal record sheet headed 'Goal'. Check that it is written in a valid way — that is, it must be specific, time bounded, measurable and achievable.

3. Give your goal a priority. Write it in the priority box.

4. Write down in the section called 'Measurement method' how you propose to measure your success in attaining your goal.

5. Plan the activities you need to carry out to achieve your goal. Think them through. This is the heart of the method. Stay with it until you know how to achieve your goal.

6. Now start writing down these activities on the goal record sheet. Write them in sequential order, so that you are doing in a logical, planned way what needs to be done to reach your goal.

7. Number your activities from 1. Give each activity a sequential number. Place the number in the column headed 'Item'.

8. Write the activity you plan to do in the column called 'Plan to achieve objective' alongside its activity number.

9. Decide the date by which you will finish each activity. Write the date under the heading 'Proposed completion date'.

10. As you complete each planned activity, sign it off in the column headed 'Date completed by'. Sign it off by entering the date on which you completed the activity and initialling the date. This will be a constant check on whether you are completing your activities as planned.

GOAL RECORD SHEET

Jack Collis   **Period covering next 3 months**

Goal   **Priority 1**
Complete by end of 3 months from today 30 sales of
new product X.

Measurement method
Sales recorded in monthly sales analysis and sales progress sheets.

Item	PLAN TO ACHIEVE OBJECTIVE	Proposed completion date	Date completed by
1	Prepare myself to achieve the objective by:		
	(a) Preparing a first-class sales story	1/8	1/8
	(b) Preparing a first-class visual to back up my sales story	3/8	2/8
	(c) Learning the answers to likely objections	5/8	5/8
	(d) Seeking help from a top salesperson and the sales manager	7/8	6/8
2	Prepare a list of prospects to whom I can make an offer.		
	(a) Go through my current clients who will be interested in this product. Rate them on a scale of 1–10	10/8	10/8
	(b) Prepare a list of current clients who may be interested in this product. Rate them on a scale of 1–10	10/8	10/8
	(c) Make a list of my current clients who could help me with referred leads. Rate them on a scale of 1–10	10/8	11/8
	(d) Identify current business classifications that could be interested in this product. Rate them on a scale of 1–10	10/8	11/8
	(e) Prepare a list of 50 prospects from other sources. Rate them on a scale of 1–10	11/8	11/8

	(f) Tie my activity into my company advertising to get additional prospects if possible. Rate them on a scale of 1–10	11/8	11/8	✍
3	Consolidate my list from all sources. Check all details are complete (source of prospect, address, contact numbers, etc.). Rate them on a scale of 1–10	11/8	12/8	✍
4	Prepare a work plan.	12/8	12/8	✍
	(a) How many calls will I make each day?	12/8	12/8	✍
	(b) Will they be by letter, phone or face-to-face?	12/8	12/8	✍
	(c) Prepare a story to suit each approach.	12/8	13/8	✍
	(d) Learn the answers to the most likely objections to an interview.	12/8	13/8	✍
5	Make the calls.	13/8	13/8	✍
6	Keep detailed records of my results.	(dates progress on daily basis)		
7	Review my progress weekly.			
8	If necessary seek prospects from other sources.			
DON'T WALK, DON'T RUN, GALLOP!				

and a method for measuring the successful completion of the goal. You now have a list of activities designed to successfully achieve your goal. All that remains to be done is to do the same for each of the goals you have decided are important to you. Fill out a separate record sheet for each goal, and at the end of the entire operation place the sheets in a folder in order of priority. You now have a game plan for life.

Above is an example of a completed goal record sheet which you can use as a guide to lay out your own sheet. The example used in the goal record sheet is a simple and straightforward real-life exercise based on logical sequence and creative thinking, although item 1 in the list was a creative exercise and required a separate goal record sheet of its own. The activities on your goal record sheet should appear in a logical order and should be signed off as you complete them.

You don't have to work on one item or goal at a time. Sometimes it is possible to do many of your activities at the one time. Go for it! You have the plan, now all that is needed is the desire to see it happen. Select your 'A.1' goal and work on it now.

Unfortunately, this is where most game plans finish: on paper, relegated to the office drawer, or forgotten amongst the problems of the day and it's back to crisis management. What you need now is a daily list, a 'to do' list, to make sure that your daily activity plan is carried through and completed by the date you have set.

Almost everyone I know who achieves great effectiveness in their life uses a 'to do' list in one form or another. Some use a card, some a diary system, but the principle remains the same. In my view, the most effective way is to write on the 'to do' list only those things that have a high priority today and might not get done unless you give them special attention. When preparing your list, don't forget your long-term goals. Their activities have to be put on the list well in advance of them becoming a necessity. This is what planning is all about.

Whether you will ever successfully carry out all the activities you have defined will be decided by the extent of your desire to achieve your dream. The main factor in motivation is desire. When you desire, above everything else, to achieve a particular goal or dream, then that desire will push your motivation towards working and doing what needs to be done to ensure that you achieve the goal. Nothing will be too difficult. You will try and try again until you achieve success. Desire is a key motivator. Go for it!

CHAPTER 27

MANAGING
YOUR TERRITORY

*Managing a territory is a lot like farming.
The better you sow the better you reap, but it
helps to know what to sow, where to sow it
and when to reap.*

THIS CHAPTER WON'T tell you how you should manage your territory in a specific way. It will simply bring to your attention a number of well-proven principles which can make your work easier and more productive. A sound knowledge of your territory is necessary for effective planning. Some of the key things you need to know about your territory are:

◆ Its geographic makeup.
◆ The number and location of your customers.
◆ The number and location of prospects you would like as customers.
◆ The dollar value of the sales you must raise from this territory.
◆ The dollar value of your present customers.
◆ The names and locations of your competitors and who represents them in your territory.
◆ Anything else that will be of value to you in terms of local knowledge, especially about what you sell.

◆ Any time factors that have to do with buying patterns. These may be seasonal or organisational. For example, if you sell school supplies, the main buying times will occur at certain times of the year.

When all this information is available, you can plan to get the best value for your time by way of productive work. It is acknowledged that country territories are usually more geographically oriented, while city territories are more customer or product based. However, the challenge for you is to organise your sales activities in a way that will be the most productive for you and your company.

DEVELOPING A REGULAR CALL PATTERN

Divide your territory into five parts, and, if possible, work in a different part each day. This will spread your activities and your influence over a large area and get people talking about you. This in turn will give your competitors the impression that you are very active, while also giving you the opportunity to monitor their activities. You may say, 'But I have to go where the work or prospects are.' I agree. You may say, 'I'm at the mercy of my customers. I can't regiment myself. If they call, I have to respond.' I agree. However, unless you want your life to become a continual episode of chaos and uncertainty, you should try to organise and manage your territory in a disciplined way.

If you divide your territory into workable parts, it makes it possible to ensure that you are seen in most parts on a regular basis. It also means you can develop a regular call pattern which gives your customers some flexibility in dealing with matters that require your attention. If they expect you tomorrow, they will be less likely to insist that you call today.

Develop key contacts throughout your territory, so that you can refer to them if you need a testimony about your work or your company.

Place a map of your territory on a wall in your office and mark the locations of your customers with coloured pins. Identify key customers and show sales values by using different colours. It won't be long before you see a pattern emerging as to your most valuable customers and the most productive parts of your territory. This method is also effective for showing rates of conversion of competitor's customers to your customers by location, as well as for giving life to other statistics.

USING YOUR TIME EFFECTIVELY

It isn't always easy to understand precisely what is happening in your territory, but good records intelligently used will improve your chances. If you can't be seen in all parts of your territory on a regular basis, you need to consider a phone campaign for those parts that are not easy to get to. If the phone isn't practical, then try direct mail. Otherwise, you have to be content with those prospects and customers you can see in person. See first those people who give you the greatest chance of improving your productivity. The 80/20 rule is always at work: 20 per cent of your customers will make up 80 per cent of your sales. They are easily identified and should get most of your attention. Twenty per cent of your customers will make 80 per cent of the complaints, and these customers are not always your top 20 per cent, but they are important because if they are not dealt with they become your bad-news brigade. If you solve their problems, they generally become more loyal than those who don't complain.

Reduce your travelling time wherever possible. The less time you spend travelling each day is a bonus, as long as you can use that time in asking prospects and customers to buy what you sell. Don't do administration in A-class selling time, and don't let the mail dictate your life; stick to your work plan. Only change it if it is absolutely imperative. Learn to say 'Later, not now', or otherwise it's goodbye to planning.

Organise next week before you have finished the current week. Try to set aside a time at the end of the current week to prepare all your presentations for next week. Work your ratios to get your sales. It is important to understand that your territory, apart from being a geographic area in which you work, is really you. Your territory, your activity, your planning and decision-making all reflect your thinking in terms of what is important and productive at any given time. If you finish with a disorganised, chaotic, low-producing territory, it is probably because that is the way you approach the matter of territory management. There is no territory in reality. There is only you. How well you organise, administer and farm it will decide how good the territory is. This isn't as easy to do as it might seem. I know only too well that there are highs and lows, but if you organise your territory on the basis of sound planning, then the lows will be fewer, the highs will be bigger and occur more often, and the payoff will be tremendous. In the end, all of this is a reflection of you — how you think and what you believe in — and it will demonstrate quite clearly what you are willing to do about getting what you want.

MARKET SEGMENTATION

You don't have to become a specialist in market segmentation. It is only necessary to be able to match your selling performance against your results in each of your segmented markets.

Market segmentation starts with your own clients. Have a clear understanding of who you currently do business with and who else you want to do business with. Go back through your records and classify your business into broad markets. They could be consumer markets or industrial markets, or both, depending on what you sell. Here are some broad market groups:

- Manufacturing
- Agriculture
- Financial services
- Health care
- Education
- Tourism
- Real estate
- Computers.

Now break down these broad markets into small segmented groups. For example, health care is a broad market which can be broken down into perhaps 50-plus subgroups. It is in the subgroups that you will find the opportunities.

The health care market could be divided into doctors — both general practitioners and specialists — working in private practice or in organisations such as hospitals, clinics and health resorts, as well as everyone else involved in health care. The list is vast.

By segmenting your market, you may discover that your results are perfectly matched to your territory or that, say, doctors make up 20 per cent of the total health care market in your territory, but you only get 7 per cent of your business from that market segment. There may be very good reasons why this is so, but you need to examine the result and make sure you are getting your share of the business.

Now you know where you have been working. Each market or segment should be shown as a percentage of your total production. Get your office to supply you with the same information about your territory population. This information is readily available from a number of sources and is based on the last available census reports.

APASCO is a company that specialises in market information based on geographical location and will provide the information according to postcodes, income, etc. You should have no real difficulty in identifying the size and makeup of the markets in which you are working.

Now match your percentages against your territory percentages and you will have a clear picture of whether the market segments you are targeting are increasing or declining in potential.

Once you are satisfied that you are getting your share from the markets in which you are operating, you need to look for opportunities in other major segments of the market. Match your product or service to a group you consider could use what you sell and decide if you should enter that market.

The only way to improve your performance is to know what you are doing, and the best way to do that is to constantly analyse your sales ratios to ensure that your selling performance is improving. Then test your production against the market segments to see if you are getting your share of the available business in your territory.

The easiest way to improve is to learn from past performance, but many people feel they don't have the time to analyse and learn from their mistakes or successes. In fact, very little time is needed to really understand one's business.

The marketplace is getting busier and more competitive. The age of the specialist is here, the bonanza will go to those who are prepared to handle it. If you know your sales and market statistics, you will be in a position to put together an effective plan which, if you work it, will almost guarantee that you will get the payoff.

Do you really believe that your best chance is just to work hard and hope it all turns out OK? School is never out for the professional. Never stop learning how to be better at selling. Ratios and statistics are not your master, they are your slave. Get excited about improving — it's for your benefit.

CHAPTER 28

CREATING
WEALTH

Wealth is a good servant,
but a very bad mistress.
ANON.

THE OBJECTIVE OF this chapter is not to spell out in detail how to become wealthy, although I will outline a plan of action and some concepts and principles of how and what you can do to create wealth. Why do I consider this to be of sufficient importance to include it in this book? The answer is that I believe we can reach financial independence if we consistently follow some simple wealth-creation principles. Another reason is that I believe each of us needs to become financially independent of the organisation for which we work so that we work for it because we *want* to, not because we need the money. This also encompasses the freedom to stop work any time we wish because we are financially independent.

Personal freedom is an objective I achieved many years before I became a full-time speaker and author. Personal freedom is generally dependent on the degree of financial independence we have achieved. There is also the matter of setting an example. If our work is to sell a product or service that can make other people rich, then we should also be rich. If we aren't, then it is because we didn't set out with an organised plan to create wealth.

WEALTH CREATION CONCEPTS

Here are some concepts and principles that, if applied to your life in a consistent and committed way, will enable you to create wealth.

The concepts are:

◆ You'll earn a fortune.
◆ A man or woman or a dollar at work.

The way to create money in your life is by working for it. Work equals money, and the higher the quality of the work you do the more you will be paid to do it. So the first principle of wealth creation is: *improve your abilities so that you will be paid more.* If you constantly improve your abilities and get paid more, you will have a constantly increasing amount of money to put towards wealth creation. Getting lucky is not much of an option. Winning the lottery would be wonderful, so buy a ticket each week and give yourself a chance, but the reality for most of us will be to exchange our labour for money. Then we save money and put it to work for us.

The second principle in wealth creation is: *pay yourself first.* Most people start out by looking for a certain standard of living. In order to achieve it, they pay their bills and then try to save what is left. In most cases, however, there is little or nothing left. As people's abilities and income increase, so does their standard of living and so little or nothing is left to add to savings. The unpalatable option of giving up something now for a greater reward in the future then has to be considered. Most people decline this option and so opportunities are lost.

The principle of pay yourself first is simple to execute and faultless in design. Set an amount that you want to save in order to start creating wealth in your life. It doesn't have to be a large amount, just enough to get you started. Once the start is made, it won't be long before you find ways to save more in order to get the benefits sooner. As soon as you have set your goal and made a plan to achieve it, you will find that you have a new mindset which will drive you towards your goal of creating wealth in your life.

You'll earn a fortune

In Chapter 20 I said that the concept of 'You'll earn a fortune' is powerful because it is about life. It's true: you *will* earn a fortune. The critical issue, however, is how much of it you will have left when the time comes to stop working. Too few people reach total financial independence, not because they didn't earn the money, but because they didn't have a plan for creating wealth.

Accept that you will earn a fortune. Some of you may already have earned your fortune; others may just be starting out on their working career. All of you are capable of earning a fortune; only the size of the fortune and the perception of 'enough' will differ. For some $1 million is enough; others won't be satisfied with $10 million. You must decide for yourself what is enough — after all, it's your fortune.

If you have doubts about your ability to earn a fortune, try this calculation on yourself. If a person aged 30 who is currently earning $30 000 per annum never gets a pay rise, and inflation continues to run at around five per cent, then that $30 000 will grow to $60 000 by the time they are 45 and to $120 000 by age 60. Their total earnings will grow to around $2.2 million. If we allow for pay increases due to promotions or a greater ability to earn, the total will reach $3 million plus. When we consider that most families are two-income families, you can add another $500 000. Despite inflation, there will be dollars to spare. The real reason that much of our wealth escapes us is that we rarely take the time to think the whole matter through and establish plans and priorities for creating wealth in our life.

A man or woman at work

The only way we can earn money, other than by having our dollars at work for us, is through our own endeavours. The popular myth is that time is money. This is only true if the time is spent working. Once we accept this, we are in a better situation to make plans and set priorities.

Dollars at work

If you never put dollars to work to earn money, your chances of creating real wealth are poor. Here is some good advice: get yourself and your family a good insurance protection plan before you do anything else. It makes no sense to try and build wealth before you safeguard what you already have. There is no future in playing dice with death. One option for putting dollars to work is to deposit money in the best interest-earning fund you can find that has a low risk factor, such as a bank cash management fund. Select a short term, say one or two years, so that you have access to your investment. Short-term, get rich quick schemes are OK if you can afford the risk. It isn't difficult to get rich over the long term. The effect of compound interest working in your favour will get you there over the long haul. The problem is that the desire to get rich quick outweighs the certainty of the long term, and the short term wins with the result that one of two things happens. Either people don't have the lump sum needed to invest in get rich quick plans, so they don't do anything. They want the rewards now, not when they are too old to enjoy them (which is actually when they may most need them), so they live for today and leave the future to look after itself. Or they raise the necessary lump sum but suffer losses because the risks are many and varied. For these people, it's back to square one, but in worse financial shape than before they began their investment program.

As your investment in your cash management fund grows, take some of this money and invest it in shares. Again, follow the pattern of low risk when selecting shares. Discuss your needs with a sharebroker who can give you advice on what to buy that will meet your criteria of low risk and the best returns. As most shares will pay dividends as well as having the prospect of capital gain, select those that are fully franked to gain tax advantages and reinvest your dividends by buying more shares. You may wish to consult a financial adviser who can help you to devise an overall plan with the objective of maximising your options in terms of tax and other government benefits. The laws affecting these options are complex and constantly changing, so expert advice is necessary.

The returns from shares, whether by way of direct purchase or through a managed fund, generally outperform other types of investments, but it is advisable to spread the risk and not have all your funds in one type of investment. While I write this chapter I am looking at a comparison of different investments over the last 12 years. It shows that Australian shares returned an average of 15.3 per cent compound over that term, which means that had you been following the advice given above, you would have doubled your money in 4.7 years. Over that 12-year term, if you had invested $10 000 it would have grown to approximately $55 000. If the return of 15.3 per cent had stayed constant over the next 4.7 years, your $55 000 would have doubled to $110 000, which means you would have been on your way to making real progress after only 17 years. From then on your progress would have been dramatic and your options would have expanded because you would have had a much larger fund with which to explore those options.

Once your investment fund starts to grow, however, so will the desire to spend it now. Resist the desire unless it is a life or death emergency. Remember: the $10 000 initial investment that has turned into $110 000 in 17 years will, if you continue investing at 15.3 per cent, turn into $1 million in 15 years. In 32 years, your $10 000 will have grown into $1 million. Imagine how quickly you would have reached your target if you had sent a few more thousand dollars each year on a journey of earning your wealth. Instead of 32 years, it could have been 20 years. You won't always get this high a return, and sometimes you will get more. But whatever you get from however you invest will be a fantastic return on doing nothing.

The $10 000 you frittered away last year is not just $10 000; it is also the $110 000 it could have been in 17 years and the $1 million it would have become in 32 years. Every time you spend a dollar on anything, it could have been $100 down the track. Creating wealth is about work. It means working at making decisions and carrying out your plans.

CONCLUSION

The objective of this chapter is not to discourage you from living now. It is to help you see that becoming wealthy is within the grasp of most of us if we are willing to trade off a little of today in return for a great deal more in the future. All our tomorrows become today, and each today is as sweet as any other. You may be a little older, perhaps a little wiser, and you will probably think differently, but the day will be just as precious, exciting and wonderful as any other. It is a fallacy to think that only the days of your youth are exciting and wonderful. Perhaps one of the big differences is that you will have created wealth, which may enable you to do many enjoyable and interesting things which otherwise would not have been possible.

The impact on our self-esteem of successfully creating wealth is very positive. We live in a society that values material possessions, and as a result when we accumulate what society as a group values, the judgment of being successful flows to us. While there are those who focus on the quality of life to the exclusion of wealth, there is no reason to believe that wealth in itself is a problem or that quality of life excludes the possession of wealth. Logic says that as long as wealth does not possess us and that we possess it, then wealth should be capable of improving the quality of our life.

As you progress in your career of selling, the quality of your thinking and the value of your contribution to your prospects and customers will determine much of their perception of you. That perception will be based not only on your contribution, but also on the confidence you display in your own ability not only to do your work to a world-class standard, but also to achieve success in the life you live. Your confidence will grow enormously as you create wealth in your life, not only in financial terms but also in a maturity of vision based on self-acceptance that you have made it and that you are by any measure a person of value.

It is my pleasure to provide you with an interview I recently conducted with David Koch especially for this book. David is one of our foremost media financial commentators. His views on financial and business matters are heard and read daily by hundreds of thousands of Australians. He is a very successful author and a major figure in the business world. I asked him about creating wealth in our lives.

◆

JC: David, in your opinion, what is the most important issue for people who want to create wealth in their life? What should they do first?

DK: The most important issue, Jack, is letting time work for you. The sooner you start creating wealth the easier it will be, and if you start doing it in a constant manner over a long period of time you will always succeed. The first step is to start thinking about creating wealth and about what you want your money to do.

The second step is to pay off your debts — it's the simplest form of wealth creation. Pay off all your high-interest debts because no matter where you invest you won't earn as much as you are paying for your mortgage, credit cards and the like. Why go out and invest money when you have 10.5 per cent mortgage? That invested money will have to earn you at least 17.5 per cent return each year to match what you would save by simply paying off the principal of your mortgage, which, by the way, doesn't incur capital gains tax.

The third step is to look at how you are paid and whether you are paying tax effectively. For example, if you can live on current remuneration and are offered extras by way of incentive bonuses, why not take those bonuses in your superannuation? Superannuation is still one of the most tax-effective and, from a personal point of view, one of the most rewarding ways to save and create wealth. It has the added advantage that you don't get it until you retire so it is a disciplined way to create wealth in the future. The current salary sacrifice is certainly worth the effort.

The fourth critical issue in creating wealth is to invest for the medium and long term in areas that are popular at the time. It is important to understand that investment markets run in cycles — they will have their boom periods and their bust periods. The people who create wealth most effectively are those who take advantage of the busts. At such times they don't panic or run with the herd; instead they see a bust as a buying opportunity. A study by IPAC Research looked at two investors who invested $10 000 a year over a 10-year period. They divided the investment market into 12 categories: for example, Australian shares, property and international shares, and so on. The first investor invested $10 000 a year in the previous year's best-performing investment sector; the second invested $10 000 a year in the previous year's worst-performing sector. The second investor finished up with triple the amount of wealth of the first investor. So, you see, investing successfully is a matter of understanding how investment cycles work and taking advantage of the downturns.

JC: David, have you any further advice?

DK: I think that salespeople work in a volatile industry in which normal remuneration can vary quite a bit, particularly if you work on a commission basis. The sales profession is higher risk than many other professions and, for that reason, you should be more conservative in your investments. If you are in a safe sales job and have a constant income, you can take more chances. However you probably don't get any of those large increases in income which are possible for salespeople. During a good year, the income of an excellent salesperson can go through the roof! My advice to salespeople during those good years is to invest their increased earnings in conservative investments because their income may fluctuate. The best rule to follow is: The more volatile your income the more conservative your investments. If you have an income which is subject to unpredictable increases or decreases, don't increase your risks by investing in unstable investments.

There is absolutely no magic to building wealth, it is all about creating assets over the long term and creating them slowly. Myths of fortunes being made overnight because someone's next-door neighbour had a nephew who was a geologist in the backblocks of Western Australia and passed on information of another Poseidon are few and far between. If you want to create long-lasting wealth follow the example of those who accumulate wealth slowly and consistently and don't lead extravagant lifestyles. The most successful people are those who balance their lifestyle to their income.

Jack, my last piece of advice to your readers is this: if you want to create more wealth in your life then do it. Don't think about it; *do it.*

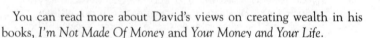

You can read more about David's views on creating wealth in his books, *I'm Not Made Of Money* and *Your Money and Your Life.*

PART 3

REACHING

YOUR POTENTIAL

CHAPTER 29

MAKING PERSONAL PROGRESS

by Dr Alec Dempster

THE REWARDS OF overcoming your personal barriers are business and material success and, more importantly, improvements in your competency, self-esteem and confidence. This will bring you enormous benefits in every facet of your life — your personal experience will be enriched and you will enjoy greater contentment and happiness.

You may be one of many who is not looking for substantial material or financial success, but is seeking a moderate lifestyle while placing priority on meeting responsibilities and living a productive, creative and meaningful life. You must ultimately define your purpose in life for yourself. There are countless avenues for expressing yourself in life, so you must define the type of successes you are looking for and what you think will bring you the happiness you want.

SETTING YOUR GOALS

Start with some perspective. There is a worldwide myth that money brings happiness, but you can be rich and unhappy at the same time. For many of us financial security is psychologically very important, even if it is a form of security that can be easily lost. Each of us needs to figure out for our own peace of mind where we are truly at on this issue. The good news is we are free to choose and then to use the power of our mind to pursue these goals.

Many self-help gurus promise you can always have whatever you want in life if you go about it the right way. In my view, many unpredictable circumstances or difficulties often come into play and unexpectedly alter your direction. A more realistic view of life is that you will most likely succeed at your goals if you have the right approach. Certainly if you have a positive approach you will end up achieving some positive outcome, even if it is unexpectedly different from what you planned. But if your approach is laden with negatives you will create a negative future for yourself that you will not enjoy.

If you want to overcome the negatives in your life and achieve positive outcomes you do have to be careful. After clearly setting your goals you must constantly observe your behaviour and progress. At intervals you need to re-evaluate your goals and refocus your direction. You must remain aware *in the present* of what you are doing and where you are heading. You cannot afford to worry too much about the past or the future. It is the effort you make *today*, not tomorrow that counts. In reality, you only have today in which to make your effort. You also need to know how to keep your life simple and avoid too many complexities which can be crippling in the time, effort and distraction they cause you. Keep the problems in your life to a minimum.

This chapter is about overcoming personal limitations, including the apparently complex psychological barriers you experience in yourself and others. Often the psychological factors that hold you back may seem complex, but they are not too difficult to understand if you give them careful consideration.

OVERCOMING PERSONAL LIMITATIONS

Overcoming personal limitations in your life depends on simple fundamentals. You need to learn to live new habits, new attitudes and values, new methods of emotional expression and control. Your path in life will then become one of maturing and progressing. You need to decide whether you are going to make your life active or passive in this regard, because this decision can substantially determine your fate. Unfortunately many adults, although they project a sophisticated facade, are struggling with the same amount of anger, stress and negativity as they did when they were children. They may pay lip-service to life values which they theoretically believe in, but in practice they haven't substantially changed their body–mind behaviours. They have not forgiven or forgotten the past or fully committed to a new way of being.

If you are sincerely interested in overcoming personal limitations, you need to understand the simple basics. These basics — the real barriers to an individual's success — are a constellation of common, negative, personal factors. These negative factors are inter-related and reinforce one another. They are:

◆ fear
◆ guilt
◆ anger
◆ impatience
◆ greed
◆ selfishness
◆ insensitivity to others
◆ low self-esteem
◆ lack of belief in oneself
◆ lack of belief in the possibilities of life (faith), energy, concen-tration, self-discipline, consistency, honesty, trust, mature detach-ment, responsibility; and
◆ lack of knowledge.

These are central difficulties that you may find in your life or in other people's lives. They are key barriers to all areas of achieve-ment — interpersonal relationships, financial management, creating positive visions and courage or doing successful business.

There are many guide books on personal development in bookstores today. They emphasise affirmations, positive attitudes and changing the way you think. Yet sometimes these books encourage optimism while not realistically addressing the work you need to put in to understand the negative factors or barriers within you. You do need to understand how your inner barriers operate. The knowledge presented here will help you break through these barriers.

DEEPENING YOUR SELF-KNOWLEDGE

This chapter explores how some of the basic factors mentioned operate as barriers to your effectiveness. By addressing these factors in yourself you will improve your abilities in sales work and in every other aspect of your life. By gradually overcoming them you will experience a feeling of being set free from the hassles of life. You will begin to sense inwardly that you are on a solid, realistic path to personal success. Your self-esteem, attitudes and personality are all closely related. Everybody has some inner personal limitations. The conflicts, worries or concerns you create within yourself reflect the level of maturity you have reached. Mastering yourself is the critical issue.

Techniques are fundamentally important in selling or any other occupation, and learning improved sales techniques may be essential for you. But success in life's endeavours does not flow just from mastering techniques. Techniques are only part of what it takes for success. A technique is only as good as the way you master and apply it in your own way. You probably realised this long ago, yet all too easily you can lose perspective in a busy life. In the final analysis the total person you are is the ultimate foundation of your achievements. So deepening your personal knowledge is vital. This chapter discusses many important personal issues that influence your performance. Some of these are:

◆ habits and personality
◆ fears and resistances
◆ conscious and unconscious mental processes
◆ low self-esteem
◆ concentration, awareness and vitality
◆ a clear focus in life and in work

Embrace this knowledge, use your common sense, use ordinary language rather than technical jargon, and you will progress.

HABITS AND PERSONALITY

Personality is not generally well-understood, but most people intuitively know that poorly-adjusted personality habits will 'cause' repetitive difficulties for them. Many people ask me about personality. It is artificial, and ultimately impossible, to separately consider self-esteem, attitudes, habitual inner conflicts or behavioural obstacles without reference to the total package that is your personality. Each of these is a different angle on interdependent parts of your nature. 'Personality' refers to the total collection of these parts that comprise the unique person you are. 'Character' refers to moral aspects of your personality. The importance of your 'morality' is widely under-rated, as your moral beliefs — that is, the standards or values you believe in regarding behaviour — play a very large part in directing your own behaviour.

Personality has been defined in many different ways by psychologists, but a widely-accepted definition is 'deeply ingrained habits of perceiving, thinking and acting in relation to oneself, others and the world, usually present since early adulthood'. The behavioural habits that form your personality are mostly deeply ingrained since childhood. They are often called 'traits', and many common traits have been described — 'introvert' and 'extrovert' are well-known examples. A description of a person's personality traits always remains imprecise, however, and although personality testing is useful it is not 100 per cent reliable.

Personality for you, like for many others, may be a sensitive, threatening topic. This is because you, like most people, probably feel a little insecure about yourself in some situations and know you have weaknesses. Naturally you may be cautious about having personal weaknesses exposed — it is not only embarrassing, but opens up the possibility of your weaknesses being exploited. This is why so many people find organisational psychology tests threatening. Personality testing often seems an invasion of privacy. By revealing possible weaknesses, such testing potentially threatens your ability to secure or direct your own career. Also you know that the tests won't be collecting all the facts about yourself.

Your own personality has fairly fixed basic characteristics, although aspects of it will change slightly as you mature. This maturing means that your abilities will become more integrated into an overall capacity to be more stable, to cope better and be more effective in what you choose to do in life. On the other hand, destructive habits will, sooner or later, cause disintegration of your personality. To gain maturity and achieve success in life you must understand your own particular personality traits, both strengths and weaknesses, and gradually modify these. Specific personality issues such as habitual attitudes, amount of fear or self-discipline will be discussed later in the chapter.

Any habitual or characteristic difficulties you have with sales may reflect a particular personal trait which misguides your thinking and actions in certain situations. In other words, your goals, and your habitual method of attaining them are not compatible. You may need to find the solution by examining your personality behaviour patterns. You may need to get professional advice. This problem with one or two traits expressing themselves as repeated patterns of failure or difficulty might only be a minor matter. Perhaps it arises only in special situations and not in other aspects of your usual life. But carefully looking at yourself to improve the minor problems of your life can greatly benefit you. Seriously pursue this self-improvement and you will discover, like many others, the untapped potential you really have.

COMMON PATTERNS OF DIFFICULTY IN SALESPEOPLE

Behavioural patterns in salespeople reflect their personality, including their limitations. Catchy, humorous descriptions such as 'creatives', 'logicians', 'nice-guys', 'heavies', 'naturals' 'senior-statesmen', 'comfort-zoners' and 'hard-workers' provided by Tony Iozzi (in *You Can Sell Anything*, Business & Professional Publishing, Sydney, 1995) are sometimes useful. If you are more serious, then explore beyond these simple concepts to see how your behavioural patterns relate to the basic psychological factors of self-esteem, self-awareness, determination, fears, worries, selfishness, inner conflicts and your particular basic habits and attitudes.

The three common patterns of difficulty for salespeople identified by Jack Collis are:

1. Fear
2. Resistance
3. Reluctance

He attaches great importance to each of these basic patterns, which include various subcategories:

◆ fear of rejection
◆ fear of failure (including possible punishment)
◆ fear of success (including fear of raised quotas or extra pressure)
◆ fear of being seen to be pushy

- ◆ resistance to setting and achieving objectives
- ◆ resistance to training and self-development
- ◆ resistance to getting organised and reporting on progress
- ◆ call reluctance (including low self-esteem)

I have added a fourth pattern: stress.

Any thoughtful sales professional will benefit by carefully examining these four basic areas of difficulty.

CAUSES OF THESE DIFFICULTIES

Are you pretending you're 'OK'? It is not surprising that we often do not fully admit that we have these sorts of difficulties — we are often too embarrassed, or too frightened to address them honestly and openly. Yet psychological insecurities occur one way or another in all of us with various situations in business and personal life. When you feel a reluctance about something in your work you need to examine it carefully, or talk about it with someone to find out what it really means. Then you can decide if it is a problem you ought to fix.

It is important to realise that a single simple factor is rarely sufficient to cause any of these persistent patterns of difficulty. Such patterns usually result from a combination of various experiences. Sometimes one or two particularly bad experiences may have provoked a particular fear in a person who was already inwardly predisposed to react this way. For example, a person who has been subject to even minor physical abuse as a child can have a particular sensitivity to aggression and violence. Encountering aggressive people, perhaps in a particular industry, may lead to difficulty with sales calls in general but especially calls to that specific industry.

Identifying precise incidents and sequences of events that might have caused your difficulties is interesting, but not always necessary or worthwhile. Often, you need to avoid navel-gazing and focus on the present to modify your habits and actions. On the other hand, making links between the present triggers of your responses and the past events which sensitised you can be helpful. This can be important in assisting people who are deeply emotionally distressed. The discovery and release of your suppressed feelings can sometimes enable you to tackle more directly the conflicts within you. During the process of self-discovery the experience of a positive relationship with a support person can contribute greatly to your gaining of confidence. This can often be more valuable than discovering explanations of your past.

TACKLING FEAR, RESISTANCE, RELUCTANCE AND STRESS

It is a pity that many people lack the inspiration and motivation in their lives to really tackle personal issues. I have often seen such people. The obstacle can be laziness, fear, lack of energy, poor concentration or lack of psychological insight. All too often, lack of self-belief is the close companion of these factors. This is the everyday reality, reflecting the state of mind of many. You have to decide if this will be you too, or will you really persist with the progress you might wish to make?

It is extremely important to try to understand your personal barriers or limitations in your work, yet many people never take up these challenges seriously. Sales difficulties are of varied seriousness, but here we are really talking about the difficulties of the 'average' person. If you are like the average person then you have various fears, resistances, reluctances and stress, and these may become evident when facing the various steps required in selling. Yet your fears and resistances are usually subtle, ingrained and complex, not simple and obvious.

Self-development solutions are not a 'piece of cake'. If they were, very few people would be troubled by difficulties! The majority of sales people have occasional confidence difficulties because that is the way most of us are. It is rare to 'get it all together' in your work or private life and keep it that way! But you will always lack confidence and will-power if you are without a strong personal philosophy that prizes effort, self-improvement and purpose in life. The following personal history shows what can be achieved when you truly commit yourself to overcoming your fears.

Personal history: Frank

Frank, a 24-year-old university graduate, gained work in a bookshop as a salesperson after suffering severe psychological depression two years before. His depression was originally precipitated by a combination of lack of direction in life, the end of a six-year relationship with a girlfriend and excessive use of marijuana. His failure to cope caused him to cease his postgraduate studies and feel he was destined for a life of inferiority and inadequacy. He decided to stop aiming for fulfilment in life, and his belief in his lack of future was reinforced by bitterness at events in his childhood where he felt he had been badly treated.

After some counselling Frank began to realise that perhaps he had reached a false conclusion about himself and decided that he would risk trying again to aspire for success in life. This involved the frightening task of facing his fears of failing again. He changed to a job which involved working more closely with his employer, requiring him to practise new skills of personally asserting himself with both his employer and clients. Initially it was very difficult and stressful, but, to his surprise, he succeeded in gaining his employer's respect as he continued to apply the advice given to him during counselling. Success boosted his confidence to a such degree that within two years he obtained a highly sought-after position in another industry, against interstate candidates, which involved learning to teach self-confidence to others. He wrote to me saying that he now realised that he had been mistaken. His experience proved to him that it was true that you can overcome major fears. Frank now understood fear as something he created within his own mind and then believed in, regardless of the realities of his prospects.

OVERCOMING FEARS

Fears are self-created imaginations which make negative associations of ideas. Fear is your projection about the future in your imagination. Fear is possible because of ignorance — if you don't know the future, you might fear it because you are not sure whether you will like it. You might imagine or believe the future will be bad, that you won't get or keep what you want. People live in fear in the present, but their fear is about what they think will be the outcome in the next few minutes, hours or years. Unless we have an overwhelming attitude of faith that we are capable of accepting events, we tend to fear the future and what it will bring.

For a mature person, fear is unhelpful. It causes nervous system and bodily changes, psychological anxiety and, eventually, ill-health. The psychological processes of fear actually create a bad future — your fear can easily lead you into disastrous self-fulfilling prophecies. Consider the case of the man called in to see his boss. Assuming the worst, believing his fears had come true and that he was to be dismissed, he abused the boss and precipitated dismissal, even though the boss hadn't originally planned to dismiss him! You've seen it in TV sitcoms, yet unfortunately our behaviour in life is frequently similar to a sitcom, but in a less obvious way. We act according to our beliefs. We often don't succeed because we don't believe we can, and therefore don't act as if we *will* succeed. Are you doing this in sales? Is your thinking strongly dominated by your fears?

It is rare to find someone who is basically fearless. Your own fears about yourself and your successes in life may seem mild in comparison to the fears that were present in Frank's personal history, yet even our mild fears can be troublesome and cause us unpredictable difficulties. Fear leads to avoidance behaviour, which could be affecting your sales work. Fear mostly arises from memories and wishes within our subconscious mind and for much of the time we are not really conscious of our subtle fears, except when we are in a serious situation. You need time and patience to work on modifying the deeper roots of your fear. You must use your conscious mind to reprogram your unconscious or automatic thoughts.

Fear of rejection

Every salesperson knows that rejection and negative judgements by others is a part of selling and a part of life. You need to accept that this is so, and not let it convince you that you are a failure. Sometimes you might feel that you are not good enough at present, and have trouble comfortably accepting your limitations. Feeling unsure of your social competence, your personal maturity and your understanding of others can lead you to fear of rejection, which can develop into a major problem. A vicious cycle of deteriorating confidence and performance can develop, so that, eventually, you regularly bring to yourself, by your lack of confidence, the rejection you fear from others.

Lack of self-understanding can lead you to believe yourself to be inadequate or inferior. Your lack of confidence and negative judgements cause you to lose perspective and to overlook the fact that many other people have similar difficulties. You develop the habit of projecting scenarios of being rejected in your imagination and in your actions. This fear greatly expands if you really want to be liked personally by prospects in your search for sales success. It only needs a few rejection experiences to make you begin to fear that you may not achieve your precious dreams, or even a basic living.

When you feel personal rejection you are certainly not coping well. When you respond to apparent rejection from others by feeling upset and rejected you are really rejecting yourself. Although the prospect may be very 'rejecting' (sometimes as a clever strategy), you do not need to take the next step by internalising or personally relating to their rejecting attitude. Your fear of rejection is a sign that you do not understand enough about yourself, other people, or what to do in rejection situations. If you sense personal feelings of rejection you should always start by reminding yourself that the other person is doing you a favour by giving you an opportunity to practise self-development!

To tackle fear of rejection you must first admit that it is a problem, be aware that is holding you back, and consciously decide to work on it. Before and during a sales situation, keep in mind a clear strategy and attitude towards the possibility of rejection. Realise that what happens to you is not all-important — it's what happens for your *client* that is vitally important.

An attitude of service helps to overcome fear of rejection. First, you must make sure that you are honest to yourself by identifying your own essential needs. If you can't look after yourself, then you probably won't look after others too well either. But if you can't look after others, you won't be doing very well for yourself in the long run. For example, one of your basic needs might be to have the freedom to set your own weekly program in order to efficiently match your activities with your energy peaks. You might have to sort out many little personal needs before you can work with others effectively.

Having thought out a basic and balanced approach to your own needs, you can then concentrate on finding ways to meet the needs of others. Do not make selling an exercise in getting a pat on the back from others. Try to change this sort of attitude and, within fair and reasonable limits, see yourself as a salesperson serving others. If you realistically cannot meet the needs of others, then don't waste everyone's time — bow out graciously and be productive elsewhere. But if you believe you may be able to meet their needs, then point this out honestly and confidently. Most people will appreciate you being honest with them.

Mentioning your attitude of service can be reassuring for clients if you do not labour or embellish the point. Promise no more than you can deliver. Be alert that the more selfish a person is, the less he or she will believe in sincere service. Extreme selfishness does not co-exist comfortably with genuine attitudes of service, yet lives easily with cynicism. Regardless, try to hold your constructive attitudes consciously at the front of your thinking. Handle rejectors or cynics with dignity, calm objectivity and belief in yourself!

Interestingly, an attitude of genuine service to others does not put you in a completely subservient position. Instead it gradually gives you an equal, or even an upper, hand. Because you know your own motivation, you can build a sense of confidence in yourself and your motives. Eventually, with maturity, this confidence, together with your clearly-held ideas of the goals you are pursuing, puts you in a position to effectively guide and persuade others. You become a leader and earn respect if you genuinely and knowingly serve the interests of those you lead. You won't understand leadership issues until you find the maturity to provide such leadership. If you want to be a good sales team leader you need to sort out the considerations involved in properly serving others in your team, as well as your prospects.

Adopting new attitudes takes time and involves repetition and making mistakes. Think carefully about the opportunities you can create to practise and incorporate into your life these stronger attitudes. Discuss your new approaches with other people who really understand what you are attempting to do, who like your ideas and are practising something similar. Go over your new approach often in your own mind, write notes about it, visualise it until it starts to happen almost automatically. Read books on these issues. Imagine specific situations and variations on them. Practise repeatedly, both mentally and in the real world. Tackle fear of rejection and you will find your self-esteem improves in business and in your personal life. If, despite these strategies, you still find that rejection is a major problem in your life, you may benefit from seeking psychological advice.

Fear of being seen to be 'pushy'

A tendency to be 'pushy' can quickly ruin a relationship. Are you one of those people who are good at starting positive relationships, but cannot sustain them so positively? If you are a person whose characteristic is to push or pressure people to do things, you are probably harbouring substantially impatient, insensitive, aggressive or selfish attitudes. Interestingly, you may also conceal these traits with a polite veneer. These characteristics cause difficulties in relationships. It is easy to be friendly and relaxed for a short while at the beginning of a relationship, however your underlying negative or dishonest attitudes will eventually have an impact, making people wary of you.

Fear of being too pushy can arise because, at some level, you know from experience that you have this bullying potential and fear the effect it can have on your relationships. Fundamentally, being pushy usually means you are not showing due sensitivity and respect for others. If we want a healthy society and healthy personal relationships, we must allow others the freedom, within reasonable limits, to make their own decisions, enjoy their personal rights and meet their personal needs.

Interestingly, the opposite also happens: some individuals fear being pushy, but never actually are. If you are an individual who is very timid, you probably find pushy people very threatening. Due to your own fear of pushy people, you may avoid any trace of pushiness in yourself. This seems to be 'niceness', but is really a fear of losing face or appearing unlikable. It also can be an excuse for lack of courage to tackle your more difficult responsibilities. You may feel that being assertive could jeopardise existing or future acceptance, especially by someone you are close to. Yet behind timidness hides unhappy, defensive or guilty attitudes, which you probably hope will not surface or be noticed. If you are a timid person, try to be honest about your fears and feelings towards others, and stand up for yourself more.

If you really are a pushy person, you may do better to settle down a bit. Impatience, greed and anger are prime culprits in pushiness. These particular traits create an undisciplined approach which, at its roots, is disrespectful of other people. You will do better in life by giving genuine respect to others rather than habitually pushing them. Personality habits of impatience, ready anger and underlying disrespect for others are weaknesses that need to be confronted and changed.

The typically pushy person finds such changes threatening to their basic *modus operandi*. If you are used to getting results from others, especially weaker personalities, by being pushy, it's time you realised that being pushy is a double-edged sword. Reassess whether you are getting the results you really want. Don't just look at sales figures — look at the depth and quality of your relationships as well. Are you facing greater resistance and barriers from others? How is your own health and self-respect? Look carefully at the effects you could be having on the mental and physical health of others around you. Look at the sincerity of responses of others to you. Look at the effects that being pushy could be having on your family life.

Strong-minded people, whether they are friends, family or clients, will not be interested in being pushed around. Eventually they will leave you. Dependent personalities will tend to stay around until they become a burden for the pushy or aggressive person. Your overall success and happiness could substantially increase if you temper your pushiness and develop more poise.

A mature salesperson will use pushiness selectively, where it seems appropriate. For a client who is being evasive or misleading or is procrastinating, a little extra questioning, persuasion or push may be exactly what they need to help them reach a decision. They might even be hoping for this help from you! The line between being acceptably persuasive and uncomfortably pushy is a fine one. It varies according to the personalities and preferences of the individuals involved. Less mature salespeople lack a feel for the fine line between comfortable assertiveness, acceptable persuasiveness or unpleasant pushiness. Developing your insight into pushiness, and giving it serious thought as you work with others, will improve your capacity to exert appropriate influence with people.

Fear of failure and punishment

If you have low-self-esteem , you typically tend to see yourself as not as successful as you would like to be. You probably also fear failure. Failure is only an attitude. You only become a failure when you pronounce that judgement on yourself. If *you* don't think you are a failure, it doesn't matter what other people say. They might pronounce you a success or a hopeless failure, but the real issue is — do *you* feel you are a failure? Subconsciously you might be one of many people who believe they are failures. Sometimes it takes a lot of conscious effort to identify and change this belief, which can often be deeply ingrained in your underlying basic views on yourself and your life.

Even if you are one of the hard-working people in this life, you might still never achieve your goals if you are so bogged down by fears of failure that you cannot take risks when necessary. In other words, being excessively strongly concerned with achieving successful results is an unhelpful attitude that builds fear of failure and eventually leads to actual failure.

Let's use the analogy of breaking a rock with a hammer. You wouldn't consider yourself a failure if you hit the rock once or twice and it didn't break. You might have to hit it many times before it cracks and eventually disintegrates. You might even need to ask for someone else to help you blow up the rock with dynamite. But if you keep trying, there is every chance that you will find a solution if you are determined enough. In the same way, just because you have to tackle the major problems of life several times before you succeed doesn't mean that you should consider yourself a failure.

Do your job in the best and most sensible way you can. Be prepared to accept any outcome without believing that lack of success should bring loss of face. This attitude will help you to sustain a more positive approach and bring you more likelihood of success.

Fear of success and its consequences

Success brings reponsibilities and demands and, as a result, you will be asked to carry more responsibility for yourself and for others. If you want to be successful, you need to prepare yourself to handle success and accept the responsibilities and even the suffering that success might bring to you. It is naïve to be surprised at or fearful of the high price and the suffering associated with life's successes. Ultimately, success is about who you have become, and the basic principles you have chosen to build your life on.

Consider the troublesome role of the unconscious mind in success. It often sabotages our efforts. It may lead us to become anxious and unable to control our desire to escape from the larger risks we are faced with. This is the downside of taking on greater responsibilities. Even after trying hard to overcome such unwanted anxieties, we might still be deeply fearful. This is because our subconscious holds the painful memories and experiences of the past which we associate with getting into trouble. It takes a lot of will and effort to overcome deep-seated fears. The same applies for overcoming resistances, which is discussed next. Unless we are very self-observant, we can easily become preoccupied by fears or negative mental projections which typically develop into fears about particular issues. This can be sufficient to stop us progressing as we try to hold the status quo, and may even bring our progress to a halt.

Psychologists often use structured problem-solving or cognitive-behavioural approaches to tackle major problems related to fear, anger, depression and other emotions. Such approaches involve defining the problems clearly and carefully, taking into consideration both external stress factors and internal personal reactions or automatic thoughts. Once the problem has been defined, various possible solutions to each aspect of the problem are listed and ranked in order according to ease or usefulness. From this list, a written, staged plan is prepared for implementing the solutions in logical order. Next, a list of the situations which provoke the particular emotional difficulty is drawn up in order of significance and each situation is targeted for attention. A number of small, graded, sequential steps are identified which the client is then required to complete in each troublesome situation.

The plan is implemented and progress is monitored according to a rating scale. The aim is to build the client's confidence through tackling, repeatedly practising and gradually achieving success in each task. Eventually the client is able to master the difficult situation. For example, fear of speaking in meetings can be tackled by giving the client exercises of various graded levels of difficulty, which might eventually culminate in giving a full-scale public address.

There are many serious self-help books written by psychologists on managing anxiety or managing anger which can be very helpful. Alternatively, consult a psychologist for more specific and individual help.

OVERCOMING RESISTANCES

Resistance to change often arises from a tricky part of ourselves called the 'ego' which holds much of our arrogance and associated negative attitudes and feelings. Most of this negativity and resistance is unconscious; it is not deliberate, but is part of our egotism. We can be perverse, so exploring our mental blocks or resistances is an important part of overcoming our personal limitations.

Our self-image is strongly influenced by the psychological processes which we commonly call our ego. The ego creates a facade of 'I' — a picture of ourselves we are conscious of. But ego processes have their limitations, to a greater or lesser degree in each of us. Because we lack awareness of certain things about ourselves and our mental processes, we call them collectively the 'unconscious'. We often seem to prefer to keep some things, including ideas, wishes, conflicts and feelings, hidden in our unconscious. Our ego is closely tied up with our defensiveness, or defence mechanisms. Sometimes people call this egotism and see it as excesses on the part of the ego, which often leads to defensiveness, arrogance and associated negative attitudes and feelings.

We are continually influenced in subtle ways by our memories of the past, including feelings and thoughts that we are hardly conscious of. Our conscious mind seems focused on other more immediate things. We become so preoccupied with our thinking, beliefs or feelings in situations that we lack awareness of the important underlying factors. For example, when we are criticised by someone, we tend to spend a lot of time justifying our actions and overlook the fact that our response may be dominated by anger, rather than being rational, well-judged and objective. Then we typically create further trouble for ourselves.

Resistance to change, to advice or to learning new skills is often a psychological reaction which is more deep-seated than we realise. We are often not fully aware of why it happens. Some people harbour deep-seated anger and resentment towards others who are successful, or towards people who let them down, or even towards people who try to advise them to change or do things differently. This may be because they were let down or pushed around a lot by their parents in childhood. Yet they often don't realise this, or deny that it makes any difference to them. They are also denying that they should or could change.

Another example: I know a woman who gets very angry when she hears any talk about positive attitudes. She says her childhood was so bad that she is entitled to be angry and negative. She is arrogant, critical and blames others for her problems. Naturally she has difficulties in her personal and work relationships. She doesn't see that her anger is due partly to her negativity about herself. I told her that she is entitled to be angry and miserable, and to live every day with her resentment, if that is what she wants. Paradoxically, she is always visiting counsellors to help her cope. She wants to be happier, but is resistant to the price of forgiving or forgetting the wrong done to her. She has an inner conflict which is holding her back: the wish to change, versus fear and the wish not to let go of the attitudes she has adopted as her crusade in life — attitudes she really needs to let go of. Although one can be sympathetic towards such a person, their arrogance harms their future prospects. Psychologists are often faced with individuals who want to improve their life but who simultaneously, mostly unconsciously, resist making the necessary changes in themselves. That is the difficult nature of human beings, and it is no different in training people for the workplace.

Inner conflict of desires is typically encountered in resistance. Many of us have conflicts about our relationships, work, success or money. For example, we wish not to have money problems, but we also think things like 'There are more important things in life than work or money' and so justify our careless use of our time or money. But you cannot be irresponsible in your self-management and still expect to be happy. This inner conflict of desires often leads to resistance to progress. We are often reluctant to give up immediate desires and pleasures for longer-term discipline and progress.

The main difficulty is that we usually cannot see our own resistance. When we are advised by others to look at our negativity, arrogance, anger or defensiveness, we sometimes find it hard to see clearly. Lack of honest self-appraisal and negative, selfish attitudes that together comprise arrogance are common in people who see themselves as 'failures'. This prevents them from admitting fully and honestly why they are not as successful as they wish, and from being able to change.

Resistance and defensiveness is unlikely to solve most problems, and you probably know deep down that this is the wrong approach. Take a mature approach and train yourself to avoid being defensive, denying your problems, or projecting them onto and blaming other people. Practise using humour to defuse your difficulties, or rechannel your destructive impulses into creative activity. You may need to find an experienced support person who can help you resolve your difficulties. Whatever approach you take, always remember to focus and build on your existing strengths and positive qualities. Maintain a balanced perspective in your efforts towards progress.

OVERCOMING CALL RELUCTANCE

The reluctance to make sales calls is a very basic problem. If it is a problem that you frequently experience, you need to look at it hard and square to find the solution. Call reluctance arises from underlying negativity and half-heartedness or indecisiveness in some aspect of your commitment, and may indicate that you have significant career difficulties. You may only suffer repeated call reluctance with one client or situation, or it may undermine all your work. Either way, it's a basic handicap that you certainly don't need.

A combination of factors may contribute to this negative attitude — fears of rejection, continual tiredness, dissatisfaction with your employment conditions, unhappiness with your business or career direction, and so on. Review these factors, identify any which apply specifically to you, and address them honestly. Review your situation carefully — you really cannot afford this basic problem which will destroy your initiative, energy and success.

Low self-esteem is the most common cause of call reluctance. Low self-esteem is a very widespread problem and has a pervasive influence on our lives. It tends to lead to failure, depression, anxiety, becoming preoccupied with yourself, becoming withdrawn and resentful of others who seem happier. Sometimes low self-esteem drives individuals into excessive socialising in an unfulfillable search for happiness via the attention of others. Paradoxically, low self-esteem also underlies the development of ruthless ambition, arrogance or excessive, unbalanced attempts at success.

Low self-esteem usually becomes established during the childhood years. Lack of close communication, love and acceptance from parents and guardians causes you to doubt your own worthiness of respect and love. Even children who receive parental love can still doubt themselves. Gaining acceptance, admiration or reassurance from others becomes the fickle, frail foundation on which self-esteem is built. Strong self-esteem is based in the sense of your own inherent self-worth and your own personal integrity. This is reinforced by a sense of your own self-discipline. Children need to be encouraged to acknowledge their own self-worth and integrity and to develop the capacity for self-discipline.

Low self-esteem is frequently unconscious, so you do not sense or realise how much it is affecting you underneath. Even people with lots of money or fame can still doubt or dislike themselves. Success, ambition, sensory pleasures, social involvements or material possessions and gadgets are not sufficient to solve the fundamental problems of inner self-acceptance. The solution is to realise and find respect for your fundamental human qualities by developing a consistent ability to give and receive care and love through personal discipline and maturity. If you have strong self-esteem, you can afford to be graceful, humble and unassuming because you already have underlying psychological strength and self-respect, so you don't need or worry about the admiration of others, nor do you need to gain power over others.

A salesperson with poor self-esteem has an innate lack of confidence in handling other people in a variety of situations. With self-esteem comes a different approach: 'I don't mind what the other person thinks about me because I feel happy about myself as a person. I know my motives are constructive and honest. I know I may get anxious at times or make mistakes, but that does not diminish my self-worth or belief in myself, regardless of what others might think.'

Overcoming call reluctance often means building your self-esteem. The old adage, 'Practice makes perfect' applies to making calls as well, but no matter how many calls you make, you need to focus deliberately on resolving low self-esteem. You can start with a simple change of your conscious attitudes. Read books about self-esteem, and write out statements about self-esteem and yourself. Identify both constructive and destructive attitudes that you hold towards yourself and write them down. Read those statements to yourself every day, and practise the new attitudes to make them a part of your habitual thinking. Transforming your attitudes so they become a deeply-ingrained part of your personality, your automatic thinking patterns and your everyday behaviour takes a lot of repeated practice and thought over a long period of time. It requires a really serious look at your problems and your commitment to making the effort to change them.

If you are working on your self-esteem, you can accept some limitations if you commit to overcoming them through repeated daily effort, even if it takes years. Clearly define personal goals for each area of your life — family, marriage, employer, employees, health, social life, financial future, self-education, religion and so on. Recognise that you are honestly working towards these goals and living your life better. You have begun the process of defining who you are or want to be, and your progress will ultimately bring with it self-esteem.

Start right now by listing each of the steps described in the two paragraphs above on a sheet of paper. Address each point in turn, with the help of other sections in this book, and from other books and courses, or discussion with family or friends. You *can* make a difference if you really decide to.

OVERCOMING STRESS

Repeated stress adversely affects the nervous system. This effect is subtle at first — you may not notice your lowered performance. But, gradually, you will cease to function effectively. Without realising it, you will become slightly less mentally aware, less clear-thinking and less relaxed, sharp and intuitive. Without a fully concentrated mind, you cannot sustain your decisiveness as accurately or effectively. It is easy to get caught in a vicious cycle of stressful external demands, personal limitations and poor job performance.

Some of the main stressors of today which could be affecting you are the demands of adapting to rapidly changing business environments and practices, higher levels of performance expectations and advancing technology. Your susceptibility to these stressors arises from your personal difficulties of fear, resistance and low self-esteem. Your stress comes from your inner limitations in interacting with the demands of the external world. As a result, your anxiety, fears, impatience, disappointment and other emotional disturbances increase.

The inner pressures that you experience as 'stress' are often a result of your own inner functioning. Driving inner desires, psychological attachments to outcomes, or your weak response to pressures from others can mean that you lose objectivity and balance in your approach. Additionally, it is easy to waste too much energy and time on multiple pleasures, distractions or inefficiencies in an attempt to escape stress, however these can often leave you more tired and less able to concentrate. And the less concentrated you are, the more time and energy you waste. Loss of objectivity and poorly planned escapist activities both contribute to the vicious stress cycle that you can get trapped in if you do not stop to consider to what extent this process is affecting your life. It is worth asking yourself now, 'How much of this stress am I creating myself?'

You can learn to manage stress by carefully looking at the predicament you are caught up in. Identify your important responsibilities and priorities. It is vital that you allow regular time for reflection, self-organisation, quiet and physical and mental relaxation. Conserve your energy. Where you must apply it, apply it effectively. It is especially important to develop an attitude of patience. Start by carrying with you a brief reminder list of these points to refer to during the day.

Many individuals need help to learn to cope with pressures and avoid becoming excessively stressed. The common habit of blaming others for your stress is simply an excuse for the fact that the stress is your problem and the solutions are up to you. You are free to take charge of your own life. Your decision to learn to change stress-producing factors in yourself is an important first step in leaving the rat-race behind and beginning your personal journey towards maturity, happiness and 'peak performance'.

THREE PERSONAL HISTORIES

I invite you now to examine more deeply the psychological problems of average people. Our particular examples are related to the ability to sell, but even if you are not a sales professional there are countless situations in everyone's life where some sort of selling is needed. Teachers have to sell their skills to their employer and their subject to students. Lawyers or doctors sell their practice and services to potential clients; politicians sell their views to an electorate. These situations are highly influenced by basic factors such as the self-esteem of the individuals concerned, and the amount of training and experience in promotions they have. Yet only a small percentage of us achieve a strong personal sense of success in our lives. This applies regardless of definitions of success, and regardless of the level of education or type of professional qualifications we have.

To go backstage and see how these dramas are produced in daily life, actual case histories of reasonably 'average' people are presented here. Each has been modified to protect the anonymity of those concerned. To some readers these cases may not seem to be those of 'normal' people, but remember that every person needs to seek personal help at some time in their life, and it is now much more common and acceptable to see professional advisors. More than one in five Australians sees a psychologist or psychiatrist for help during their lifetime. If 'normal' means a person who has had no periods of difficulty in his or her private or business life, there are very few 'normal' people in our society.

Personal history 1: Ron

Ron, aged 30, was surprised to find, through counselling, knowledge about himself and other people of which he hadn't been previously aware. This led to a promotion in his work, and helped him to gain insight into how he could become very successful in his career and in his relationships. He also began a new and important friendship.

Ron was coping reasonably well as a computer services sales manager, but found interpersonal relationships difficult both at work and in his private life. He had low self-esteem and had been, at times, quite depressed about his inability to form successful relationships, which was something he greatly desired. His interest in a management and marketing career could not be pursued fully until he sorted out this problem. Ron was puzzled by other people's reactions towards him — they seemed unpredictable, and sometimes aggressive, cold and untrusting. This reinforced his lack of confidence. He initially sought help to cope with extreme distress about being abandoned by a girlfriend, and then sought advice about his social skills in general.

Ron's childhood life was often not happy. An only child, his parents separated when he was five and for the next 10 years he lived with his father who largely ignored him. His father was part of a circle of drug-abusing friends, who were frequently at his home. Consequently Ron spent much time at home, by himself, without the company of other children his age. However he was intelligent, did well at school and in sports, and became determined to succeed in life.

Ron discovered, through counselling, the importance of sorting out his basic personal values, his attitudes to others and to himself. He had to become more detached in his relationships at work by being more objective and worrying less. He needed to believe in his own personal commitment, as well as that of the people he supervised, and he needed to become realistically tolerant of the failings of others. He realised that being honestly informed about himself and others was crucial.

During the time he was attending counselling, Ron met a new girlfriend. He was able to discuss the importance of finding sensible, balanced ways of properly looking after his new friend, without being overly intrusive or suffocating. After six months of this type of discussion and support, Ron had a new sense of personal commitment and confidence. He began to believe in himself and his future possibilities. He became much more effective at work and was promoted to supervisor of all the contract staff.

An unexpected benefit was a new, more meaningful and open relationship with his father. He was also able to comfortably meet his mother, whom he had avoided for five years. I am sure that Ron will progress to even further success in life, and will have far less trouble in the future in selling himself to others or in representing his company well.

Personal history 2: Julie

Julie's story shows how we sometimes need to openly express and courageously confront our hidden emotions and fears.

Julie is a 35-year-old insurance agent with a successful sales career. In the past four years she has not coped well with stress and has needed to take a few weeks off as stress was affecting her work performance. She sometimes felt anxious and panicky without obvious cause, and conversations in the office about the success of others irritated her. Visits to her parents were upsetting because her mother showed great disrespect for her father. Julie had hated her mother, who was an aggressive alcohol-abusing woman, since childhood. She had recently begun to feel terrified that she was not coping in her everyday life, and that her anxiety was out of control.

Julie felt reassured at being carefully listened to during counselling. After a realistic, supportive discussion about symptoms, treatment options and possible outcomes, she could see herself progressing with her problems. Anti-anxiety medication helped at first, and she gradually ceased the medication while continuing to work on a program of identifying and modifying her personal attitudes and behaviours and implementing the changes in her life.

Gradually, Julie became more open. She did not like admitting her fears about herself, her low opinion of herself, or feeling less strong than others and would get angry at people who wanted to help. She became extremely annoyed when she felt unfairly dealt with by others, but tended to suppress this aggression and frustration. However, she could become extremely abusive and reckless when driving her car. She also had an explosively angry side when sufficiently provoked, although fortunately this was rarely evident.

The root of Julie's problem was revealed when she recollected the severe distress she experienced in childhood caused by her mother's continual aggression. She had felt trapped in a terrifying, powerless and demeaning position. Subsequently, she always felt anxious to please people and to be polite and friendly within genuine relationships. However, she does have a limited capacity for patience with stressors, and has always been very anxious about being successful.

Despite her fears of not succeeding, Julie adopted a more detached attitude to success and acknowledged her good potential. She stopped being 'helpful' and doing unnecessary jobs for her work colleagues, and allowed herself the dignity and authority appropriate to her seniority. Privately, she began regular walking to relax instead of relying on a few drinks, and enlisted her husband's support. She acknowledged her need to please others and to have complete control, and she began to modify these attitudes.

Julie learned to visualise herself becoming a person with a new primary purpose of a stable, balanced and relaxed approach to living. This actively replaced her negative self-doubts. As a result, she changed some key goals and attitudes, which led to behavioural changes in her private and business life activities. After five months, feeling fully recovered from the episode of anxiety, she had learned vital information about herself and had a new positive approach to her life and her career.

(*Note*: Recent evidence shows that the popular theory of 'anxiety' as an inherited biological problem has been overstated. The personal psychology of an individual has always been vitally important in working with anxiety problems.)

Personal history 3: Peter

In this case, we see how top professional performance requires good personal balance. Peter, a successful 36-year-old corporate accountant, seems competent and very personable. A year ago, during a meeting with a potential new client of substance, Peter observed how his colleague handled the client successfully and with confidence, openly saying 'No' and correcting the client where appropriate. Peter was impressed, but also worried that he could not have handled the client as confidently as his colleague did. Peter finds that he automatically avoids potential conflict by tending to agree on everything. Peter has received indicators that promotion to partnership in the next few years is an option, however he feels that he needs to increase his abilities before he can function effectively in a senior position. He needs to attain high-level performance skills, especially in relating to and managing other people. He has to be really fantastic at client negotiations and selling his firm. Overall, he sees himself as satisfactory, with no major flaws, but he feels that he lacks the mark of the top professionals — a confidence and competence that seem 'natural'.

Peter had always believed that his background was very average and normal. He has fairly conservative parents of reasonable means and had attended an excellent private school. But his wife began to point out his shortcomings. She said that everyone in his family was polite, but no-one said what they really felt. Discontent was only expressed obliquely, in coded language. Extremely judgmental attitudes were masked by self-righteous niceness and hypocrisy, especially in relation to his family. Peter's wife's direct confrontation of this lack of honesty caused the family extreme offence. Initially Peter judged his wife's views to be unrealistic and irrational and their marriage became strained. However, he eventually realised that his wife was raising very important, real issues. The conflict between Peter's wife and his mother became intense and Peter then became deeply upset by his parents' refusal to discuss their attitudes honestly. After encouragement from his maternal uncle over a period of several years, Peter was eventually able to constructively confront his parents to discuss these issues.

You could say that Peter's family suffered from reasonably normal family tensions. Social pretentiousness and anxiety about social acceptance and material security *was* apparent in the family, although this is common enough in some circles. However, Peter grew up defensive, guarded and wary of putting a foot wrong and incurring his mother's hostility. He could not honestly express his feelings. Being subjected to somewhat stifling and over-controlling house and school rules contributed to make him feel hostile towards people who tried to control or challenge him. Until recently he avoided sharing his real feelings in any relationship and automatically tried to be nice and agreeable, or to make himself busy to avoid difficult issues. He regretfully suspects that this may even have caused him to avoid acting assertively in the best interests of a client.

The overall effect is that insecurity, hidden anger and lack of trust have subtly inhibited Peter's ability to have fully effective relationships with others. He now realises that he is less than fully confident, honest or trusting, and, to some extent, doesn't respect himself. Most people would never see his shaky inner self because, despite some egotism, he has a pleasant, clever, hard-working professional facade. But he is not psychologically free enough to be a truly 'natural' performer.

Happily, Peter has already become more aware of his issues. He is working on them by seeking a more self-aware, concentrated mind, using daily relaxation, and focusing his thoughts through writing a diary.

He is refining his goals, values and priorities and is being encouraged to use these to guide himself in structuring each day. This is helping him to maintain more positive attitudes, especially towards his wife. He is learning to put more trust in himself and other people through being more honest, open and direct about his thoughts and feelings, as well as learning more about how to handle matters of trust in business.

Achieving this sort of personal progress is a fairly subtle task, which must be tackled gradually. Eventually Peter will be able to say confidently: 'I respect myself because I have been taking a more mature, honest approach to myself and others in my life, and doing what I believe in.' After 12 months of personal work, he is already much less defensive, and more naturally self-confident both at home and work.

SUMMARY COMMENTS ON THE PERSONAL HISTORIES

We each have our own story, our own issues, limitations, family problems, etc., regardless of our pretences. Common basic issues affect most of us: hidden self-esteem and confidence problems, impatience, anger, depression and anxiety about life, poor emotional control, lack of mental alertness and concentration, lack of a clear set of balanced priorities and values, lack of clear goals because we haven't defined our values, lack of commitment and motivation, selfishness and lack of thoughtfulness to others, etc.

When seeking solutions to our work-related problems, we often overlook or misunderstand the importance of the basic essentials we need to help us mature: self-awareness, controlling our negative thinking, developing honesty, trust, patience, finding belief in ourself, living in the present and having fun in life. Some of us feel the need to address these issues; others don't. Some of us know that we *need* to, but can't face up to it for various reasons. Some people's lives are so complicated, and they have become so confused and demoralised, that they have great difficulty in just trying to realise what is happening to them, let alone changing it. Yet I have seen people with quite extreme psychological disturbances make major changes in their attitudes which have changed their lives for the better.

I have presented the basic ideas that seem to me to be important in these histories, taking a common sense approach and minimising the complex theory. I avoid pushing people to follow my professional advice or opinions, but through discussion present my points of view, respecting others' independence and freedom to follow their own views. They must choose without psychological tricks or exploitative persuasion or 'selling' being used on them. It shows out in the end-result. You must carry the final responsibility for your own individual progress in achieving what you want from your life.

SUGGESTIONS TO HELP YOU DEVELOP AND PROGRESS

Develop a concentrated mind.

Review the section in this chapter on stress and its destructive effects on concentration and awareness. If you are able to properly concentrate, you should have no difficulty in settling down to summarise this chapter with pencil and paper. Select the main points you need to work on, identify your problems and clearly target them for resolution. Practise being more observant of your own attitudes and habits and those exhibited by others.

Plan to include in your daily schedule several rest periods of a few minutes each. During these rest periods review the attitudes you have observed so far. Spend five minutes at the end of each day writing notes on your attitudes during the day. Use a diary to plan and track your progress. List both positive and negative attitudes, including specific new attitudes that you intend to adopt in place of the old ones. Mentally rehearse and practise these new attitudes in various situations. Seek feedback and support from others with this. Have a regular daily period for quietening your mind and practising inner contemplation. If you want to improve your concentration, it is essential to practise a deep relaxation exercise or meditation. You can discipline your mind to rest from its overactivity, wandering and continual preoccupation with endless thoughts.

Believe in and seek improved personal integration

Very few people can 'get it all together'. We may be good at technical ideas but not skilled at being sensitive to others' feelings, or we may be able to excite others by our creative ideas but not carry through with the practical work on time. Do you know many people who have got themselves and their life working in a way where they are consistently relaxed, happy and successful in all of their involvements?

Make a committed decision to work consistently towards balancing time and concentration across the various facets of your life. Enjoying your personal and family life, business projects, running your personal finances successfully, sustaining good personal health and having very positive social involvements outside of business and family all requires planning and attention. Make lists of your objectives, your real dreams in life, the top 10 things you value most (health or a happy family, for example), your practical goals for the next one, three and five years. Read self-help books about this, or seek professional advice.

Write a detailed description of the practical changes you believe you can implement to make your business and personal life coexist in greater harmony. Carry that description with you each day in your diary and review it often. Plan how you can enlist the support of several people or mentors who can help you with advice on making balanced changes. Remember, the task is to change aspects of your *own* behaviour and thoughts, rather than trying to change the other people in your life.

It takes a great deal of personal development and maturity to be able to progress substantially to successfully integrate all the aspects of your life. There are many forces, both internal and external, that can repeatedly upset your consistency. Be patient, and do not lose sight of your ideal. Explore, and incorporate within yourself, the broad combination of knowledge and skills needed to achieve an overall integrated life.

Consciously develop a sustained will

The combination of poor concentration, imbalances in various facets of our lives, and lack of energy makes it difficult for us to maintain stability and equanimity while coping with every day, year in and year out. Combine this with a lack of precision about our fundamental beliefs or motivations, and we are really hampered in sustaining a strong will.

Your ability to mentally 'project' yourself into achieving your goals — that is, to mentally sustain and develop your ideas and wishes and translate them into courageous action — varies dramatically according to your state of mind. Negative feelings, doubts and uncertainties seriously limit your ability to keep a strong will in action, and without a strong will, you will rarely get strong results.

Commit yourself to developing a stronger will. This is a special part of any lifelong commitment to making the absolute best of your life and your potential. However, do not take on or promise yourself too much will-power at once — this could lead to you becoming disillusioned, or an unbalanced fanatic. Be careful and patient. It is tempting to suddenly feel enthusiastic and strong-willed, but your untrained will can weaken just as suddenly. Developing a strong, unwavering determination requires deep thought and a lot of practice at maintaining positive attitudes throughout your ups and downs in life.

Practise improving your will-power gradually by setting yourself minor tasks. For example, you could decide to give up for a month one or two pleasures that you really like. Try not watching any TV or stop eating your favourite food for exactly one month. You might commit to doing at least 15 minutes of a relaxation exercise every day without fail for one month. Once you have done this, you might continue such disciplines, perhaps with some variations.

Develop a precise knowledge of your approach to selling

Two main factors lie behind a lack of precision in selling. The first, and most important, is a lack of precision about the fundamental principles of our own personal approach to life, including beliefs and attitudes we bring to selling as one facet amongst all aspects of our life. The second factor is a lack of precision in learning and applying specific steps and techniques used in the process of selling. These are addressed thoroughly in the other chapters of this book. Neither factor can work consistently in a balanced, practical way without the other. 'Knowledge', more than technical details about products or markets, means a clearer perspective on the fundamentals of what we are doing and why.

Decide to become very clear-minded about your approach to selling and how it fits into your personal values. Review whether your selling role is part of your personal commitment. If it is, how great a part is it? Make every hour of your life as personally meaningful as you possibly can. You don't have to spend your life doing things that you're not enthusiastic about. You can adopt a more creative outlook on your life.

Think carefully and honestly about why you are selling a particular product or service. Look beyond the immediate reasons to your deeper feelings. For example, maybe you enjoy selling a particular product because it makes people like you or brings you companionship which you enjoy. Or, you might be selling in the way you do out of fear of changing, or fear of not succeeding at something else. A variety of motivations might be helping you to be successful, but if your motivations are out of balance or negative they will bring other complications. Think carefully to see if you have deeper motivations which may be creating difficulties for you. When you are dealing with sophisticated clients, your approach to selling and service has to be soundly based and very precisely thought-out, or they could outsmart you.

Examine your particular motivations carefully. Motivation, according to Michael Le Boeuf, can be summed up as 'reward', which means: 'What's in it for me?' Don't misinterpret this as 'What's in it for others doesn't matter', because you really do need to understand others. But you can't understand others if you first don't understand yourself. So what does being 'rewarded' mean for you?

Decide how altruistic you can be while still feeling comfortable. You may feel that you should be altruistic, but if you are pretending to be altruistic towards others, or to society, this can create resentment, stress and unhappiness within you which will eventually show through in your results. Pretending to be nice to your customer and then taking out your frustrations on your colleagues or family later in the day will lead to complications that will eventually affect your ability to work successfully.

Always seek more precision and knowledge in your life. Knowledge removes fear and reluctance and frees you psychologically to act with inner conviction and to be more powerful and effective in your work and your life.

POSTSCRIPT ON SUCCESS

Where is the peacefulness in our life? Deep down inside, many of us are driven by fears, desires and wishes to the point where we have little or no personal peace. Life becomes a continual merry-go-round of demands. And without as much peace as we deeply wish for, we find it hard to really have a strong self-belief. We subconsciously feel our inner imbalance. We know we are not fearless. A fearless approach to life is rare. Personally, I seek it, but I have a lot of progress to make yet. It doesn't arise with arrogance. Arrogance may masquerade as fearlessness, but it arises from deeper fears and suppressed feelings of insecurity. We can see the advantages in being fearless. On the other hand, we fear not satisfying our desires. These psychological attachments in life mean that we rarely or only briefly feel calmness and peacefulness.

If anyone, in sales or any other walk of life, seeks less fear and more self-esteem, they need inner relaxation without arrogance. The result tends to be more effective actions and interactions that are sensible, to the point, direct and efficient.

Arrogant self-confidence and subtle intimidation works in persuading people, but mainly weaker personalities. Many people see and admire 'arrogant' qualities as a sign of strength, and as a bold, successful means of getting what you want. To some extent, this is the unfortunate 'politics' of contemporary life. It reflects a selfish outlook and the lack of a deeper spirituality.

More mature persons are less susceptible to arrogance and intimidation. They prefer something different: well-balanced humility, neutrality, honesty and unselfishness. They prefer a happy, calm and competent approach. There are a lot of hyped-up salespeople in the world. There are relatively few who are deeply relaxed. You have to be highly trained in self-discipline to have this. Gradually develop a little more maturity for yourself in your sales work, in your family life, and in your personal approach to everything. This is success.

CHAPTER 30

GO FOR IT!

*Every day, remind yourself of your own ability, of
your good mind, and affirm that you can make
something really good out of your life.*
NORMAN VINCENT PEALE

BECAUSE YOU HAVE the power to choose, you can
influence your own destiny. Choice is what separates you from all
other known forms of life in our universe. Choose you can and choose
you must, for it is a basic function of human life. No one is exempt.
From the beginning of life to its end, you are required to make choices.
Even not choosing is a choice. You cannot escape making choices,
everything is a decision, a choice. In your sales career, your choice is
to say 'yes' or 'no' to outstanding success.

A major step forward in life is to accept that your decisions are yours
to make and that you are responsible for their outcomes. There is no
escape from the responsibility of building your life by the choices you
make. Even when something happens to you that is completely
outside your control, you must choose how you will react to what has
happened. Will you choose to respond in a positive, determined
manner, or will you choose to let it affect your life in a negative way
and pay undue interest of worry, anger, sorrow by adopting an attitude
of mind that will prevent you from making choices that can turn a
short-term setback into a long-term gain? Ita Buttrose offers some

excellent advice: 'Only a loser finds it impossible to accept a temporary setback. A winner asks "Why?".' Unforeseen events may prove to be a blessing in disguise if you embrace them and consider the positive possibilities they represent.

Each of us was born with all we will ever need in order to accomplish all we want to become. So, go for it! If you don't, you are choosing to give up the opportunity to become the best possible you. The difference between great success and average performance is the drive to make the extra effort needed to be your best. It's that little extra in everything you do. It's the drive to find added value in what you sell, and the grim determination to keep on trying when everyone else is giving up. There is no better advice than that given by Harry M. Miller, who says: 'All the successes that I have had, and that I have watched other people have, have come from keeping on going when everyone else has dropped dead or gone to bed.'

There is no limit to what you were given at birth: a divine gift with one condition attached. You have to discover it within yourself and bring it into your own life. No one else can give it to you; they have to find it for themselves. You were also given the means to bring what you want into your everyday life through the power of the self-fulfilling prophecy which is at work in your life every second of your existence. It is the source of all human accomplishment and of the divine power given to each and every one of us the day we were born. Today, millions of people around the world, from every walk of life, are discovering and using this great power in their life. If you are to become what you want to become, you must learn to use and direct this power in your life. Chapter 24, 'The Mindpower Advantage', showed you how to use the self-fulfilling prophecy to create the life you want and to bring you unlimited happiness and success.

Each person's journey is different, and the results may vary from outstanding success to bitter disappointment, confusion and chaos. There will be times when you ask, 'Why me?' and 'What did I do to deserve this?'. These questions suggest that you believe someone or something else is responsible for your life, and that you are just playing a role and have no control over your destiny. It would be more productive to accept that you are in charge and that by your thinking you create the life you have. Then you are able to ask the right question, which is: 'How can I give myself the best chance of achieving a successful outcome in my search for self and becoming the salesperson I want to be?'

It is here that all who face the challenge have common goals, for the attitudes, skills and habits that win for one will win for all. The only difference will be in the application. If you want a lot you have to give a lot, but if you want little then you only have to give a little. It's not good enough to give only enough to get only enough. The competition in the sales marketplace is swiftly sorting those who want to win from those who are unwilling to try. Remember: winning isn't everything, but wanting to is. So, go for it! Become everything you want to be.

Becoming is the act of changing from what you are to what you can become through self-development applied in a constructive and continuous way. The fact that you are reading this book is evidence that you are willing to set your sights on more than being average. Becoming is a lifelong process of change, but it doesn't mean you have to wait a lifetime for either success or happiness. You may achieve both of those goals in a short space of time, and then it is only a matter of the degree of success or happiness you continue to work for. Irrespective of the outcome of your efforts, there is constant change taking place within you and around you. The process doesn't stop until you die, and that may be the time when you undergo the greatest change and make the most progress.

When you are considering those actions that can best help you to become happy and successful, you should take account of three things that will decide most of your future. They are: what you see, what you hear and who you associate with. Each of them is within the scope of your power to choose, and each of them will have a major influence on your life for they are factors which decide your attitude of mind.

You decide what books you read, what films you watch, what videos you hire, what sports you follow. Very few of these decisions are forced upon you. You make choices about all sorts of issues that are shaping your life. Your choices imply who you want to become. You decide who you will associate with, so you should choose people who will have the most beneficial impact on your life and future. You can make the popular choice, blindly follow the herd, and adopt their values and habits, but in doing so you will build a life in common with theirs. Or you can choose the actions and habits of highly-successful people and journey further along the path of self-development and fulfilment of your goals.

What you think is deciding your future every second of your life, and the greatest influences on what you think come from what you see, what you hear and who you associate with. It is also true that who you are and what you do and say will be influencing others, because the same laws of life apply to them. So always give your best and be an example of the good things in life. Your example and encouragement will not only help to build better lives for those you associate with, but you will at the same time build a better life for yourself and those you love and care for. Give yourself every chance. Life is not a lottery; it is an opportunity to choose what you will do and what you will become. It's a never-ending process of change, and the key to unlocking the life you want is already in your hands. Remember, the law of destiny applies to everyone: 'Glory may be fleeting but obscurity is forever.' So make your choices, set your plans and go for it!

Work Smarter
Not Harder

We need people like Jack Collis to kick us out of our
mental ruts, to lift our sights and put us on track for the
breakthroughs we're looking for.
MICHAEL KIELY, EDITOR, MARKETING MAGAZINE

Work Smarter, Not Harder has been used as the basis for
our internal training for both our Sales Team, and
Operation and Administration Support. It provides easy-
to-follow steps to demonstrate that your destiny is of your
own making.
**GORDON ATKINS, NATIONAL MANAGER,
FINANCIAL MARKETING SERVICES,
TOYOTA AUSTRALIA**

Work Smarter, Not Harder is a book that is required
reading for all who aim to achieve their full potential.
You will enjoy every chapter.
DOUG NETTLESHIP, EDITOR, *BUSINESS BULLETIN*

Throughout my business career I have read many books
on selling, motivation and time study, most of which
have been written by celebrated international 'experts';
but I can say in all honesty that I have gained far more
from this book than all others put together.
PETER ALLEN, MANAGING DIRECTOR, IMAGE SPORTS

Working too hard? Not getting the fulfilment and rewards you want? With a little guidance from Jack Collis and Michael LeBoeuf you can find the perfect balance. It's simple. Just work smarter, not harder. *Work Smarter, Not Harder* is more than just a business book. It is a clear and effective personal strategy that can help you to get the most out of your life.

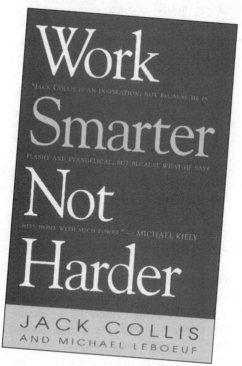

When Your Customer Wins, You Can't Lose

*Let's take the war out of customer relationships and create a
little peace and harmony plus increased productivity and profit.*
— Jack Collis

When Your Customer Wins, You Can't Lose is a book with
a big message — your customer is your business. If you
want to be more profitable and more successful than your
competitors, you need to turn your business into a
customer driven organisation. Put simply, the difference
between success and failure can be the quality of your
relationship with your customers.

The rewards of customer loyalty are enormous.
Customers quickly tire of businesses that offer the same old
quick-fix solutions, but always respond positively to
professional, creative, individually tailored solutions.
Businesses that exceed the expectations of their customers
are the winners.

In this indispensable book, Jack Collis shows you how to:

- win customers more easily and more often
- generate and increase customer satisfaction
- keep customers coming back
- create strategies to increase staff effectiveness
- create a highly motivated team
- become more productive and profitable

When Your

"JACK COLLIS HAS CORPORATIONS FOR CUSTOMERS. HE WORKS FOR SMALL

Customer

BUSINESS, AND OWNS HIS OWN. NO ONE UNDERSTANDS CUSTOMERS LIKE

Wins, You

JACK COLLIS." — LOWELL TARLING, EDITOR, FRANCHISING MAGAZINE

Can't Lose

JACK COLLIS

BESTSELLING AUTHOR OF THE GREAT
SALES BOOK, YES YOU CAN AND CO-AUTHOR
OF WORK SMARTER NOT HARDER

The Great Sales Book